高校英语选修课系列教材

Selected Readings of American and British News Publications

(The Second Edition)

美英报刊选读

第二版

主 编◎郭 印 毕纪芹
副主编◎张 艳 张 苑 刘舒展
编 者◎高公社 马 岩 李 娇
　　　刘晓茜 任翌平

清华大学出版社
北京

内 容 简 介

本教材共10个单元,以美英报刊基本知识为经线,以主流报刊代表性文章题材为纬线,涵盖时政新闻、财经资讯、科技导航、生活百科、体坛风云、文娱在线、艺术名家、教育视窗、旅途人生、全球热点等主题,内容丰富,解析深入。每单元均配有思考题,读练结合、难易适中,有助于培养学生美英报刊阅读能力、跨文化交际能力和思辨创新能力。本教材另配有参考答案和PPT课件,读者可登录"清华社英语在线"(www.tsinghuaelt.com)下载使用。

本教材适合高等院校英语专业本科生使用,也可用作高校英语选修课系列教材。

图书在版编目(CIP)数据

美英报刊选读 / 郭印, 毕纪芹主编. -- 2版.

北京:清华大学出版社, 2025. 2. -- (高校英语选修
课系列教材). -- ISBN 978-7-302-67778-9

Ⅰ. H319.4

中国国家版本馆CIP数据核字第20256YX456号

责任编辑:李星霖
封面设计:李伯骥
责任校对:王荣静
责任印制:刘海龙
出版发行:清华大学出版社
    网 址:https://www.tup.com.cn,https://www.wqxuetang.com
    地 址:北京清华大学学研大厦A座   邮 编:100084
    社 总 机:010-83470000   邮 购:010-62786544
    投稿与读者服务:010-62776969,c-service@tup.tsinghua.edu.cn
    质量反馈:010-62772015,zhiliang@tup.tsinghua.edu.cn
印 装 者:三河市少明印务有限公司
经 销:全国新华书店
开 本:185mm×260mm 印 张:15 字 数:296千字
版 次:2017年8月第1版 2025年3月第2版 印 次:2025年3月第1次印刷
定 价:65.00元

产品编号:087076-01

第二版前言

本教材第一版于2017年8月出版以来，前后重印多次，受到广大高校师生的欢迎，也收到了不少读者的积极反馈。

自第一版出版以后，教育部又相继颁布了多个文件，对英语专业的培养目标和教学标准做了明确要求。2018年颁布的《普通高等学校本科专业类教学质量国家标准（外国语言文学类）》要求，教学应"融合语言学习与知识学习，以能力培养为导向，重视语言运用能力、跨文化能力、思辨能力和自主学习能力的培养"。2020年4月，教育部高等学校外国语言文学类专业教学指导委员会出版《普通高等学校本科外国语言文学类专业教学指南（上）——英语类专业教学指南》提出：在培养目标方面，英语专业学生应具有"较强的跨文化能力"；在素质要求方面，应具有"中国情怀与国际视野"；在知识要求方面，应"了解主要英语国家的历史、社会、政治、经济、文化、科技等基本情况"。同时，近年来，国际政治、经济、文化、科技等方面发生了很大变化，第一版有些内容已经显得不合时宜。

以上是我们决心对教材再版的主要原因。本版延续了第一版的基本框架和体例，主要对以下内容做了更新：

- 对报刊知识部分相关内容做了更新，更换了绝大部分例句。

- 更换了部分课文及课后练习题：Unit 1 Text A、Unit 1 Text B、Unit 2 Text A、Unit 5 Text A、Unit 6 Text A、Unit 7 Text A、Unit 10 Text A 和 Unit 10 Text B。

- 应广大读者要求，制作了教学课件。

- 对第一版使用中发现的错误进行了更正，个别语言表述做了调整。

- 本版单词的音标以《牛津高级学习者词典》（*Oxford Advanced Learner's Dictionary*）为参考标准，统一采用英音标注。

第二版编写过程中的组织、联络、统稿、修改等工作仍由郭印、毕纪芹主要负责。

具体分工如下：郭印负责 Unit 1、Unit 2；毕纪芹负责 Unit 9、Unit 10；张艳负责 Unit 4、Unit 5；张苑负责 Unit 6、Uint 7；刘舒展负责 Unit 3、Unit 8；高公社、李娇、刘晓茜、任翌平等负责语言材料搜集和文字润色。

欢迎广大师生在使用过程中，继续提出宝贵意见与建议。

郭印　毕纪芹

2024 年 12 月

第一版前言

教育部《高等学校英语专业本科教学质量国家标准》（征求意见稿）中对英语专业的培养目标、知识要求、教学要求等方面做了明确规定：在培养目标方面，"教学过程强调实践和应用，人才培养突出人文素质教育，注重开阔学生的国际视野"；在知识要求方面，要"了解英语国家的历史和当代社会的政治、经济、文化、科技、军事等基本情况"；在教学要求方面，"教学应以能力培养为导向，突出语言综合运用能力和思辨能力的培养"。

要达到以上标准，学生应该能较好地理解、诠释、评价原汁原味的英语文本，能以包容的态度、思辨的方法和客观的立场对待英语文本所体现的多元文化现象；提高与拥有英语文化背景人士进行有效沟通的能力。对此，《美英报刊选读》有助于帮助学生实现以上目标。

《美英报刊选读》是英语专业本科阶段的"美英报刊选读"课程的通用教材。此课程设立的直接教学目标在于培养学生阅读美英报纸杂志的能力，长远教学目标在于拓宽学生视野，更多地了解英语国家的文化。本教材服务于英语专业的本科学分制教学改革，与课程建设紧密结合。其内容涵盖美英报刊的基本知识、新闻报道和文化背景介绍，旨在帮助学生：理解美英报刊文章的文体和语言特点，培养阅读美英报刊的能力；拓宽视野，深入了解西方文化，提高跨文化交际能力；加强思辨训练，培养独立思考能力和创新能力。

本教材的编写博采众长，选取的文章原汁原味、难度适宜、趣味性强，相配的报刊常识和背景知识由浅入深、循序渐进。主要特色可总结如下：

1. 知识性与趣味性相结合。阅读报刊文章的根本目的是提高英语学习效果，而良好的学习效果需要依托于学习者的兴趣与动机。因此，本教材内容的选取不仅注重结合当前热点，而且注重与学生现有的知识结构和认知水平相结合，从而减少阅读疲劳，激发学习兴趣。

2. 广泛性与深刻性相结合。阅读报刊文章既是语言学习，又是文化学习，其中更难的是对文化背景的理解。因此，本教材选材广泛，文章涉及西方国家政治、经济、科技等诸多方面，每个专题配有较为深入的文化背景介绍与相关知识解读。

3. 时效性与稳定性的平衡。新闻报道的重要评定指标之一就是时效性，正因为如此，报刊教材需要常换常新。为了保证教师上课的质量与效度，报刊文章还需要保持相对的稳定性。因此，本教材在内容设置上，兼顾了"软新闻"和"硬新闻"，平衡了时效性与稳定性。

4. 思辨能力与创新能力并举。报刊文章直接选材于西方报刊，自然会涉及意识形态问题。因此，本教材在选篇时一方面注重对学生的正面引导，另一方面注重保持文章的完整性，保持原文的风貌；尽可能给学生提供事实性和批判性的文章，以提高其阅读能力和分析能力，同时兼收一些观点不同的文章，以锻炼学生独立思考的能力。教师授课则需要坚持以学生为中心，鼓励学生结合课后思考题，慎思明辨，勇于发问，想人未想，见人未见，提高学生主动探索和获取知识的能力。

5. 线上与线下学习相融合。随着新闻媒体的网络化，《纽约时报》《泰晤士报》《经济学家》《时代周刊》等诸多美英主流报刊均免费提供网络版内容。因此，为了扩大阅读题材范围，本教材介绍了一些网站，课后学生可以根据个人兴趣，"无缝"延续报刊阅读，并凭借网络即时答疑沟通，将线上线下阅读活动融为一体。

每单元的内容框架如下：

● 报刊语言特点介绍：本部分旨在帮助学生熟悉了解报刊文章的语言特点，提高该类文体的阅读能力。

● 课文导读与思考：针对本单元的专题和课文进行导入式介绍，启迪学生深入思考。

● 课文：每单元课文集中体现本单元主题，分 A、B 两篇，每篇在 1000 词左右。

● 课文注释：针对课文中的词汇、习语、语法、文化知识的难点给予解释。

● 背景知识延伸阅读：围绕本单元主题筛选材料，帮助学生进一步了解美英文化精髓。

● 课后练习题：练习题的客观题环节主要目的是检验阅读质量，主观讨论环节旨在培养学生的思辨和创新能力。

● 著名报刊介绍：每单元精选并推介一份美英报纸或杂志，帮助学生培养阅读原文的习惯。

本教材围绕时政新闻（Politics）、财经资讯（Finance）、科技导航（Technology）、生活百科（Lifestyle）、体坛风云（Sports）、文娱在线（Entertainment）、艺术名家（Artists）、教育视窗（Education）、旅途人生（Travel）、全球热点（Global Spotlight）等十个主题

展开，全部文章均选材于西方主流媒体。在课文基础上，本教材对美英两国的政党制度、经济情况、科技革命、饮食文化、体育赛事、影视产业、艺术展馆、教育体制、人文景观、宗教影响等专题逐一补充了背景信息，以便于学生深入了解。

在美英报刊知识介绍方面，本教材对当今美英的著名杂志，包括《纽约时报》《华盛顿邮报》《今日美国》《华尔街邮报》《泰晤士报》《读者文摘》《新闻周刊》《时代周刊》《卫报》《镜报》等予以详细介绍。在报刊阅读技巧方面，本教材对报刊英语的阅读方法、语言特色、文体风格、修辞手段、话语权力等逐一展开讲解，内容的安排体现出英语语言知识的层次性、语言技能的系统性以及语言与文化的关联性。

广大师生在使用本教材时，还需要注意以下几点：

- 在编写过程中，为了保持原汁原味，本教材保留了美式英语和英式英语的原貌，而没有做统一处理。
- 本教材的编排格式较多地保留了报刊英语的行文格式和特点，比如标题往往仅首词首字母大写、单引号多于双引号等。
- 每单元的教学内容大约需要三个课时，加上考试复习，全书共需 32 学时，供英语专业本科教学一学期使用。

参与本书编写的郭印、毕纪芹、高公社、马岩、刘舒展、张艳均为青岛理工大学人文与外国语学院教师，刘晓茜为齐鲁工业大学（山东省社会科学院）外国语学院教师，吕慧、李文平为青岛理工大学琴岛学院教师。

所有参编人员都是从事英语专业一线教学工作的高校教师，具有丰富的教学经验和良好的敬业精神，但是由于时间仓促和水平有限，疏漏舛误在所难免，敬请广大师生和专家同仁批评指正。

郭印　毕纪芹

2017 年 6 月

Contents

Unit 1
Politics

报刊英语阅读的方法和技巧

　　在第二语言习得过程中，阅读是获取知识和信息的重要手段。其中，美英报刊文章因其题材广泛、体裁多样、内容鲜活、语言表达生动自然，为学习者搭建了一个获得各种语言信息的平台。一方面，通过美英报刊阅读，学习者可以扩大报刊词汇量，培养和提高阅读外刊的基本能力，增强语言感知的敏锐性，提高英语综合应用能力；另一方面，学习者可以了解西方文化背景知识，提高社会认知能力，进而培养跨文化交流意识，提高综合人文素质，以满足国家和社会对于大学生应具备较高人文素养的要求。

　　社会科技发展日新月异，社会生活各个方面的新事物和新动态迅速涌现，新的词语和表达法也在源源不断地出现。报刊英语除兼具时效性和鲜活性以外，其内容丰富多彩、实用性强。可以说，有效阅读美英媒体报刊是准确把握现代英语脉搏的一条捷径。由于报刊英语在遣词造句、文章结构、题材体裁等方面都具有鲜明的特点，这决定了报刊文章的阅读策略和方法技巧与其他种类的阅读会有所不同。

　　下面就报刊英语阅读的方法和技巧方面提出几条建议。

一、学会阅读版面

　　阅读报纸之前，首先要了解报纸的不同版面及各版面的主要内容。版面是每期报刊内容编排布局的整体产物，通过熟悉版面能够了解每种报纸的主要内容的分布位置，使进一步的阅读具有针对性。美英主流报刊每期都在固定位置刊示报纸内容的索引，对比索引就可以看出报刊之间不同的版面安排。比如，我们对比《卫报》（*The Guardian*）、《华盛顿邮报》（*The Washington Post*）和《基督教科学箴言报》（*The Christian Science Monitor*）的内容索引，就可以看出三者办报风格的异同：

《卫报》	《华盛顿邮报》	《基督教科学箴言报》
News; Opinion; Sport; Culture; Lifestyle	Politics; Opinions; Style; Investigations; Climate; Recipes; Well+Being; Business; Tech; World; D.C., Md., & Va.; Sports; Crosswords & Games	News; Culture; Books; Commentary
其中，News 主要包含以下模块：World; US politics; UK; Climate crisis; Middle East; Ukraine; Environment; Science; Global development; Football; Tech; Business; Obituaries		其中，News 主要包含以下模块：Economy; Education; Environment; Foreign Policy; Law & Courts; Olympics; Politics; Science; Security; Society

有些报纸的时事新闻部分会视重要性程度提供不同的要闻索引，以方便读者快速了解时事。例如，我们选择不同日期对比了《华盛顿邮报》头版上方的要闻索引，可以看出时事变化：

- Jul. 30, 2021: Politics; Opinions; Investigations; Tech; World; D.C., Md. & Va.; Sports; Race & Reckoning; Arts & Entertainment; Business; Climate & Environment; Climate Solutions; Coronavirus
- Aug. 9, 2021: Politics; Coronavirus; Tokyo Olympics; Race & Reckoning; Opinions; Tech; Investigations; World; D.C., Md. & Va.; Sports; Arts & Entertainment

这样，读者可以根据自己的需要和兴趣来选择不同阅读版块的内容，从而减少盲目性，提高阅读效率。

二、准确把握标题

标题是新闻报道的点睛之笔，用以精要概述全文重点，通常会以不同颜色和字体表示，凝练醒目。快速而高效地理解标题对整篇新闻的领悟起到提纲挈领的作用。新闻标题在词汇、语法等方面均有显著的特点。比如，在语法方面有两个显著特点：一是某些语法功能虚词的省略现象；二是标题时态的特定习惯用法。由于新闻报道的是新近或刚刚发生的事情，新闻语言倾向于使用能让读者感受到时效性的表达形式。常见标题的时态用法可以概括为以下四种：一般现在时表述新近发生的事实；一般过去时表述往事或历史事实；现在分词表述正在进行的动作；不定式表述未来发生的行为。例如：

- New York's Transit Agency Quits Sharing Updates on Twitter (*The New York Times*, Apr. 29, 2023)
- A contest encouraged children to hunt feral cats—until the backlash (*The Washington Post*, Apr. 19, 2023)

- Trump Pressed Justice Dept. to Declare Election Results Corrupt, Notes Show (*The New York Times*, Jul. 31, 2021)
- Going to the Moon via the Cloud (*The New York Times*, Aug. 9, 2021)
- Canada to Reopen Border to Vaccinated U.S. Travelers (*The New York Times*, Jul. 20, 2021)

关于纽约交通局停止在推特上共享更新的新闻标题用了历史现在时（historical present）来表述新近发生的事实，让读者感觉这件事情的发生近在眼前。关于"一竞赛教唆孩子捕猎夜猫——遭强烈反对"的新闻是陈述往事，因此使用了一般过去时。新闻 Going to the Moon via the Cloud 使用进行时态表达"正在飞向月球"之义。关于"加拿大将向打过疫苗的美国游客开放边境"的新闻则使用动词不定式 to reopen border 表示将来的行为。

三、了解新闻体裁

英语报刊的体裁包括消息报道、特写及专栏、社论和广告。消息报道就是通常意义上的"硬新闻"，结构上一般采用典型的"倒金字塔"，即最重要的信息出现在导语中，其他信息的重要性依次降低。特写着重在某一方面，既要提供事实，又要引起读者的兴趣，因此在文笔上比较讲究。特写包括新闻特写（news features）和一般特写（general features）（廖维娜等，2008），可专门写一人、一事、一情、一景，也可就专门问题写个人的看法，并由此发展成定期发表文章的"专栏"。特写通常以独特的思想、趣味、观点、风格来吸引读者。报刊上的社论代表报纸或杂志的立场、观点，常是对某件事做出表态、提出问题或发出号召，对某行为或某人物进行臧否褒贬。社论的篇章结构与一般议论文相同，即"论点—论证—论据—结论"。广告是商业宣传的手段，通过大量使用照片及图画，做到图文并茂、形式活泼。其中，文字部分语言凝练、善用修辞、表现力强，与广告意图紧密结合。

四、正确处理生词

在报刊英语阅读中，读者会不可避免地遇到一些新词和生词。正确的处理方法包括利用构词法、上下文语境、时事和百科知识等进行合理猜测释义。

首先合理利用构词法。"词缀＋词根"的构词法在英语中非常普遍，在理解基本的词缀和词根含义、熟练掌握构词规律之后，理解由这些词根和词缀组成的单词意思也就容易多了，如 un-employ-ment、con-tribu-tion 等。除"词缀＋词根"构词法之外，缩略词是美英报刊文章的另一个常用构词手段。例如：

- ADB: Asian Development Bank（亚洲开发银行）
- APEC: Asia-Pacific Economic Cooperation（亚太经济合作组织）

- ASEAN: Association of the Southeast Asian Nations（东南亚国家联盟）
- IAEA: International Atomic Energy Agency（国际原子能机构）
- IEA: International Energy Agency（国际能源机构）
- IMF: International Monetary Fund（国际货币基金组织）
- IOC: International Olympic Committee（国际奥林匹克委员会）
- NATO: Northern Atlantic Treaty Organization（北大西洋公约组织）
- OPEC: Organization of Petroleum Exporting Countries（石油输出国组织）
- SALT: Strategic Arms Limitation Talks（限制战略武器会谈）
- UNESCO: United Nations Educational, Scientific, and Cultural Organization（联合国教科文组织）
- WTO: World Trade Organization（世界贸易组织）

其次通过上下文猜测单词意义。任何新闻都是一个语篇，都有一定的语域（register）。在特定的语域内，语言的使用是紧密相关的。单词的意义通常和语域是相契合的，具有可推测性。根据上下文正确推测贴合具体语境的单词意义，是阅读的重要方法之一。例如，对于"Boris Johnson won't need to quarantine, his office says, despite a positive test on his team." (*The New York Times*, Aug. 7, 2021)，虽然读者有可能对 quarantine 一词有些陌生，但是通过上下文语境不难猜出 quarantine 为"隔离检疫"之义（to place into enforced isolation, as for medical reasons）。

最后合理利用时事和百科知识进行推测。熟知国际政治经济和人文地理等方面的专有名词，以及一些知名企业和组织的中英文对应名称，对报刊阅读能力的提高会很有帮助。例如，White House（白宫，即美国政府）、No.10 Downing Street（唐宁街 10 号，即英国首相官邸和办公处，指代英国政府）、Élysée（爱丽舍宫，即法国总统官邸和办公处，指代法国政府）、Capitol Hill（美国国会大厦，指代美国国会）、Buckingham（白金汉宫，即英国君主在伦敦的主要寝宫及办公处，指代英国皇室）、Pentagon（五角大楼，指代美国国防部）、Walmart（沃尔玛）、J. P. Morgan Chase（摩根大通银行）、AIG（American International Group，美国国际集团）等。

五、养成良好的阅读习惯

在报刊英语阅读中，除特殊需要之外，一般应努力避免指读、笔读、唇读、默读，以及过于依赖辞典等阅读习惯。指读或笔读是指用惯用手或笔指着文章逐词阅读。但因为眼球的运动远比手指灵活，速度也更快，所以指读和笔读在一定程度上会迫使眼睛跟着手指移动，势必会降低阅读速度。同时，眼睛涉及的阅读范围不应是单个词语，而应是一些意群（sense group）。由于一个句子通常由若干结构不同的意群构成，阅读意群可以提高阅读效率。如果英语学习者过于依赖有声朗读练习，忽略速读、泛读练习，逐渐养成出声朗读、动唇拼读或在心里默默拼读的习惯，这些都会降低大脑处理语言信息的速度。另外，阅读过程中碰到生词是正常的，频繁查单词不仅会影响阅读兴趣，而且根据语境猜词义的阅读技能也得不到锻炼和提高。

　　总之，语言的学习是一个漫长的实践过程。通过阅读英语报刊，可以有效培养英语学习者的语感，提高阅读理解能力，增强精读、略读等阅读技能。同时，阅读英语报刊能使英语学习者在信息激增的时代，积极有效地获取并积累有价值的信息，了解西方文化，培养正确的跨文化交流意识。

导读

本文源自《周末画报》与《纽约时报》合作出版的2020年年度特刊《转折点》，旨在探讨本年度的关键时刻对未来的象征意义。2020年，在日益恶化的全球新冠疫情大流行中，美国前副总统、民主党人乔·拜登以创纪录的得票数在美国总统大选中胜出，这标志着共和党人唐纳德·特朗普政府谋求连任失败。然而，时任总统特朗普甚至在竞选结果公布之前就公开声明，如败选则拒绝和平移交总统权力。

本文评论了特朗普政府的执政目标、执政手段，以及对美国民主带来的负面影响；分析了美国当下民主制度的弱点以及面临的危机；认为社会两极分化加剧，良性制衡体系陷入了僵局和对抗；指出美国面临着强化民主这一艰巨任务，亟须直面种族不平等、经济不均衡等问题，只有这样才有可能增强互信、凝聚民心，进而修复民主制度的裂痕。

A Chance to repair the cracks in our democracy

By Joseph E. Stiglitz[1]

Our norm-shattering president has taught us not to take our norms for granted.

Like many of my fellow Americans, I was aghast when President Trump[2] refused to commit himself to a peaceful transfer of presidential power if he were to lose in the Nov. 3 election. And he revealed this in October, while consistently trailing the eventual victor, former Vice President Joseph R. Biden Jr.[3], in the polls.

Then, to make matters worse, Senator Mike Lee[4] of Utah, a Republican who sits on the

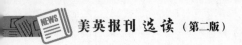
Senate Judiciary Committee[5], followed that up with this tweet: "Democracy isn't the objective; liberty, peace, and prosperity are. We want the human condition to flourish. Rank democracy can thwart that." Rank democracy? The only saving grace for such a pronouncement is that, at last, a Republican politician was being honest about his or her intentions, and this could well be a turning point in the narrative of our country and our national discourse.

If there is to be no peaceful, or even smooth, transition of power, and if people like Senator Lee have their way, and we turn our backs on democracy, then our lives and our conception of the United States as a bastion of popular representation and respect for human rights will change forever.

Over a year ago, in my book *People, Power, and Profits: Progressive Capitalism for an Age of Discontent*, I mused over the quandary facing the Republican Party. It has supported a set of policies that are opposed by the majority of Americans, who have expressed their belief in universal access to health care, better access to education, higher minimum wages, tighter gun control and so on. The only way the Republican Party can hold on to its power is through anti-democratic policies—disenfranchisement (voter suppression), disempowerment (gerrymandering voting districts) and packing the Supreme Court in order to constrain what a Democratic-majority Congress or president might have the ability to do.

We've watched what the Republicans have actually been doing, as incongruous as it might be, with their flag-waving and constant appeals to the U.S. Constitution. Now they have begun to speak more openly about their intentions. Now, perhaps, we can have a real conversation about what kind of country we want America to be. Do we agree with Senator Lee on the ends? Do the ends justify the means? Are we willing to give up on our democracy to get them? And would giving up on democracy really get us there? Certainly, history provides us with many warnings.

The past four years have made us aware of just how exquisitely fragile our institutions—such as those ensuring equality, political freedom, a quality Civil Service[6], a free and active press and the rule of law—are. When I was chief economist of the World Bank[7] some 20 years ago, we would lecture countries about creating good institutions, and at the time we looked to the United States as a model and paragon. We weren't certain how you created good institutions; we couldn't even define what the term meant precisely, but you knew it when you saw it. It involved norms as well as laws. Well-performing societies had both—the rule of law was necessary, but norms respected by all citizens had greater flexibility. One couldn't encode in laws everything implied by "good behavior". The world was just too complex and ever-changing.

A little while later, I was chair of an international group called the Commission on the Measurement of Economic Performance and Social Progress[8]. Our objective was to assess healthy economies, where citizens enjoyed a high level of well-being, and discern what went into the making and sustaining of these societies. One ingredient we focused on, often left out in earlier analyses, was *trust*—the trust of citizens in one another and in their common institutions.

When I was growing up in Gary, Ind., we learned in school about the strengths of America's democracy, about our systems of checks and balances, and the rule of law. We talked about a democracy in which the voice of the majority was heard clearly, but the rights of the minority were respected, too. We didn't talk about trust—it was taken for granted—or institutional fragility, which was the sort of thing that afflicted banana republics[9]. We looked down at other countries where money stained the political process. We hadn't yet had Supreme Court decisions like Citizens United v. the Federal Election Commission[10], which enshrined the role of corporate dollars in our politics. And we couldn't even have conceived of an America permanently dominated by a political minority that paid no respect to the rights of the majority.

Well, for the past few years we've had a norm-shattering president. He has taught us not to take our norms for granted, and made it clear that we may have to translate long-established behaviors—such as respect for the role of inspectors general, avoidance of conflicts of interest, and disclosure of tax returns—into laws.

I hope this pivotal juncture in our national discourse will not be a turning point in the course of the nation. If those who disdain democracy like President Trump and Senator Lee continue to call the tune, history tells us where it will lead, and we have already seen hints. The abduction of peaceful protesters by inadequately identified security personnel in unmarked cars in Portland, Ore., last summer instills in us an ugly sense of foreboding, and carries with it the sour odor of Hitler's Brownshirts[11]—as do the claims of a president that he is, quite simply, above the law, or the results of a free and fair election.

Assuming, however, that our democracy survives, this pivot point may turn us in quite a different direction: We will now face the even more daunting yet invigorating task of reinforcing our democracy. We've seen the weaknesses, the fragility in its structure. We've seen the destructive dynamic of money in our politics, how it undermines trust and creates conditions that exacerbate societal inequalities. We've seen how this process leads to greater polarization, transforming a virtuous system of checks and balances into one of gridlock and confrontation.

We won't succeed in restoring trust and a sense of social cohesion until we confront, head on,

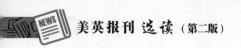

our intertwined racial, ethnic and economic inequalities. These schisms inevitably divide us and undermine the solidarity democracy demands.

（From *The New York Times*, Dec. 8, 2020）

NOTES

1. **Joseph E. Stiglitz**：约瑟夫·斯蒂格利茨（1943—），美国经济学家，哥伦比亚大学教授，2001 年诺贝尔经济学奖得主。他曾任美国总统经济顾问委员会成员及主席，世界银行副行长兼首席经济学家，国际经济学协会主席。

2. **President Trump**：第 45 任美国总统唐纳德·特朗普（Donald Trump）。特朗普生于 1946 年，美国共和党人、房地产商，2016 年当选美国总统。2020 年 11 月 7 日，民主党候选人约瑟夫·拜登赢得 2020 年美国总统大选，特朗普败选。

3. **Joseph R. Biden Jr.**：第 46 任美国总统小约瑟夫·罗宾内特·拜登。拜登生于 1942 年，1970 年开始从政，1988 年、2008 年竞选美国总统未果，2008 年、2012 年辅助美国前总统奥巴马并出任美国副总统，2020 年赢得美国总统大选。

4. **Senator Mike Lee**：迈克·李（1971—），时任美国犹他州共和党参议员。

5. **Senate Judiciary Committee**：参议院司法委员会，是美国参议院历史最悠久、最有权力的立法委员会之一，负责监督参议院任命最高法院法官和联邦法官。其成员通常由民主和共和两党代表担任，在参议院占多数的政党所占席位也多。

6. **Civil Service**：政府文职机构，这里统称行政工作人员。

7. **The World Bank**：世界银行，世界银行集团的简称。世界银行是一个成立于 1945 年的联合国专门机构，包括国际复兴开发银行、国际开发协会、国际金融公司、多边投资担保机构和国际投资争端解决中心五个成员机构。其宗旨是向成员国提供贷款和进行投资，以推进国际贸易均衡发展。

8. **Commission on the Measurement of Economic Performance and Social Progress**：经济表现和社会进步衡量委员会，于 2008 年 2 月在法国前总统萨科齐的要求下成立。其主要成员包括诺贝尔经济学奖获得者约瑟夫·斯蒂格利茨、阿马蒂亚·森（Amartya Sen）及法国经济学家让–保罗·菲图西（Jean-Paul Fitouss），其任务是研究国内生产总值（GDP）作为经济表现和社会进步指标的局限性，并评估其他衡量社会进步指标的可行性。

9. **banana republics**：香蕉共和国。香蕉共和国是一个政治专有名词，通常指中美洲或南美洲的一些国家，经济上为单一经济体系（如香蕉、可可等），政治上不民主或不稳定，往往高度依赖外援。

10. **Citizens United v. the Federal Election Commission**：联合公民诉联邦选举委员会案，美国联邦最高法院 2010 年 1 月 21 日判决的一场具有重要意义的诉讼案。该案判定两党选举改革法案条款限制了商业机构资助联邦选举候选人，违反了宪法中的言论自由原则，因此判决取消了美国企业的政治献金限制。反对者认为这一判决将导致大量资金介入竞选活动，腐蚀民主政治。

11. **Hitler's Brownshirts**：冲锋队，指以阿道夫·希特勒为领袖的德国纳粹党武装组织，其队员穿褐色制服，因此也称"褐衫队"。冲锋队成立于 1921 年 8 月 3 日，宣誓为纳粹党效力并追随领袖希特勒。该组织最初主要从事破坏革命运动、冲击其他党派群众集会及进行街头殴斗等活动。

USEFUL WORDS

abduction	[æb'dʌkʃn]	*n.*	kidnapping 诱拐
bastion	['bæstiən]	*n.*	sb. or sth. regarded as providing strong defense or support, especially for a belief or cause, or a place where there are such people 堡垒；捍卫者；防御工事
confrontation	[ˌkɒnfrʌn'teɪʃn]	*n.*	~ *with sb.*; ~ *between A and B* a situation in which there is an angry disagreement between people or groups who have different opinions 对抗；对峙；冲突对抗
daunt	[dɔːnt]	*v.*	~ *sb.* to make sb. feel nervous and less confident about doing sth. 使胆怯；使气馁；使失去信心威吓
discern	[dɪ'sɜːn]	*v.*	to know, recognize or understand sth., especially sth. that is not obvious 觉察出；识别；了解
disdain	[dɪs'deɪn]	*v.*	~ *sb./sth.*; ~ *to do sth.* to think that sb./sth. is not good enough to deserve your respect 蔑视；鄙视
disempowerment	[dɪsɪm'paʊəmənt]	*n.*	失权；无力感
disenfranchisement	[dɪsɪn'fræntʃɪzmənt]	*n.*	剥夺公民选举权；剥夺穷人的权利
enshrine	[ɪn'ʃraɪn]	*v.*	~ *sth. (in sth.)* to make a law, right, etc. respected or official, especially by stating it in an important written document 把（法律、权利等）奉为神圣；把……庄严地载入
exacerbate	[ɪg'zæsəbeɪt]	*v.*	~ *sth.* to make sth. worse, especially a disease or problem 使恶化；使加剧；使加重
exquisitely	[ɪk'skwɪzɪtli]	*adv.*	in a delicate manner 精美的，精致的；剧烈的，强烈的
foreboding	[fɔː'bəʊdɪŋ]	*n.*	a strong feeling that sth. unpleasant or dangerous is going to happen （对不祥或危险事情的）强烈预感
gerrymander	['dʒerimændə(r)]	*v.*	~ *sth.* to change the size and borders of an area for voting in order to give an unfair advantage to one party in an election 不公正地改划（选区），不公正地划分（选区）（旨在使某政党获得优势）
gridlock	['grɪdlɒk]	*n.*	a situation in which people with different opinions are not able to agree with each other and so no action can be taken 僵局（因意见分歧而无法采取行动）
incongruous	[ɪn'kɒŋgruəs]	*adj.*	unsuitable or out of place in a specific setting or context; not in accord or consistent with sth.; strange because of being very different from other things that happen or exist in

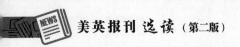

			the same situation 不合适的；不相称的；不协调的
instill	[ɪnˈstɪl]	v.	to impress ideas, principles, or teachings gradually on sb.'s mind；to make sb. have a particular feeling or belief 慢慢灌输
intertwine	[ˌɪntəˈtwaɪn]	v.	to be connected so as to be difficult to separate （使）紧密关联
invigorating	[ɪnˈvɪɡəreɪtɪŋ]	adj.	making sb. feel healthier, less tired, and more energetic 令人充满活力的；使人精力充沛的
juncture	[ˈdʒʌŋktʃə(r)]	n.	a particular point or stage in an activity or a series of events 特定时刻；关头
pack	[pæk]	v.	to ensure that a group such as a jury or committee is made up wholly or mainly of supporters of one side 打包；包装（使其利于一方）
paragon	[ˈpærəɡən]	n.	a person who is perfect or who is a perfect example of a particular good quality 典范；完人
pivot	[ˈpɪvət]	n.	the central or most important person or thing 最重要的人（或事物）；中心，核心
pivotal	[ˈpɪvətl]	adj.	of great importance because other things depend on it 关键性的；核心的
polarization	[ˌpəʊləraɪˈzeɪʃn]	n.	the condition of having or giving polarity 产生极性；极化
quandary	[ˈkwɒndəri]	n.	a state of uncertainty or indecision as to what to do in a difficult situation 困惑；进退两难；困窘
schism	[ˈskɪzəm]/[ˈsɪzəm]	n.	a division into two groups caused by a disagreement about ideas, especially in a religious organization 宗派，派别，派系；（特指教会的）分立

EXERCISES

I. Vocabulary

Choose among the four alternatives one word or phrase that is closest in meaning to the underlined part in each statement.

1. Like many of my fellow Americans, I was <u>aghast</u> when President Trump refused to commit himself to a peaceful transfer of presidential power if he were to lose in the Nov. 3 election.

    A. horrified   B. pleasant   C. interested   D. satisfied

2. Over a year ago, in my book *People, Power, and Profits: Progressive Capitalism for an Age of Discontent*, I <u>mused over</u> the quandary facing the Republican Party.

    A. listened to   B. reminded of   C. took over   D. thought about

3. Our norm-<u>shattering</u> president has taught us not to take our norms for granted.

A. bringing   B. breaking   C. shaking   D. slapping

4. Over a year ago, in my book *People, Power, and Profits: Progressive Capitalism for an Age of Discontent*, I mused over the <u>quandary</u> facing the Republican Party.

A. amusement   B. surprise   C. dilemma   D. amazement

5. The only way the Republican Party can hold on to its power is through anti-democratic policies—disenfranchisement (voter suppression), disempowerment (gerrymandering voting districts) and packing the Supreme Court in order to <u>constrain</u> what a Democratic-majority Congress or president might have the ability to do.

A. hold back   B. control   C. exclude   D. give up

6. We want the human condition to flourish. Rank democracy can <u>thwart</u> that.

A. encourage   B. facilitate   C. frustrate   D. promote

7. If those who disdain democracy like President Trump and Senator Lee continue to <u>call the tune</u>, history tells us where it will lead, and we have already seen hints.

A. call up   B. be in charge   C. obey the rule   D. call on

8. The past four years have made us aware of just how exquisitely <u>fragile</u> our institutions—such as those ensuring equality, political freedom, a quality Civil Service, a free and active press and the rule of law—are.

A. successful   B. delayed   C. freak   D. weak

9. We didn't talk about trust—it was taken for granted—or institutional fragility, which was the sort of thing that <u>afflicted</u> banana republics.

A. conflicted   B. bothered   C. insulted   D. charged

10. And we couldn't even have <u>conceived of</u> an America permanently dominated by a political minority that paid no respect to the rights of the majority.

A. imagined   B. created   C. provided   D. accepted

II. Comprehension

Decide whether the following statements are true (T) or false (F) according to the information given in the press clipping. Mark T or F for each statement.

1. President Trump refused a peaceful transfer of presidential power when he lost in the Oct. 3 election.

2. It can be inferred from Senator Mike Lee's remarks that democracy is much more important than liberty, peace, and prosperity.

3. According to the author, peaceful transition of power and national discourse has a great impact on democracy in America.

4. The majority of Americans supported a set of policies enforced by the Republican Party, such as higher minimum wages, tighter gun control, and so on.

5. In order to keep its power and restrict the Democratic Party, the Republican Party carried out

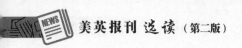

anti-democratic policies and packed the Supreme Court.

6. Twenty years ago, the United States was viewed as an excellent example of creating good institutions which involved norms as well as laws.

7. According to the author, America's democracy was satisfactory in the good old days when he grew up.

8. The author implies that politicians like President Trump and Senator Lee may harm American democracy.

9. According to the text, even if America's democracy survives, there is still a lot to do to fix the crack.

10. As long as we confront racial discrimination, we will succeed in restoring trust and a sense of social cohesion.

III. Topics for Discussion

1. Please briefly explain why the author was aghast when President Trump refused to commit himself to a peaceful transfer of presidential power if he were to lose in the Nov. 3 election.

2. Donald Trump was voted out after a single term in 2020. What do you think are the causes of his failure in the re-election bid?

3. According to the author, what are the schisms that inevitably divide the U.S. and undermine the solidarity democracy demands?

4. What do you know about the COVID-19 pandemic in America in 2020? Surf the Internet and exchange the information you get with your partners.

5. "Black Lives Matter" is an anti-racism campaign in America. Make a reference to the Internet and present your view about racial inequality in America.

美英政党简介

一、美国

美国是世界上最早出现政党的国家之一，也是实行两党制的代表性国家之一。民主党和共和党是两大主要政党，主导着美国各个层面的政治生态（表 1.1）。美国的两党制，与其政治选举制度、国会制度、行政管理制度、司法制度等的联系都非常密切。美国大选期间，报纸上经常出现两党的党徽：驴和象。前者象征民主党，后者则象征共和党。人们通常将两党的这一政治交锋称为"驴象之争"。两党制在一定程度上对于维护美国的政治稳定、保证公民参与政权等方面发挥了较为积极的作用。

民主党（Democratic Party）起源于 1792 年由托马斯·杰斐逊（Thomas Jefferson）创立的民主共和党（Democratic-Republican Party）。初期主要由种植园主、农民和一些与南方奴隶主有联系的资本家组成。1828 年，该党正式改为现名。民主党在经济上的立场偏左派。1932 年，富兰克林·罗斯福（Franklin Roosevelt）实施"新政"以来，民主党的自由派色彩比较浓，强调国家干预社会经济生活，主张建立更完善的福利保障制度。民主党的选民基础是城市中产阶级、蓝领工人、有色人种等（周鑫宇，2020）。哈基姆·杰弗里斯是民主党的现任执政领袖。

共和党（Republican Party）于 1854 年成立，初期主要由反对扩大奴隶制的北方工商业资本家组成。前身亦为民主共和党。该党于 1825 年发生分裂，其中一派组成国家共和党（National Republican Party），1834 年改称"辉格党"（Whig Party）。共和党的保守派形象更突出，被视为"社会保守主义""经济古典主义"。共和党更多地主张发挥市场的作用，强调个人自由，反对国家干预，反对国家承担过多的福利保障职能，在外交、国防问题上则采取强硬的右派态度。共和党的选民基础主要是保守的基督教白人和工农商阶层（周鑫宇，2020）。

近年来，全国性政党在代表选举和总统竞选中所起的作用逐渐增大。全国代表大会是政党的最高权力机关，每四年举行一次。大会提名下届总统和副总统的候选人，并通过该政党的纲领。民主党和共和党的全国委员会是两次全国代表大会期间的主要管理实体，其主要任务是为该党的总统候选人进行选举筹款、开展选情调研、从事政策研究等。该委员会还设有外围组织，如妇女联合会和青年联合会（周淑真等，2010）。

表 1.1　美国历任总统及所属党派

任数	姓名（英文）	姓名（中文）	任期	所属党派
1	George Washington	乔治·华盛顿	1789—1797	无
2	John Adams	约翰·亚当斯	1797—1801	联邦党
3	Thomas Jefferson	托马斯·杰斐逊	1801—1809	民主共和党
4	James Madison	詹姆斯·麦迪逊	1809—1817	民主共和党
5	James Monroe	詹姆斯·门罗	1817—1825	民主共和党
6	John Quincy Adams	约翰·昆西·亚当斯	1825—1829	民主共和党
7	Andrew Jackson	安德鲁·杰克逊	1829—1837	民主共和党
8	Martin van Buren	马丁·范·布伦	1837—1841	民主党
9	William Henry Harrison	威廉·亨利·哈里森	1841—1841	辉格党
10	John Tyler	约翰·泰勒	1841—1845	辉格党
11	James Knox Polk	詹姆斯·诺克斯·波尔克	1845—1849	民主党
12	Zachary Taylor	扎卡里·泰勒	1849—1850	辉格党
13	Millard Fillmore	米勒德·菲尔莫尔	1850—1853	辉格党
14	Franklin Pierce	富兰克林·皮尔斯	1853—1857	民主党

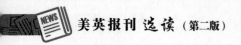

续表

任数	姓名（英文）	姓名（中文）	任期	所属党派
15	James Buchanan	詹姆斯·布坎南	1857—1861	民主党
16	Abraham Lincoln	亚伯拉罕·林肯	1861—1865	共和党
17	Andrew Johnson	安德鲁·约翰逊	1865—1869	民主党
18	Ulysses Simpson Grant	尤利西斯·辛普森·格兰特	1869—1873	共和党
19	Rutherford Birchard Hayes	拉瑟福德·伯查德·海斯	1877—1881	共和党
20	James Garfield	詹姆斯·加菲尔德	1881—1881	共和党
21	Chester Alan Arthur	切斯特·艾伦·阿瑟	1881—1885	共和党
22	Grover Cleveland	格罗弗·克利夫兰	1885—1889	民主党
23	Benjamin Harrison	本杰明·哈利森	1889—1893	共和党
24	Grover Cleveland	格罗弗·克利夫兰	1893—1897	民主党
25	William McKinley	威廉·麦金莱	1897—1901	共和党
26	Theodore Roosevelt	西奥多·罗斯福	1901—1909	共和党
27	William Howard Taft	威廉·霍华德·塔夫脱	1909—1913	共和党
28	Woodrow Wilson	伍德罗·威尔逊	1913—1921	民主党
29	Warren Gamaliel Harding	沃伦·盖玛利尔·哈定	1921—1923	共和党
30	Calvin Coolidge	卡尔文·柯立芝	1923—1929	共和党
31	Herbert Clark Hoover	赫伯特·克拉克·胡佛	1929—1933	共和党
32	Franklin Delano Roosevelt	富兰克林·德拉诺·罗斯福	1933—1945	民主党
33	Harry Truman	哈里·杜鲁门	1945—1953	民主党
34	Dwight David Eisenhower	德怀特·戴维·艾森豪威尔	1953—1961	共和党
35	John Fitzgerald Kennedy	约翰·菲茨杰拉德·肯尼迪	1961—1963	民主党
36	Lyndon Baines Johnson	林登·贝恩斯·约翰逊	1963—1969	民主党
37	Richard Milhous Nixon	理查德·米尔豪斯·尼克松	1969—1974	共和党
38	Gerald Rudolph Ford Jr.	杰拉尔德·鲁道夫·福特	1974—1977	共和党
39	James Earl Carter	詹姆斯·厄尔·卡特	1977—1981	民主党
40	Ronald Reagan	罗纳德·里根	1981—1989	共和党
41	George Herbert Walker Bush	乔治·赫伯特·沃克·布什	1989—1993	共和党
42	Bill Clinton	比尔·克林顿	1993—2001	民主党
43	George Walker Bush	乔治·沃克·布什	2001—2009	共和党
44	Barack Hussein Obama II	巴拉克·侯赛因·奥巴马	2009—2017	民主党
45	Donald John Trump	唐纳德·约翰·特朗普	2017—2021	共和党
46	Joseph Robinette Biden Jr.	小约瑟夫·罗宾内特·拜登	2021—2025	民主党
47	Donald John Trump	唐纳德·约翰·特朗普	2025—	共和党

二、英国

英国是世界上最早确立政党政治的国家，是现代政党政治的发源地，也是实行两党制的典型国家（表 1.2）。

17 世纪复辟王朝时期，英国诞生了辉格党和托利党（Tory Party）这两大政党，当时辉格党代表新兴资产阶级和新贵族的利益，主张限制王权、提高议会权力；托利党代表地主贵族利益，维护君主特权。随着资产阶级的发展，辉格党以自由贸易的工厂主为核心，在原来的基础上组成自由党（Liberal Party）。托利党以土地贵族为核心，在原来的基础上组成保守党（Conservative Party）。19 世纪末 20 世纪初，自由党逐步衰落。1924 年后，工党（Labour Party）取代自由党，与保守党轮流执政。到 20 世纪 80 年代末，英国除保守党和工党两大政党之外，还有自由民主党（Liberal Democrat Party）、苏格兰民族党（Scottish National Party）等。其中，自由民主党是比较重要的第三政党，通常能够获得 20% 左右的选票。虽然这样的支持率不足以组建政府，但往往能够对保守党和工党的执政前景产生决定性影响。

1979 年，保守党在撒切尔夫人（Margaret Thatcher）的带领下赢得大选后，致力于反对国有化，削弱工会权力，倡导经济自由主义。与之相对，工党推动政治体制改革比较积极；经济上推行国有化，强调一定程度的国家干涉，主张建立福利型国家。现任首相基尔·斯塔默（Keir Starmer）是工党的党魁。

表 1.2　英国历任首相及所属党派

任数	姓名（英文）	姓名（中文）	任期	所属党派
1	Robert Walpole	罗伯特·沃波尔	1721—1742	辉格党
2	Spencer Compton	斯宾塞·康普顿	1742—1743	辉格党
3	Henry Pelham	亨利·佩勒姆	1743—1754	辉格党
4	Thomas Pelham-Holles	托马斯·佩勒姆 – 霍利斯	1754—1756	辉格党
5	William Cavendish	威廉·卡文迪许	1756—1757	辉格党
6	Thomas Pelham-Holles	托马斯·佩勒姆 – 霍利斯	1757—1762	辉格党
7	John Stuart	约翰·斯图尔特	1762—1763	托利党
8	George Grenville	乔治·格伦维尔	1763—1765	辉格党
9	Charles Watson-Wentworth	查尔斯·沃森 – 文特沃斯	1765—1766	辉格党
10	William Pitt	威廉·皮特	1766—1768	辉格党
11	Augustus Henry Fitzroy	奥古斯都·亨利·菲茨罗伊	1768—1770	辉格党
12	Frederick North	腓特烈·诺斯	1770—1782	托利党
13	Charles Watson-Wentworth	查尔斯·沃森 – 文特沃斯	1782	辉格党
14	William Petty	威廉·配第	1782—1783	辉格党

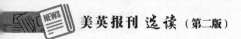

续表

任数	姓名（英文）	姓名（中文）	任期	所属党派
15	William Bentinck	威廉·本廷克	1783	托利党/联合内阁
16	William Pitt	威廉·皮特	1783—1801	托利党
17	Henry Addington	亨利·阿丁顿	1801—1804	托利党
18	William Pitt	威廉·皮特	1804—1806	托利党
19	William Wyndam Grenville	威廉·温德姆·格伦维尔	1806—1807	辉格党/联合内阁
20	William Bentinck	威廉·本廷克	1807—1809	托利党
21	Spencer Perceval	斯宾塞·珀西瓦尔	1809—1812	托利党
22	Robert Banks Jenkinson	罗伯特·班克斯·詹金逊	1812—1827	托利党
23	George Canning	乔治·坎宁	1827	托利党
24	Frederick John Robinson	弗雷德里克·约翰·罗宾逊	1827—1828	托利党
25	Arthur Wellesley	阿瑟·韦尔斯利	1828—1830	托利党
26	Charles Grey	查尔斯·格雷	1830—1834	辉格党
27	William Lamb	威廉·兰姆	1834	辉格党
28	Arthur Wellesley	阿瑟·韦尔斯利	1834	保守党
29	Robert Peel	罗伯特·皮尔	1834—1835	保守党
30	William Lamb	威廉·兰姆	1835—1841	辉格党
31	Robert Peel	罗伯特·皮尔	1841—1846	保守党
32	John Russell	约翰·罗素	1846—1851	辉格党
33	Edward Smith-Stanley	爱德华·史密斯－斯坦利	1852	保守党
34	George Hamilton-Gordon	乔治·汉密尔顿－戈登	1852—1855	保守党/联合内阁
35	Henry John Temple Palmerston	亨利·约翰·坦普尔·帕麦斯顿	1855—1858	辉格党
36	Edward Smith-Stanley	爱德华·史密斯－斯坦利	1858—1859	保守党
37	Henry John Temple Palmerston	亨利·约翰·坦普尔·帕麦斯顿	1859—1865	自由党
38	John Russell	约翰·罗素	1865—1866	自由党
39	Edward Smith-Stanley	爱德华·史密斯－斯坦利	1866—1868	保守党
40	Benjamin Disraeli	本杰明·迪斯雷利	1868	保守党
41	William Ewart Gladstone	威廉·尤尔特·格莱斯顿	1868—1874	自由党
42	Benjamin Disraeli	本杰明·迪斯雷利	1874—1880	保守党
43	William Ewart Gladstone	威廉·尤尔特·格莱斯顿	1880—1885	自由党
44	Robert Gascoyne-Cecil	罗伯特·盖斯科因－塞西尔	1885—1886	保守党

续表

任数	姓名（英文）	姓名（中文）	任期	所属党派
45	William Ewart Gladstone	威廉·尤尔特·格莱斯顿	1886	自由党
46	Robert Gascoyne-Cecil	罗伯特·盖斯科因－塞西尔	1886—1892	保守党
47	William Ewart Gladstone	威廉·尤尔特·格莱斯顿	1892—1894	自由党
48	Archibald Philip Primrose	阿奇博尔德·菲利普·普里姆罗斯	1894—1895	自由党
49	Robert Gascoyne-Cecil	罗伯特·盖斯科因－塞西尔	1895—1902	保守党
50	Arthur James Balfour	阿瑟·詹姆斯·贝尔福	1902—1905	保守党
51	Henry Campbell-Bannerman	亨利·坎贝尔·班纳曼	1905—1908	自由党
52	Herbert Henry Asquith	赫伯特·亨利·阿斯奎斯	1908—1916	自由党
53	David Lloyd George	大卫·劳合·乔治	1916—1922	联合内阁
54	Andrew Bonar Law	安德鲁·博纳·劳	1922—1923	保守党
55	Stanley Baldwin	斯坦利·鲍德温	1923—1924	保守党
56	James Ramsay MacDonald	詹姆士·拉姆齐·麦克唐纳	1924	工党
57	Stanley Baldwin	斯坦利·鲍德温	1924—1929	保守党
58	James Ramsay MacDonald	詹姆士·拉姆齐·麦克唐纳	1929—1935	工党/国民内阁
59	Stanley Baldwin	斯坦利·鲍德温	1935—1937	保守党/国民内阁
60	Arthur Neville Chamberlain	阿瑟·尼维尔·张伯伦	1937—1940	保守党/国民内阁
61	Winston Leonard Spencer Churchill	温斯顿·伦纳德·斯宾塞·丘吉尔	1940—1945	保守党/联合内阁过渡政府
62	Clement Richard Attlee	克莱门特·理查德·艾德礼	1945—1951	工党
63	Winston Leonard Spencer Churchill	温斯顿·伦纳德·斯宾塞·丘吉尔	1951—1955	保守党
64	Robert Anthony Eden	罗伯特·安东尼·艾登	1955—1957	保守党
65	Harold Macmillan	哈罗德·麦克米伦	1957—1963	保守党
66	Alec Douglas-Home	亚历克·道格拉斯－霍姆	1963—1964	保守党
67	Harold Wilson	哈罗德·威尔逊	1964—1970	工党
68	Edward Heath	爱德华·希思	1970—1974	保守党
69	Harold Wilson	哈罗德·威尔逊	1974—1976	工党
70	James Callaghan	詹姆斯·卡拉汉	1976—1979	工党
71	Margaret Hilda Thatcher	玛格丽特·希尔达·撒切尔	1979—1990	保守党
72	John Major	约翰·梅杰	1990—1997	保守党

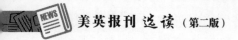

续表

任数	姓名（英文）	姓名（中文）	任期	所属党派
73	Anthony Charles Lynton Blair	安东尼·查尔斯·林顿·布莱尔	1997—2007	工党
74	Gordon Brown	戈登·布朗	2007—2010	工党
75	David William Donald Cameron	戴维·威廉·唐纳德·卡梅伦	2010—2016	保守党/联合内阁
76	Theresa Mary May	特雷莎·梅	2016—2019	保守党/联合内阁
77	Boris Johnson	鲍里斯·约翰逊	2019—2022	保守党/联合内阁
78	Elizabeth Truss	伊丽莎白·特拉斯	2022	保守党/联合内阁
79	Rishi Sunak	里希·苏纳克	2022—2024	保守党/联合内阁
80	Keir Starmer	基尔·斯塔默	2024—	工党

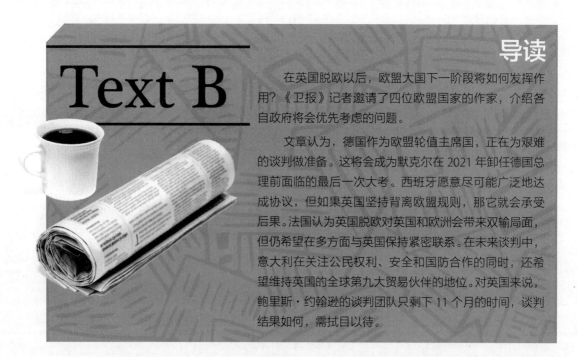

Text B

导读

在英国脱欧以后，欧盟大国下一阶段将如何发挥作用？《卫报》记者邀请了四位欧盟国家的作家，介绍各自政府将会优先考虑的问题。

文章认为，德国作为欧盟轮值主席国，正在为艰难的谈判做准备。这将会成为默克尔在 2021 年卸任德国总理前面临的最后一次大考。西班牙愿意尽可能广泛地达成协议，但如果英国坚持背离欧盟规则，那它就会承受后果。法国认为英国脱欧对英国和欧洲会带来双输局面，但仍希望在多方面与英国保持紧密联系。在未来谈判中，意大利在关注公民权利、安全和国防合作的同时，还希望维持英国的全球第九大贸易伙伴的地位。对英国来说，鲍里斯·约翰逊的谈判团队只剩下 11 个月的时间，谈判结果如何，需拭目以待。

Europe's British question: How will the EU's big powers play the next phase?

By Stefan Kornelius, Xavier Mas de Xaxàs, Sylvie Kauffmann, Philippe Ricard,

Francesca Sforza, Alberto Simoni and Patrick Wintour

The UK and EU must now work out their future relationship. We asked writers in four EU capitals what their governments will prioritise.

Berlin: The political class is divided on how harsh to be

The German government is bracing itself for tough negotiations. Berlin sees the UK's decision to put a 31 December time limit on the process as a tactical manoeuvre by Boris Johnson[1], calculated to step up the pressure on the EU towards the end of 2020. Germany holds the EU presidency until the end of December and will have to oversee negotiations on the next EU budget, which will involve juggling increasingly difficult demands. It will also be the last major test for Chancellor Angela Merkel, coming shortly before she leaves office in 2021.

According to officials, a bare-bones EU-UK trade agreement that obviates only the introduction of customs duties and import quotas is fully negotiable within this time. If the agreement touches only on areas the EU has sole responsibility for, it will be quickly ratified. Greater difficulties arise in what are known as "mixed" agreements, where member states themselves also retain power. Here, national or even regional parliaments must agree, and ratification can take at least two years.

The German government no longer expects agreement on the "level playing field" provisions (outlawing competition by undercutting EU standards). London is unlikely to automatically submit to EU rules. Still, Berlin is determined not to allow EU environmental protection standards, social policies or data protection to be undermined.

Stefan Kornelius writes for Süddeutsche Zeitung[2]

Madrid: Looming on the horizon is Gibraltar

Spain knows the road ahead won't be easy. The levels of bilateral economic interdependence, both trading and financial, are intense. Both nations have hundreds of thousands of citizens working and living in each other's territories. Tourism—some 19 million British tourists visit Spain every year, where they spend about €13.3bn—fishing, agriculture and aviation are all big sectors. And of course, looming large is the Rock of Gibraltar[3], the British colony that Spain aspires, some day, to recover.

The UK withdrawal agreement seems to have shielded the rights of these people, including their professional qualifications, pensions and health coverage, but many questions remain around labour and mobility rights. "Spain will be very forceful in protecting these rights," says its foreign affairs ministry. Spain, as a new net contributor to the EU, will have more power to flex its muscles on this point in the coming year.

From now, however, everything depends on how the UK plays its cards. Madrid is willing to

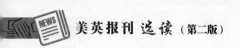

make the agreement as broad as possible, but if London insists on diverging from EU rules—for instance, by making it difficult for people to move back and forth, undercutting regulations and detaching from the internal market—Spain will stand firm with Michel Barnier's[4] position. And if that happens, the British will find it very difficult to move, sell their services and do business on the continent.

Xavier Mas de Xaxàs writes for La Vanguardia[5]

Paris: Macron[6] won't allow anything that helps Le Pen[7]

Far from having any sense of schadenfreude, the French view the UK's departure from the EU with sadness, convinced, as Michel Barnier says, that this is a lose-lose situation: bad for the UK and bad for the rest of Europe, just when it needs to be strong in an unstable world.

Yet a certain sense of relief is tangible on this side of the Channel[8]: the Brexit saga went on for too long, monopolising the EU's time for three and a half years when there were so many other urgent matters to deal with. It had to be resolved.

The French would like the future relationship to be as close as possible, while at the same time leaving the UK in no doubt that being a "third" (or non-EU) country is always less advantageous than being a fully paid-up member. In Paris, there are fears that a successful Brexit will be seized on by French Eurosceptics, starting with Marine Le Pen—something that would augur badly for Macron in the presidential election in 2022. This is an argument against rushing the negotiations, even if it means rejecting the timetable that Boris Johnson seeks with his self-imposed deadline of 31 December 2020.

At this point, given the inability of Johnson's team to provide the rest of Europe with much precision on what he wants the UK to look like once Brexit is "done", the French can only speculate. Paris will seek to revive bilateral ties not covered by the trade agreement. In defence and security in particular, the French believe they can maintain strong links with the UK. This year marks the 10th anniversary of the Lancaster House defence treaties[9], and neither side's military has any desire to part company with the other.

Sylvie Kauffmann and Philippe Ricard write for Le Monde[10]

Rome: Cutting Britain adrift totally won't help anyone

The Italian strategy on Brexit has three pillars: the rights of 600,000 Italian citizens living in the UK, protecting trade, and security and defence cooperation. Over the next 11 months of negotiations on the future relationship, Rome doesn't intend to budge from these priorities.

However, Italy will seek to advance its interests, according to sources in the foreign ministry, while avoiding "predatory attitudes". Italy wants to keep things in balance. Peronaci[11] emphasizes that cutting London adrift wouldn't help anybody.

Italy was the UK's ninth biggest trading partner globally in 2018, a position that Rome plans to defend, if not improve. So doing the least possible to disrupt the current state of affairs is of fundamental interest. "What we want," diplomats say, "is a balanced agreement: zero dumping, and import and export quotas stripped to the bone." Business activities and credit facilities, conditions for the roughly 1,000 Italian companies based in the UK, financial channels and Milan stock exchange's membership of the London Stock Exchange Group must not be interrupted, not now and not after the negotiations—which won't be easy.

Francesca Sforza and Alberto Simoni write for La Stampa[12]

London: It's frictionless trade versus full political sovereignty

Britain knows it has taken a leap in the dark by ending its 47-year relationship with the EU. The divorce took more than three years, but Boris Johnson has given his negotiating team only 11 months to forge an enduring new settlement.

Johnson has never truly revealed his brand of Euroscepticism. In order to secure the withdrawal agreement, he largely accepted the form of Northern Ireland backstop[13] first offered by Brussels[14]. But that episode only revealed his pragmatic determination to achieve Brexit.

For the first few months of this year, before the talks start in earnest in late spring, Johnson will be able to avoid hard choices. But at some point he will have to acknowledge that frictionless trade and full political sovereignty are incompatible. Downing Street believes its diplomatic cards will produce compromise. Brussels will not want a deregulated behemoth on its doorstep. The collective discipline the EU showed in the first round of talks may be tested. The UK also believes that Germany and France, needing British defence assets, want to cooperate with the UK on defence. On foreign policy the EU 3 group, deployed in policymaking over Iran and Libya, makes Britain a necessary partner for Europe.

（From *The Guardian*, Feb. 5, 2020）

NOTES

1. **Boris Johnson**：鲍里斯·约翰逊（1964—），出生于美国纽约，英国国会保守党籍议员，保守党领袖。2019 年 7 月 24 日，鲍里斯·约翰逊正式接任特雷莎·梅，成为英国首相。2022 年 9 月 6 日，约翰逊辞去首相职务。

2. *Süddeutsche Zeitung*：《南德意志报》（又译为《南德日报》），德国的一份全国性报纸，由南德意志出版社发行，总部位于慕尼黑。

3. **Rock of Gibraltar**：直布罗陀巨岩，磐石山。它是指地处地中海西南端的一处悬崖，位于西班牙南部直布罗陀港城附近。

4. **Michel Barnier**：米歇尔·巴尼耶（1951—），曾任法国环境部长、外交部长等职，时任欧盟首席谈判代表，负责与英国就脱欧事宜展开谈判。

5. *La Vanguardia*：《先锋报》，西班牙的一份综合性报纸，成立于 1881 年，总部位于巴塞罗那。

6. **Macron**：埃马纽埃尔·让－米歇尔·弗雷德里克·马克龙（Emmanuel Jean-Michel Frédéric Macron，1977—），法国政治家，曾任法国经济部长，现任法国总统。马克龙毕业于巴黎第十大学哲学系，后进入巴黎政治学院、法国国家行政学院学习。2012 年任总统府副秘书长，2014 年 8 月出任法国经济、工业和数字事务部长。2017 年 5 月 7 日，马克龙赢得总统选举，成为法国历史上最年轻的总统。2022 年 4 月 27 日，马克龙在法国总统选举中获得连任。

7. **Le Pen**：玛丽娜·勒庞（Marine Le Pen，1968—），法国国民阵线（Front National）主席（2012—2017）。2018 年，国民阵线更名为国民联盟（Rassemblement National）之后，她担任国民联盟主席（2018—2022）。

8. **the Channel**：英吉利海峡（the English Channel）的简称。该海峡将英格兰南部和法国北部分隔开，通过东北端的多佛海峡与北海南部相连。英吉利海峡长约 560 公里，宽度在 34 公里至 240 公里，是世界上最繁忙的航运区之一。

9. **Lancaster House defence treaties**：《兰开斯特宫防卫条约》，一般称为《兰开斯特宫条约》（Lancaster House Treaties），是英法两国签订的关于国防和安全合作的两项条约，由时任英国首相卡梅伦（David Cameron）和时任法国总统萨科齐（Nicolas Sarkozy）于 2010 年 11 月 2 日签署。

10. *Le Monde*：《世界报》，创刊于 1944 年，目前是法国第二大全国性日报，也是法国在海外销售量最大的日报。

11. **Peronaci**：此处指 Marco Peronaci（马可·佩罗纳奇，1965—），曾任意大利外交部脱欧特使（2018—2020）。2020 年 2 月起，佩罗纳奇任意大利驻布鲁塞尔欧盟政治和安全委员会常驻代表。

12. *La Stampa*：《新闻报》，创刊于 1867 年，面向意大利及其他欧洲国家发行，总部在意大利都灵。

13. **Northern Ireland backstop**："北爱尔兰后盾计划"，是英国政府和欧盟于 2017 年 12 月制订并于 2018 年 11 月敲定的"退欧协议草案"的失效附录，旨在防止英国脱欧后爱尔兰共和国和北爱尔兰之间出现有海关管制的边界。2019 年 10 月，约翰逊新政府重启谈判，于 2020 年 12 月签署"北爱尔兰议定书"（Northern Ireland Protocol），取代了"北爱尔兰后盾计划"。在新的协议中，整个英国作为单一关税区脱离欧盟关税同盟。

14. **Brussels**：布鲁塞尔，比利时首都。由于欧盟总部设在布鲁塞尔的贝尔莱蒙大楼（Berlaymont Building），布鲁塞尔常用于代指欧盟。但需要指出的是，并非所有欧盟机构都设在布鲁塞尔，比如欧洲中央银行总部设在德国的法兰克福，欧洲法院、欧洲统计局、欧洲审计处、欧洲投资银行等重要机构设在卢森堡。

📰 USEFUL WORDS

aviation	[ˌeɪvi'eɪʃn]	n.	the designing, building and flying of aircraft 航空制造业；航空；飞行
behemoth	[bɪ'hiːməθ]	n.	a very big and powerful company or organization 超级公司（或机构）
deploy	[dɪ'plɔɪ]	v.	~ sb./sth. to move soldiers or weapons into a position where they are ready for military action 部署，调度（军队或武器）
diverge	[daɪ'vɜːdʒ]	v.	~ from sth. to be or become different from what is expected, planned, etc. 偏离；背离；违背
dumping	['dʌmpɪŋ]	n.	selling goods abroad at a price below that charged in the domestic market （向国外）倾销
loom	[luːm]	v.	to appear important or threatening and likely to happen soon 显得突出，逼近
manoeuvre	[mə'nuːvə(r)]	n.	a clever plan, action or movement that is used to give sb. an advantage 策略，手段；花招，伎俩
monopolise	[mə'nɒpəlaɪz]	v.	~ sth. to have or take control of the largest part of sth. so that other people are prevented from sharing it 独占；垄断；包办
obviate	['ɒbvieɪt]	v.	~ sth. to remove a problem or the need for sth. 消除；排除；打消
predatory	['predətri]	adj.	(of people) using weaker people for their own financial or sexual advantage （人，在金钱或性关系上）欺负弱小的，压榨他人的
provision	[prə'vɪʒn]	n.	a condition or an arrangement in a legal document （法律文件的）规定，条款
quota	['kwəʊtə]	n.	the limited number or amount of people or things that is officially allowed 定额；限额；配额
ratify	['rætɪfaɪ]	v.	~ sth. to make an agreement officially valid by voting for or signing it 正式批准；使正式生效
retain	[rɪ'teɪn]	v.	to continue to have that thing 保留；保持
saga	['sɑːgə]	n.	a long story, account, or sequence of events 长篇小说，长篇故事；一连串事件
schadenfreude	['ʃɑːdnfrɔɪdə]	n.	a feeling of pleasure at the bad things that happen to other people 幸灾乐祸

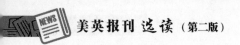

EXERCISES

I. Vocabulary

Choose among the four alternatives one word or phrase that is closest in meaning to the underlined part in each statement.

1. According to officials, a bare-bones EU-UK trade agreement that <u>obviates</u> only the introduction of customs duties and import quotas is fully negotiable within this time.

   A. obligates   B. regards   C. removes   D. obtains

2. The German government no longer expects agreement on the "level playing field" provisions (<u>outlawing</u> competition by <u>undercutting</u> EU standards).

   A. permitting; shortcutting   B. illegalizing; undermining

   C. outrunning; undergoing   D. implementing; overcoming

3. The Brexit <u>saga</u> went on for too long, monopolising the EU's time for three and a half years when there were so many other urgent matters to deal with.

   A. long story   B. sage   C. deep sorrow   D. song

4. In Paris, there are fears that a successful Brexit will be seized on by French Eurosceptics, starting with Marine Le Pen—something that would <u>augur</u> badly for Macron in the presidential election in 2022.

   A. August   B. indicate by signs   C. anger   D. remove entirely

5. "What we want," diplomats say, "is a balanced agreement: zero dumping, and import and export quotas <u>stripped to the bone</u>."

   A. removed entirely   B. insulting   C. stopped   D. increased

6. It's <u>frictionless</u> trade versus full political sovereignty.

   A. imperfect   B. fictitious   C. affectionate   D. smooth

7. The divorce took more than three years, but Boris Johnson has given his negotiating team only 11 months to <u>forge</u> an enduring new settlement.

   A. force   B. make   C. fork   D. abandon

8. But at some point he will have to acknowledge that frictionless trade and full political sovereignty are <u>incompatible</u>.

   A. comparable   B. uncompetitive   C. ill-sorted   D. incomputable

9. Brussels will not want <u>a</u> deregulated <u>behemoth</u> on its doorstep.

   A. an animal   B. an ugly man   C. a giant   D. a moth

10. On foreign policy the EU 3 group, <u>deployed</u> in policymaking over Iran and Libya, makes Britain a necessary partner for Europe.

    A. deprived   B. used   C. displayed   D. deputed

II. Comprehension

Decide whether the following statements are true (T) or false (F) according to the information given in the press clipping. Mark T or F for each statement.

1. Berlin sees the UK's decision to put a 31 December time limit on the process as a tactical manoeuvre by Boris Johnson, calculated to step up the pressure on the EU towards the end of 2020.

2. To oversee negotiations on the next EU budget is a challenge for German Chancellor Angela Merkel.

3. The Spanish government was optimistic about the prospects of Europe after the Brexit.

4. It seems that Spain is waiting to see the UK's stand.

5. The French consider the UK's departure from the EU with more delight than disappointment.

6. In defence and security matters, the French believe they can still cooperate with the UK.

7. Italy seems to be indifferent to the Brexit, for these two countries are geographically and financially aloof.

8. Italy plans to maintain trading partnership with the UK.

9. In order to secure the withdrawal agreement, Boris Johnson largely accepted the form of Northern Ireland backstop first offered by Brussels.

10. Sometimes Boris Johnson will have to acknowledge that smooth trade and full political sovereignty are incompatible.

III. Topics for Discussion

1. Why did British people decide to depart from the EU? Do you think that the Brexit is advantageous to the economy of the UK?

2. How would you predict the relationship between the UK and the EU? And why?

3. What are the major issues that the German government is considering in confrontation with the Brexit?

4. Is the German government for or against the "level playing field"?

5. Why did Boris Johnson largely accept the form of Northern Ireland backstop first offered by Brussels?

《纽约时报》简介

　　《纽约时报》（*The New York Times*，有时简称为 *NYT*），创刊于 1851 年 9 月 18 日，是美国三大主流报纸之一，也是美国公认的历史记录性报纸。该报历史悠久，在全世界发行，历来以信息灵通、言论权威著称。截至 2022 年 5 月，该报已荣获 135 项普利策奖（Pulitzer Prize）。《纽约时报》初期名为《纽约每日时报》（*The New York Daily Times*），其创始人是亨利·贾维斯·雷蒙德（Henry Jarvis Raymond）和乔治·琼斯（George Jones）。阿道夫·奥兹（Adolph Ochs）家族于 1896 年开始接管经营。

　　该报的宗旨是"天下新闻，宜而刊之"（All the News That's Fit to Print）。《纽约时报》在突发新闻、国际局势与政治报道方面享有盛誉，如对 1912 年豪华客轮"泰坦尼克号"撞上冰山沉没事件的及时报道；对第一次世界大战后签订《凡尔赛和约》（Treaty of Versailles）的独家刊载；对飞行家林白（Charles Augustus Lindbergh，又译林德伯格）于 1927 年单人驾驶单翼飞机飞越大西洋的报道；对 1945 年美国向日本广岛投掷原子弹的报道；等等。在美国的精英报纸中，《纽约时报》被称为"政治精英的内部刊物"，政府部门、社会团体都视其为重要的信息参考材料。其头版新闻深受美国新闻界的重视，已成为每日重大新闻的标准版本。

　　多年来，浏览《纽约时报》似乎成为美国民众生活中不可缺少的部分。由于该报风格古典严肃、拘谨保守，版面一片灰色，有时被戏称为"灰衣女士"（The Gray Lady）。

　　《纽约时报》隶属于纽约时报公司（The New York Times Company）。该报国际版原名为 *International Herald Tribune*，现称为 *International New York Times*。2012 年 6 月，《纽约时报》开始发行中文版。

Unit 2
Finance

📰 报刊英语的语言特色

美英报刊是我们了解西方世界的政治、经济、科技和社会文化诸多方面的重要窗口，也是英语学习者，特别是英语专业学生熟悉并掌握纯正英语的良好素材。美英报刊的题材广泛，内容丰富，语言地道鲜活，体裁丰富多样，通常包括新闻报道、解释性报道、调查报道、精确性报道、特写、社论、读者来信、广告等（王克俊，2007）。以新闻报道为例，受到报刊大众性、经济性、趣味性、时新性和客观性等诸多因素的制约，该类文章在语言运用上形成了独特的风格。

📖 一、英语报刊文章的标题特点

英语报刊文章的标题需要简洁明快，引人注目。为了达到这一目的，常用的语言手段有省略、缩略词、简短词、韵音词、一般现在时的使用等。

（一）省略

省略这一手段在新闻标题的撰写方面表现得尤为突出。

1. 虚词省略

新闻标题通常只使用实义词（content word）而弱化或省略起语法功能作用的虚词。省略常见于冠词和系动词，此外还有连词、介词、助动词、人称代词等。例如：

- Explosion at chemical park shakes German city, kills 1 (**An** explosion at **a** chemical park shakes **a** German city, **and** kills 1 **person**) (*The Washington Post*, Jul. 31, 2021)
- Syrian doctor in Germany charged with torture in Assad's military hospitals (**A** Syrian doctor in Germany **is** charged with torture in Assad's military hospitals) (*The Washington Post*, Jul. 31, 2021)

但需要指出的是，冠词省略不能一概而论，有时也有例外。例如：

- Black Lives Matter movement at a crossroads as Biden prepares to take office (*The Washington Post*, Dec. 2, 2020)（at a crossroads 是固定表达，意思是"在十字路口 / 处在紧要关头"）

- Obama in Athens: 'The current path of globalization needs a course correction'(*The Washington Post*, Nov. 16, 2016)（标题中有直接引语，不能省略）

2. 使用标点符号代替

在新闻英语标题中，冒号使用较多，主要有两个目的：一是取代说意动词、连系动词等；二是提炼出主题词，用冒号引出解释性语言，大致相当于"on/about + 主题词 + 逗号"。就引号而言，常用单引号代替双引号。例如：

- CNN's Cuomo Conundrum: A Star Anchor with a Brother in Trouble (*The New York Times*, Aug. 4, 2021)（用冒号取代系动词 is）

- Anthony Fauci's pandemic e-mails: 'All is well despite some crazy people in this world' (*The Washington Post*, Jul. 1, 2021)（用冒号取代 says；单引号代替双引号）

- A conversation with Trump Campaign Senior Adviser Jason Miller: Discussing the Republican National (*The Washington Post*, Aug. 20, 2021)（用冒号引出关于谈话的具体内容）

- 'No parallels': 2,300-year-old solar observatory awarded UNESCO world heritage status (*The Guardian*, Jul. 31, 2021)（用冒号引出被评价为"无与伦比"的具体事物，即被列入世界遗产名录的太阳观测台；单引号代替双引号）

3. 名词用作修饰语

用若干名词作定语的标题常常可以达到双重节省的效果——既节省了动词，又节省了连词或介词。例如：

- FBI releases Hillary Clinton **e-mail investigation documents** (FBI releases documents from an FBI investigation into Hillary Clinton's e-mails)(*The Washington Post*, Sep. 2, 2016)

- **UK aid money** spent trying to boost British role in **Malawi oil sector** (UK aid money: money of aid from the UK; Malawi oil sector: sector of oil in Malawi)(*The Guardian*, Nov. 21, 2016)

（二）缩略词

缩略词的大量涌现是现代英语的发展特点，这在词汇层面表现得尤为突出。无论是在报刊文章的标题中还是正文中，政治、军事、经济、文化、教育等重要机构的首字母缩略词的出现频率都很高（王克俊，2007）。例如：

- Amanda Pritchard to replace Simon Stevens as NHS England chief (*The Guardian*, Jul. 28, 2021) (NHS: National Health Service, 英国国民医疗保健制度)
- BBC Olympics coverage misses events after loss of TV rights (*The Guardian*, Jul. 25, 2021) (BBC: British Broadcasting Station, 英国广播公司)

此类缩略词不胜枚举，再如：

- CPI (Consumer Price Index)：居民消费价格指数
- IOC (International Olympic Committee)：国际奥林匹克委员会
- ISO (International Organization for Standardization)：国际标准化组织
- OPEC (Organization of Petroleum Exporting Countries)：欧佩克，石油输出国组织
- GDP (Gross Domestic Product)：国内生产总值
- GNP (Gross National Product)：国民生产总值

英语报刊也常用其他形式的缩略词——截短词（clipping）。例如：

- advertisement：ad（截后段 ）
- caravan：van（截前段 ）
- influenza：flu（前后均截 ）

（三）简短词

简单词和短词短小精悍、通俗易懂，能够降低读者的阅读门槛，以争取更大的读者群，同时亦能节省篇幅，因此简单词和短词常常受报刊文章标题的青睐。例如：

- Biden **vows** his support for the 'critical role' the arts play in America (vow: promise) (*The Washington Post*, Jun. 4, 2021)
- U.S. men's soccer team **backs** women in equal-pay fight, saying USWNT should have been paid more (back: support) (*The Washington Post*, Jul. 30, 2021)

类似的情况还有很多，例如：

- aid: help/assist（帮助，援助 ）
- axe: dismiss/reduce（解雇；减少 ）
- drive: campaign（运动 ）
- due: schedule（安排；预定 ）
- top: exceed（超过 ）
- slump: drop drastically（暴跌 ）

- vie: compete（竞争）
- woo: seek to win（争取，追求）

（四）韵音词

韵音词能够赋予语言灵动的乐感和韵律。在标题中使用韵音词能够达到让人赏心悦目，甚至过目难忘的效果。以下两例分别通过使用押头韵（alliteration）和押尾韵（end rhyme）的修辞手法，达到了这一效果。例如：

- Why Are India and the U.S. Sparring Over a $110 **Million Mumbai Mansion**? (*The New York Times*, Jul. 27, 2021)
- **Stay away**, or **pay, says** Victoria Police (*The Guardian*, Sept. 18, 2020)

（五）一般现在时

为强调新闻的真实性和即时性，新闻英语常用一般现在时来表示刚发生或正在发生的事情。例如：

- Judge **rules** in Bob Dylan's favour in lawsuit over $300m sale of songs (*The Guardian*, Jul. 30, 2021)
- UK minister **seeks** to calm row over France COVID travel curbs (*The Guardian*, Aug. 1, 2021)

二、英语报刊文章的词句特点

（一）使用转喻和提喻

转喻（metonymy）是指用一个与被比喻的事物有联系的词来替换被比喻事物的名称。提喻（synecdoche）是指用物体的部分名称来指代整体，或以整体名称来指代部分。在美英报刊文章中，这两种修辞手段常用于凝练篇幅，并增加行文的生动性（廖维娜、杨静，2008）。例如：

- White House appoints new director to steer key climate change report. (*The Washington Post*, Jul. 13, 2021) (White House: the U.S. government)
- Meanwhile, Paris gets ready to welcome migrants in a new urban center. (*The Washington Post*, Sept. 17, 2016) (Paris: France)

类似的用法还有很多，例如：

- Moscow：俄罗斯或俄罗斯政府

- Waterloo：滑铁卢战役
- Donkey：美国民主党

（二）语言准确具体、生动有趣

具体词汇表达的语义更准确、更生动，因此新闻报道中往往用具体词汇代替抽象词汇。例如，Quakes rattle New Zealand but no reports of major damage（*The Washington Post*, Apr. 26, 2023）中 rattle 的意思是 make nervous，但 rattle 是拟声词，较为形象具体，容易给人留下深刻的印象。又如：

- Biden must embrace his own logic on voting rights. (*The Washington Post*, Jul. 14, 2021)（embrace 由"拥抱"引申为"欣然接受"，语义比 accept 更加生动鲜活）

使用隐喻（metaphor）的新闻往往借助词汇的联想意义和情感意义来增加语言的趣味性。例如：

- sexy（性感的）：attractive（吸引人的）/interesting（有趣的）
- divorce（离婚）：break up of relationship（关系破裂）
- marriage/wedding（结婚、联姻）：close association or union（亲密的关系或联盟）
- war（战争）：conflict（冲突）、argument（辩论）、quarrel（争吵）、competition（竞争）、contest（比赛）

（三）使用新词

报刊英语常常通过借用行业词汇、旧词新用、创造新词等手段，让语言保持新鲜有趣。

行业词汇，特别是商业词汇、科技词汇等，极大地丰富了新闻词汇，新闻英语有时借用此类词汇表达某种新的含义。例如：

- Can European shuttle diplomacy avert war in Ukraine? (*The Washington Post*, Feb. 12, 2023)（shuttle diplomacy 在这里指的是"穿梭外交"，即为解决某一问题，一国代表频繁来往于有关国家和地区之间的外交活动）
- One unfortunate covect is that my favorite restaurant went out of business. (*The New York Times*, Mar. 30, 2023)（covect 用来表示"新冠疫情后续影响"）

有时旧词词义经过变化，还会产生新的用法，如 plastic 在"塑料"的基础上发生转义，可以表示"信用卡"。此外，报刊英语中偶尔会有使用俚语、行话的情况，使文章更加生动亲切。例如，DeSantis sacked me for doing my job as a prosecutor. Who's next?（*The Washington Post*, Apr. 12, 2022）一句中的 sacked 是英语俚语，表示"解雇"之义。

不少新闻记者为了增加文章的吸引力，在语言上刻意求新，不断创造新的词汇和

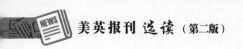

表达法，如 dawk（中间派）是 dove（温和派，鸽派）和 hawk（好战派，鹰派）的混成词。类似的还有 webinar（web + seminar，网络研讨会）、Brexit（British + exit，英国脱欧）等。

（四）使用分隔结构和套嵌结构

分隔结构（split structure）是指在句子中额外插入其他成分，或把句子中某些成分从原来的位置上移走，造成连贯句子的分裂。同位语和插入语是常见的分隔结构形式，其两端通常用逗号或破折号标识。例如：

- The interior minister, **Gérald Darmanin**, said on Twitter that 19 demonstrators were arrested, including 10 in Paris. (*The Guardian*, Jul. 31, 2021)

该句中，Gérald Darmanin 是 The interior minister 的同位语，前后均用逗号隔开。

套嵌结构（embeded structure）由于能够使语句传递多层信息，是报刊英语中的常见句式。在报刊英语中有时会将套嵌结构与分隔结构合用，以增加句式的语义容量。例如：

- Lord Digby Jones, **a crossbench peer who served as a trade minister under Gordon Brown**, hit out at the former Arsenal and England footballer in tweets on Friday night, in which he also criticised Sky News political editor Beth Rigby. (*The Guardian*, Jul. 31, 2021)

该句中，a crossbench peer 是 Lord Digby Jones 的同位语，该同位语又套嵌了定语从句 who served as a trade minister under Gordon Brown，传递了多层信息。

- The governors of three prefectures near Tokyo were due to ask the government to declare full states of emergency for their regions, the economy minister Yasutoshi Nishimura, **who leads Japan's coronavirus response**, told a parliamentary panel. (*The Guardian*, Jul. 29, 2021)

该句中，the economy minister Yasutoshi Nishimura...told a parliamentary panel 是插入语，其中又套嵌了定语从句 who leads Japan's coronavirus response，传递了多层信息。

综上，英语报刊文章题材广泛、体裁多样、内容丰富、信息即时、语言鲜活，英语学习者若能养成经常浏览阅读的习惯，"博观而约取，厚积而薄发"，必有助于掌握纯正地道的英语。

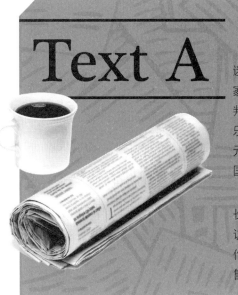

导读

美国股票未来的走向如何，是持续牛市还是渐趋低迷？普通投资者应该作何选择？本文介绍了美国经济学家伯顿·马尔基尔的观点。马尔基尔从历史的经验做出判断，未来十年的美国股市，可能不会像过去十年那样乐观。其建议之一是选持多种股票和基金债券，开展多元化的健康组合投资，而不受制于特定的行业、规模、国别等因素的影响。

时年 87 岁的马尔基尔曾担任耶鲁大学管理学院院长、先锋集团董事和美国总统经济顾问委员会成员，受访时是普林斯顿大学经济学荣休教授。他的投资经典著作《漫步华尔街》自 1973 年出版以来，已发行 13 版，售出 200 多万册（统计截至 2023 年）。

Why it's important to remember what we don't know about stocks

By Thomas Heath

The nosebleed heights of today's stock prices have me, like many other investors, a bit on edge.

Have equities become too risky? How much longer will the decade-long bull market last? Is a stock crash or a recession coming? Should I sell?

I called Burton Malkiel at his home in Florida recently to talk about the state of the stock market and what it means for average investors, people—like me—who have been stashing money in 401(k) accounts[1] or who might own stocks in taxable accounts.

Malkiel, 87, wrote *A Random Walk Down Wall Street,* the investment classic first published in 1973. He has served as dean of the Yale School of Management, as a director of the Vanguard Group and as a member of the president's Council of Economic Advisers. He is currently a professor emeritus of economics at Princeton University.

Malkiel is part of an influential cohort—along with the late John C. Bogle[2] and the legendary stock picker Warren Buffett[3]—that has warned most of us against trying to divine which stocks will beat the overall market. Most people, this persuasive line of reasoning goes, are better off investing in index funds[4] or a diversified portfolio with low fees.

But with the Dow Jones Industrial Average[5] approaching 30,000, another, broader issue arises: Have stocks, in general, become too expensive?

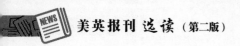

"What we can say is that relative to historical valuations, the stock market is quite richly valued," Malkiel said.

Malkiel stated the obvious: Stocks have had a tremendous run in the past 10 years, but no bull market runs forever. History tells us, he said, that the next 10 years aren't going to be quite so merry.

"We are in an era when, I think, we are going to clearly have very low returns and much lower than average stock returns," Malkiel said. "If you look at the empirical work, you would suggest the stock market over the next 10 years is likely to give you mid-single-digit returns."

As 2010s conclude, investors have enjoyed bull market for the ages—but many Americans have been left out.

Over the next decade, he said, we would be "very fortunate" to see 5 percent a year.

That's a heartburn number for pension fund[6] managers counting on 8, 9 and even 10 percent annual returns. So what's an investor to do?

Start with rebalancing, Malkiel said. "If the big rise in the stock market has put your stock holdings much higher than normal levels for you, then I would say take some out and put it in other categories."

Malkiel sits on the investment committee of Rebalance, an online financial advisory firm based in Bethesda, Md., and Palo Alto, Calif., that puts clients' money in long-term, low-cost index funds, mostly Vanguard Group's exchange-traded funds[7].

I wrote about Rebalance, then known as Rebalance-IRA, a couple of years ago. Rebalancing, in its simplest form, means buying and selling stocks and bonds annually to keep your holdings in line with your ability to tolerate risk.

"Given that asset prices[8] shift, sometimes significantly, it's normal for investors to look at their portfolio allocations periodically and rebalance, in order to avoid over- or under-weighting exposures to certain asset classes," said Shelly Antoniewicz, senior director of industry and financial analysis at the Investment Company Institute, which represents the mutual fund industry.

Take last year's U.S. stock boom, which returned 31 percent, compared with a 9 percent return in bonds.

"If you did nothing, your asset allocations will have moved to include more equity than you intended," Antoniewicz said. "If you aim for a 60-40 allocation between equity and bond fund holdings and have not yet rebalanced, your current equity allocation would be 64 percent, not 60 percent, and your current bond allocation would be 36 percent, not 40 percent. So, investors who want to rebalance back to a 60-40 split will sell stock funds and buy bond funds."

Malkiel said rebalancing a portfolio cures many ills for investors who are not—and I emphasize NOT—professional stock pickers.

"Nobody, and I mean nobody, can consistently predict the short-term moves in the stock markets," Malkiel said.

"There are a lot of people who get it right sometimes. But nobody gets it right consistently. Don't try to time the market," Malkiel said. "You will get it wrong. Ride things out. Be well diversified."

Being diversified means buying a variety of stocks across multiple industries or, better yet, holding a healthy mix of mutual funds that include large and small companies, U.S. and international stocks, and even some bonds.

I asked Malkiel whether he follows his own advice.

"Am I still holding equities? Yes," the professor said, speaking by telephone from Florida. "But I hold other things as well. I am broadly diversified. I hold fixed-income investments[9]. And I hold real estate[10]."

When asked about the likelihood of a recession or other economic pullback in 2020, Malkiel said he avoids making predictions on short-term market behavior because, well, it is just too difficult.

"The biggest threat is something that will come out of nowhere," Malkiel said. "Just think of the last few days. We have this new virus. Is it going to be contained? Is it something that affects the whole world? In [former defense secretary] Donald Rumsfeld's[11] parlance, it's not what we know now. It's what we don't know."

I can't do anything about that. But I can rebalance to make sure that I am taking a market risk that I have decided is tolerable for me.

(From *The Washington Post*, Feb. 12, 2020)

NOTES

1. **401(k) accounts**：401(k) 计划。1978 年，美国国会为鼓励国民增加养老储蓄，允许为雇员建立一种延迟纳税的储蓄计划，该计划因《国内税收法》中的 401 条第 k 项而得名。美国国税局在 1981 年发布规章，1982 年起实行。401(k) 计划是"固定分担额退休金计划"的一部分，其他还有利润分享计划、个人退休金账户、小型企业雇员配款、简易雇员退休金和货币购买计划。雇员参加 401(k) 计划时，可以告知雇主自己希望在账户中存入多少钱，缴款在计算税款前会直接从工资中扣除，因此 401(k) 是美国最方便的养老金储蓄计划之一。

2. **John C. Bogle**：约翰·博格尔（1929—2019），出生于美国新泽西州，毕业于普林斯顿大学，被称为"指数基金教父"。1974 年，博格尔以英国海军上将纳尔逊在尼罗河战役使用的船只 HMS Vanguard 为名，成立了领航集团（Vanguard Group）。1975 年，博格尔创造出世界上首档指数型基金——"第一指数投资信托"（First Index Investment Trust），之后更名为现今的 Vanguard 500。

3. **Warren Buffett**：沃伦·巴菲特（1930—），出生于美国内布拉斯加州奥马哈市，全球著名的投资家，主要投资品种有股票、电子现货、基金行业。2023 年 3 月 23 日，巴菲特以 1,040 亿美元财富位列"2023 福布斯全球亿万富豪榜"第 5 位。

4. **index fund**：指数基金。它是指按照所选指数的成分股在指数中所占的比重，选择同样的资产配置模式投资，以实现与大盘同步获利。

5. **Dow Jones Industrial Average**：道琼斯工业平均指数，又称为道指（DJIA）、道琼斯工业（Dow Jones Industrial）、工业平均（Industrial Average）、Dow 30。它是一种股市指数，由查尔斯·道（Charles Dow）和爱德华·琼斯（Edward Jones）于 19 世纪 80 年代中期创建。股指加权平均在纳斯达克和纽交所交易的 30 家最重要公司的股价，是全球追踪最紧密、关注最多的股市指数，包含了一些全球知名度最高、最成熟的公司。股指目前为标准普尔道琼斯指数公司（S&P Dow Jones Indices）所有。

6. **pension fund**：养老基金，养老保险基金。它是指企业为向退休职工支付固定生活费而投资的基金。

7. **exchange-traded fund**：交易所交易基金，又称为"交易型开放式指数证券投资基金"。该基金在交易方式上结合了封闭式基金和开放基金的交易特点，既可以在交易所买卖，也可以进行申购或赎回。

8. **asset price**：资产价格，指资产转换为货币的比例。

9. **fixed-income investment**：固定收益投资，指投资者按事先规定好的利息率获得收益投资，如银行定期存款、协议存款、国债、金融债、企业债、可转换债券、债券型基金等。一般来说，这类产品的收益不高但比较稳定，风险较低。

10. **real estate**：不动产，指由于其物理性质不能移动或者移动将严重损害其经济价值的有体物。

11. **Donald Rumsfeld**：唐纳德·拉姆斯菲尔德（1932—2021），出生于美国芝加哥，美国前国防部长。

USEFUL WORDS

category	['kætəgəri]	*n.*	a group of people or things with particular features in common （人或事物的）类别，种类
cohort	['kəʊhɔːt]	*n.*	a group of people who share a common feature or aspect of behavior （有共同特点或举止类同的）一群人，一批人
emeritus	[ɪ'merɪtəs]	*adj.*	used with a title to show that a person, usually a university teacher, keeps the title as an honor, although he or she has stopped working （常指大学教师）退休后保留头衔的；荣誉退休的

equity	['ekwəti]	n.	the value of a company's shares; the value of a property after all charges and debts have been paid （公司的）股本；资产净值
			(*pl.*) shares in a company which do not pay a fixed amount of interest （公司的）普通股
heartburn	['hɑːtbɜːn]	n.	a pain that feels like sth. burning in your chest caused by indigestion （不消化引起的）胃灼热，烧心
nosebleed	['nəʊzbliːd]	n.	*have a ~* a flow of blood that come from the nose 流鼻血
parlance	['pɑːləns]	n.	a particular way of using words or expressing yourself, for example one used by a particular group 说法；术语；用语
portfolio	[pɔːt'fəʊliəʊ]	n.	(finance) a set of shares owned by a particular person or organization （个人或机构的）投资组合，有价证券组合
pullback	['pʊlbæk]	n.	a time when prices are reduced, or when fewer people want to buy sth. 价格下跌；需求减少
stash	[stæʃ]	v.	to save up as for future use 存放；贮藏

EXERCISES

I. Vocabulary

Choose among the four alternatives one word or phrase that is closest in meaning to the underlined part in each statement.

1. The nosebleed heights of today's stock prices have me, like many other investors, a bit <u>on edge</u>.

    A. advantageous   B. worried

    C. on the periphery   D. happy

2. How much longer will the decade-long <u>bull market</u> last?

    A. bear market   B. financial recession

    C. prosperous stock market   D. bull-selling fair

3. Is a <u>stock crash</u> or a recession coming?

    A. sudden drop in stock prices   B. profitable stock

    C. accident in the market   D. stock murder

4. Malkiel is part of an influential cohort—along with the late John C. Bogle and the legendary stock picker Warren Buffett—that has warned most of us against trying to <u>divine</u> which stocks will beat the overall market.

    A. pray   B. find out by guessing

    C. worship   D. divide

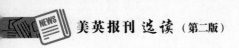

5. If you look at the <u>empirical</u> work, you would suggest the stock market over the next 10 years is likely to give you mid-single-digit returns.

    A. experimental   B. theoretical   C. ethical   D. inspirational

6. Take last year's U.S. stock boom, which returned 31 percent, compared with a 9 percent return in <u>bonds</u>.

    A. certificates of debts B. cohesion   C. relationship   D. band

7. "If you did nothing, your asset <u>allocations</u> will have moved to include more equity than you intended," Antoniewicz said.

    A. benefits   B. allowances   C. locations   D. allotments

8. "There are a lot of people who get it right sometimes. But nobody gets it right consistently. Don't try to <u>time</u> the market," Malkiel said.

    A. tame   B. doom   C. set the time of   D. save the time for

9. You will get it wrong. <u>Ride things out</u>. Be well diversified.

    A. Cycle out   B. Take a ride   C. Be stuck   D. Manage to survive

10. We have this new virus. Is it going to be <u>contained</u>?

    A. sustained   B. restrained   C. supported   D. possessed

II. Comprehension

Decide whether the following statements are true (T) or false (F) according to the information given in the press clipping. Mark T or F for each statement.

1. Stocks have had a tremendous run in the past 10 years, but no bull market runs forever.

2. According to the text, we are in an era when we are going to clearly have very high returns and much higher than average stock returns.

3. Malkiel suggested that in order to make more profits, we should bravely time the stock market.

4. Malkiel revealed that he only held equities for the sake of financial security.

5. Malkiel's suggestion to rebalance a portfolio was for professional stock pickers, rather than ordinary investors.

6. According to Malkiel, even professional stock pickers cannot consistently predict the short-term moves in the stock markets.

7. It is implied that professionally managed portfolios of equities, bonds, and other securities should be considered.

8. The profiting secret of the stock market is to stick to the portfolio you first choose and not to follow others.

9. The world is full of risks of all kinds, but the stock market is a warm harbor free from financial risks.

10. It is implied in the text that Malkiel is rather conservative about economy in 2020.

III. Topics for Discussion

1. Do you agree with Malkiel in saying that the stock market is quite richly valued? And why?

2. When looking at the year of 2020 in retrospect, do you think Malkiel's suggestions are reasonable?

3. According to the text, what seems to be the biggest threat to economy?

4. Why is it important to buy a variety of stocks across multiple industries?

5. Can you make a summary of Malkiel's opinions concerning investment in the stock market?

二战以来的美英经济概览

美国和英国分属美洲和欧洲，美国是当今世界唯一的超级大国，英国也属于世界经济强国。根据世界银行公布的数据，2023 年世界 GDP 总量为 106,171.7 亿美元，美国 GDP 为 27,720.7 亿美元，约占世界 GDP 总量的 26%，这一比例与 1960 年（40%）相比有明显下降。英国 GDP 为 3,380.9 亿美元，约占世界 GDP 总量的 3.2%，比 1960 年（5%）略有下降。对比中国的经济发展情况，2023 年中国 GDP 为 17,794.8 亿美元，约占世界 GDP 总量的 16.9%，比 1960 年（4%）有极大改善（表 2.1）。

表 2.1　美、中、英国家经济实力对比

国家	2023 年				1960 年		
	GDP 排名	GDP 总量（亿美元）	占世界总量百分比	人均 GDP（美元）	GDP 总量（亿美元）	占世界总量百分比	人均 GDP（美元）
美国	1	27,720.7	26	82,769.4	5,433	40	3,007.1
中国	2	17,794.8	16.9	12,614.1	591.84	4	88.7
英国	6	3,380.9	3.2	49,463.9	723.28	5	1,380.3
世界	/	106,171.7	100	13,169.6	13,650	100	449.6

一、美国经济概览

二战结束以来，美国作为唯一的超级大国，是经济贸易自由化的积极倡议者与推动者，同时利用自身经济优势向其他国家频繁实施单边经济制裁（economic sanctions），阻止这些国家获取经济全球化的"和平红利"（peace dividend），以实现美国利益或安全目标（储昭根，2015）。目前，美国虽然在世界经济中的相对地位不断下滑，但仍然是世界头号经济强国。其经济发展可以大致分成"经济繁荣—危机调整—持续发展—震荡前行"四个阶段。

（一）经济繁荣阶段（二战结束至 20 世纪 60 年代）

二战后初期，美国通过 1944 年确立的"布雷顿森林体系"（Bretton Woods System）、1947 年成立的"关税及贸易总协定"（General Agreement on Tariffs and Trade, GATT）、1948 年开始实施的"马歇尔计划"（The Marshall Plan）等确立了其世界经济霸主地位。从 1955 年至 1968 年，美国的国民生产总值以每年 4% 的速度增长，特别是美国西部、南部经济呈现繁荣景象。这一时期的经济发展得益于一系列因素，包括：美国政府对经济加强了干预；为应付"冷战"而加强的国民经济军事化极大地刺激了经济的增长；战后技术革命推动了经济的迅速发展；利用经济优势地位，扩大商品输出和资本输出，充分利用国外的廉价资源（特别是石油资源），以获取高额利润（张宏菊，2010）。

（二）危机调整阶段（20 世纪 70 年代至 80 年代）

1973 年 10 月，第四次中东战争（The Arab-Israeli Conflict）爆发，阿拉伯石油生产国削减石油输出量，造成油价飞涨，对包括美国在内的西方国家的经济带来了负面影响。此外，美国在外部也承担着不少压力：欧共体和日本经济的迅速发展；在与苏联展开的争霸斗争中处于劣势；第三世界国家的经济迅速发展；身陷侵越战争的泥潭。以上原因导致美国经济实力相对下降。自 20 世纪 80 年代，美国的财政赤字（budget deficit）占国民生产总值的比例不断攀升，到 1992 年，美国、德国和日本的商品出口在世界出口总额中所占比重已相当接近，分别为 12.1%、11.6% 和 9.2%。此时的美国成为世界头号负债国和贸易赤字国，在国际市场上的竞争力受到愈来愈严重的挑战（储昭根，2015）。

（三）持续发展阶段（20 世纪 90 年代至 2001 年"9·11 恐怖袭击事件"）

在本阶段，美国经济持续稳定发展，发展速度名列西方发达国家前列，进入了新经济时代。这一阶段的发展特点是由过去依赖传统产业，转化为以教育、科技为支撑的信息化，以及受跨国经济合作的有力推动。

在克林顿执政时期，美国经济有了较大发展，由高达 2,900 亿美元的财政赤字发展为国库盈余 5,590 亿美元，实现了 20 世纪 60 年代以来的最低通胀，失业率也降至美国 30 年来的最低水平。1992 年 8 月，美、加、墨签署《北美自由贸易协定》（North American Free Trade Agreement，NAFTA），该协议于 1994 年正式生效。1994 年 12 月，美国发起并建立了"美洲自由贸易区"（Free Trade Area of Americas，FTAA）。1993 年起，美国开始努力促进亚太经济合作一体化，以抗衡来自欧盟、日本和韩国经济发展所带来的挑战。

美国在重视经济自由和经济外交的同时，常常使用经济制裁的手段来应对各种竞争和挑战。据统计，仅克林顿政府时期，美国就针对 35 个国家实施了 61 次制裁。

（四）震荡前行阶段（"9·11恐怖袭击事件"以来）

"9·11事件"（2001年9月11日）是发生在美国本土的最为严重的恐怖袭击行动。对于此次事件的财产损失各方统计不一，但可以肯定的是，该事件对美国普通民众带来极大的心理冲击，严重削弱了他们因美国在经济和政治上长期一国独大而产生的安全感。

小布什时期的经济安全和经济援助政策，与反恐行动紧密联系。小布什政府敦促国会批准了《2002年贸易法》，重新确立起间断了八年的重要贸易授权（即"快速审批权"）。

奥巴马时期，美国除加大小布什政府的经济刺激力度之外，大力实施金融改革，通过改变华尔街的游戏规则以解决金融和经济安全问题。在奥巴马政府的努力下，美国国会通过了《多德—弗兰克法案》（The Dodd-Frank Wall Street Reform and Consumer Protection Act）（储昭根，2015）。奥巴马政府致力于推进全球经济再平衡，实现金融监管国际化，通过国际经济合作来解决危机，努力推动《跨太平洋伙伴关系协议》（Trans-Pacific Partnership Agreement，TPP）和《跨大西洋贸易与投资伙伴协定》（Transatlantic Trade and Investment Partnership，TTIP）两大贸易协定与机制建设，试图主导并重塑世界经济格局。

2008年9月15日，美国雷曼兄弟公司（Lehman Brothers Holdings）申请破产保护，金融危机开始席卷全球，全球经济自此步伐艰难，分化加剧。自2009年起，美国经济发展一直低于经济危机前3%~4%的增长速度，远逊于1950年至1960年和1995年至2001年的两次经济复苏。

金融危机后的美国经济增长表现出与以往诸多不同的新特征，多对矛盾并存。这一趋势的实质是美国经济处于"结构转型期"与"技术创新积聚期"两期叠加的新阶段。经济结构的调整和技术创新需要时间，其在夯实美国实体经济基础、增强发展潜力的同时，会加剧结构性失业和社会分化。页岩油气的大规模开采、大量失业及隐性失业人口压低工人工资、技术进步和数字化生产压低生产成本，令美国国内通胀缺乏上涨动力。上述新特征预计在短期内不会消失，而将成为美国经济的"新常态"，其持续时间将主要取决于美国经济何时成功转型及重大技术革命何时出现（余翔，2015）。

特朗普政府奉行经济单边主义（economic unilateralism），采取大幅提高关税和投资门槛、设置贸易壁垒等贸易保护主义措施。拜登政府上台后，公布了一揽子经济复苏计划，但仍难以根本改变美国经济所呈现的结构性衰退特征。

二、英国经济概览

英国是最早开始工业化进程的资本主义国家。1850年，英国在世界工业总产值中占39%，在世界贸易中占21%。经过两次世界大战，其经济力量遭到严重削弱。二战后，英国主要依赖美国的援助来恢复发展经济。尽管如此，由于英国工业发展历史较长，国民经

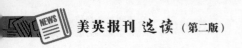

济体系和工业体系较为完整，目前仍属于经济实力较强的国家。

（一）低速稳定发展阶段（1946—1967）

1945 年至 1951 年，尽管有美国的贷款和资本支持，但是工业技术改造和工业部门建设仍需要时间，生产效率的提高并不能立竿见影，在出口贸易额没有迅速增长的情况下，英国必须进口急需的生产设备、原料和生活资料，这样就增大了国际贸易逆差。1949 年 9 月，英国政府被迫宣布英镑贬值 30.5%。从二战结束到 20 世纪 50 年代，英国从战时经济走向和平时期经济，经济领域发生了重大变化，主要表现为五个方面：（1）结束了配给制度；（2）居民实际收入得以增加；（3）消费品的国内需求扩大；（4）分期付款消费制度盛行；（5）消费者权益得到重视。

第二次世界大战结束后的 20 年，英国 GDP 低速稳定增加，私人投资的 GDP 占比有较大提高。这一阶段的经济趋势虽然是增长的，但期间出现了几次小幅衰退（如 1952 年、1955 年、1958 年、1961 年）。

（二）"英国病"的激化与缓解阶段（1967—1997）

所谓"英国病"（British Disease），是指在二战结束后，英国经济出现的滞涨状态。继 1949 年英镑贬值之后，1967 年也发生了严重的英镑危机。由于 1973 年的石油危机、1973 年至 1974 年的股市出现崩盘，英国在 20 世纪 70 年代的失业率、通货膨胀率和贸易赤字居高不下，其经济增长率在西方发达资本主义国家中相对滞后，导致英国在国际贸易和金融中的地位进一步削弱。

1979 年，撒切尔夫人当选为英国首相，率领保守党奉行新自由主义（neo-liberalism）经济主张，促使多数国有工业和公用事业在 20 世纪 80 年代都完成了私有化。随着多项宏观与微观经济政策的成功实施，英国经济开始复苏，"英国病"得到有效缓解。1988 年，英国 GDP 一度实现 5% 的增长，一跃而成欧洲经济增长最快的国家之一。在 20 世纪 90 年代，英国经济平均增速为 2.2%。

（三）震荡增长阶段（1997 年以来）

1997 年，安东尼·布莱尔率领工党，赢得大选。在布莱尔执政的十年里，英国经济连续 40 个季度实现增长，其中在 2000 年至 2009 年，GDP 每年平均增速为 1.7%，制造业每年平均收缩 1.2%，但是服务业出现了较快增长，每年平均增速为 2.6%。

不过，近年来的三件大事给英国经济带来了持续的影响。一是 2008 年的金融危机，使英国 GDP 于 2008 年和 2009 年连续两年出现负增长（2008 年为 –0.47%；2009 年为 –4.19%），虽然 2014 年（2.99 万亿美元）恢复到了 2007 年（2.97 万亿美元）的水平，但是 2015 年又降至 2.849 万亿美元。二是 2016 年 6 月，英国举行全民公投，决定退出欧盟。该事件给英国经济带来长期深远的影响。三是 2020 年以来新冠疫情带来的冲击，比如 2020 年英国 GDP 下降了 9.9%，2022 年 GDP 被印度反超。

导读

2008 年全球金融危机之后，包括美、欧在内的世界主要经济体均出现了经济恢复缓慢、长期低速增长的现象。针对此局面，2013 年，美国哈佛大学教授、前世界银行首席经济学家劳伦斯·萨默斯（Lawrence Summers）提出：美国、欧元区等西方主要经济体的经济增长可能会陷入长期停滞局面。

但与此同时，许多经济学家和政府官员并不完全同意萨默斯提出的理论。本报道是于 2015 年通过芝加哥大学布斯商学院发表的一篇质疑"长期停滞说"的论文，呈现了作者对该说法的反驳，并提供了相关论据。

Lots of economists believe in "secular stagnation[1]"—but it may be overblown

Author Unknown

Is America stuck in a rut of low growth, feeble inflation and rock-bottom interest rates? Lots of economists believe in the idea of "secular stagnation", and they have plenty of evidence to point to. The population is ageing and long-run growth prospects look dim. Interest rates, which have been near zero for years, are still not low enough to get the American economy zipping along.

A new paper published by the University of Chicago's Booth School of Business[2], however, reckons that secular stagnation is not quite the right diagnosis for America's ills.

A country in the grip of secular stagnation cannot find enough good investments to soak up available savings. The drain on demand from these underused savings leads to weak growth. It also leaves central banks[3] in a bind.

If the real (i.e., inflation adjusted) "equilibrium" interest rate[4] (the one that gets an economy growing at a healthy clip) falls well below zero, then central bankers will struggle to push their policy rate low enough to drag the economy out of trouble, since it is hard to push nominal (i.e., not adjusted for inflation) rates[5] deep into negative territory.

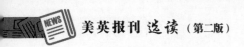
Worse, in the process of trying, they may end up inflating financial bubbles, which lead to unsustainable growth and grisly busts.

Stagnationists argue that this is not a bad description of America since the 1980s. Real interest rates have been falling for years, they note, a sign of a glut of savings. Recoveries from recent recessions have been weak and jobless.

The authors of the Chicago paper dispute this interpretation of events. Stagnationists are right, they note, that real interest rates have been falling, and have in fact been negative for much of the past 15 years. But low real rates do not necessarily imply that future growth will be weak, as many economic models assume.

The authors examine central-bank interest rates, inflation and growth in 20 countries over 40 years. They find at best a weak relationship between economic growth and the equilibrium rate. If there is a long-run link, they argue, it tends to be overshadowed by other factors.

After the Second World War, for example, government controls on rates ("financial repression") prevented the market from having its say. In recent years short-run woes have dragged down the equilibrium rate, such as the "50-miles-per-hour headwinds" that Alan Greenspan[6], the chairman of the Federal Reserve[7], described in 1991, when bad loans pushed big American banks to the brink of insolvency. The authors note that such stormy periods are usually short-lived, and that when the headwinds abate, the equilibrium rate tends to pop back up.

They also reckon the stagnationists are misinterpreting some of the evidence. Growth in the 1990s was not illusory, they argue. The stockmarket boom only really got going in 1998, after America's unemployment rate had already fallen below 5%.

The expansion of the 2000s[8] looks like a better example of secular stagnation. Rising house prices made Americans feel flush, propelling consumer spending. Expanding credit added about one percentage point to growth each year, says the paper.

Yet the behavior of the economy in this period looks more like a product of distortion than stagnation. At the time China and oil-producing states were running enormous current-account[9] surpluses with America and building up large foreign-exchange reserves[10]. Expensive oil and rising Chinese imports placed a drag on growth that more or less offset the boost from housing. The American economy would not necessarily have grown any faster or slower, just more healthily.

What about the situation now? Some of the distorting forces of recent years are slowly fading. Household finances are certainly in better shape after a long period of deleveraging. That is helping to power a consumer-driven recovery in America that will eventually lead to higher interest rates.

On the other hand, stagnationists argue that the effects of demographic change are intensifying. Baby-boomers[11] approaching retirement may be stashing more money away. Longer lifespans continue to spur saving. Experts of Cambridge University have found that the increase in life expectancy over the past 40 years in rich and middle-income countries has raised the desired stock of savings by two times GDP.

Global conditions must also be taken into consideration. The authors of the Chicago paper calculate that over the long term, America's real interest rate tracks the one prevailing across the world as a whole. Yet since about 2000 the real rate in America has generally been well below that of the world as a whole. The authors argue that thanks to the mobility of international capital that gap should soon close.

On their best estimates, America's equilibrium rate has probably fallen a little, relative to the average from the 1960s until 2007 of about 2%. But, they argue, the decline is smaller than many stagnationists believe, and the rate is almost certainly positive. Nor is a lower rate now a sign that growth will permanently fall below past averages.

That is still no reason to breathe easy. A low equilibrium rate raises the risk that central-bank interest rates will sometimes become stuck at zero, leaving an economy in a prolonged slump. Even if the risk of secular stagnation is overdone, the authors reckon that the Fed has good reason not to raise rates too soon.

(From *The Economist*, Mar. 7, 2015)

NOTES

1. **secular stagnation**：长期增长停滞。以凯恩斯理论为基础，"长期增长停滞"的说法最早来自美国经济学学会主席阿尔文·汉森（Alvin Hansen）。在 1939 年的演讲中，他认为大萧条并不是暂时的经济下滑，而是人口增长减速、储蓄过剩、投资不足引发的长期失业和经济停滞。

2. **University of Chicago's Booth School of Business**：芝加哥大学布斯商学院（原芝加哥大学商学院），创建于 1898 年，美国最好的商学院之一，以其多位学者荣获诺贝尔经济学奖而著称于世。2008 年 11 月正式更名为芝加哥大学布斯商学院，以纪念"有效市场假说"创立者尤金·法玛（Eugene Fama）的弟子、芝大商学院校友大卫·布斯（David Booth）向学院捐赠三亿美元。

3. **central bank**：中央银行，国家最高货币金融管理组织机构，在各国金融体系中居于主导地位。国家赋予其制定和执行货币政策、对国民经济进行宏观调控、对其他金融机构乃至整个金融业进行监督管理的权限，地位非常特殊。

4. **equilibrium interest rate**：均衡利率，指保持货币流通中货币供给与货币需求一致时的利率。real

interest rate 指实际利率，即剔除通货膨胀率之后储户或投资者得到利息回报的真实利率。

5. **nominal rate**：此处指 nominal interest rate，名义利率。它是由中央银行或其他提供资金借贷的机构公布的、未调整通货膨胀因素的利率，即利息的货币额与本金的货币额之间的比率，也就是包括补偿通货膨胀风险的利率。

6. **Alan Greenspan**：艾伦·格林斯潘（1926—），美国犹太人，美国第 13 任联邦储备委员会主席（1987—2006），任期跨越六届美国总统，许多人认为他是美国国家经济政策的权威和决定性人物。1998 年 7 月，格林斯潘被授予美国"和平缔造者"奖。2002 年 8 月，英国女王授予格林斯潘"爵士"荣誉称号，以表彰他对"全球经济稳定做出的杰出贡献"。

7. **Federal Reserve**：美国联邦储备委员会，美国联邦储备系统（Federal Reserve System，Fed）的核心机构，其办公地点位于美国华盛顿特区。该委员会由七名成员组成（主席和副主席各一名，委员五名），须由美国总统提名，经美国国会参议院批准方可上任，任期为 14 年（主席和副主席任期为四年，可连任）。美国联邦储备系统负责履行美国中央银行的职责，主要由联邦储备委员会、联邦储备银行及联邦公开市场委员会等组成，同时有约 3,000 家会员银行与三个咨询委员会（Advisory Councils）。

8. **the 2000s**：该表达方法有"21 世纪前 10 年""21 世纪"和"2000 年至 2009 年"三种可能的理解，其中"21 世纪前 10 年"属于通常的理解，也是本文中的意思。该阶段的世界经济处于前所未有的变化中，呈现出"新""变""乱"的特征——"新"于全球治理机构，"变"于国际力量格局，"乱"于金融危机后遗症治理。

9. **current-account**：经常账户（现金账户），反映一国与他国之间的实际资产流动，与该国的国民收入账户有密切联系，是国际收支平衡表中最基本、最重要的部分（那明，2014）。它包括货物（goods）、服务（services）、收入（income）和经常转移（current transfer）四个项目。国际收支中的经常账户（现金账户）是指贸易收支的总和（商品、服务的出口减去进口），减去生产要素收入（如利息、股息）和转移支付（如外国援助）。经常项目的顺差（盈余）增加了一个国家相应金额的外国资本净额，逆差（赤字）则恰好相反。

10. **foreign-exchange reserve**：外汇储备，指为了应付国际支付的需要，各国的中央银行及其他政府机构集中掌握的外汇资产。外汇储备的具体形式包括政府在国外的短期存款或其他可以在国外兑现的支付手段，如外国有价证券，外国银行的支票、期票、外币汇票等。外汇储备用于清偿国际收支逆差，以及干预外汇市场以维持该国货币的汇率（王明明，2009）。

11. **baby-boomer**："婴儿潮"一代，指出生于生育高峰期的一代人，此处特指美国第二次世界大战后的"4664"现象，即在 1946—1964 的 18 年间，美国出现"婴儿潮"，共有约 7,600 万人出生，约占当前美国总人口的三分之一。成长在经济大繁荣时期的"婴儿潮"一代所积累的财富极其可观，是美国社会的中坚力量。

USEFUL WORDS

abate	[əˈbeɪt]	v.	to become much less strong or severe 减弱
deleverage	[diːˈliːvərɪdʒ]	v.	(of an organization) to reduce the ratio of debt capital to equity capital （机构）减债
demographic	[ˌdeməˈgræfɪk]	adj.	of or relating to demography, the study of the changes in numbers of births, deaths, marriages, and cases of disease in a community over a period of time 人口统计学的
dispute	[dɪˈspjuːt]	v.	to say that a fact, statement, or theory is incorrect or untrue 反驳
distortion	[dɪˈstɔːʃn]	n.	the twisting or changing of facts, ideas, etc. so that they are no longer correct or true 歪曲；曲解
drain	[dreɪn]	n.	a gradual depletion 流失
equilibrium	[ˌiːkwɪˈlɪbriəm]	n.	a balance between several different influences or aspects of a situation 平衡
feeble	[ˈfiːbl]	adj.	not effective; not showing determination or energy 无效的；缺乏决心的；无力的
grisly	[ˈgrɪzli]	adj.	extremely unpleasant and frightening and usually connected with death and violence 可怕的；厉害的
illusory	[ɪˈluːsəri]	adj.	(formal) not real, although seeming to be 虚假的；幻觉的；迷惑人的
inflation	[ɪnˈfleɪʃn]	n.	a general increase in the prices of goods and services in a country 通货膨胀
offset	[ˈɒfset]	v.	to use one cost, payment or situation in order to cancel or reduce the effect of another 抵消；弥补；补偿
prevail	[prɪˈveɪl]	v.	to be larger in number, quantity, power, status or importance 胜过，获胜；占优势
repression	[rɪˈpreʃn]	n.	the use of force to restrict and control a society or other group of people 镇压；压制
rut	[rʌt]	n.	being fixed in a way of thinking and doing things, and difficult to change 惯例
soak	[səʊk]	v.	~ up to use a great deal of money or other resources 耗费（金钱或资源）
stagnation	[stægˈneɪʃn]	n.	the fact of no longer developing or making progress 停滞；不发展，不进步

EXERCISES

I. Vocabulary

Choose among the four alternatives one word or phrase that is closest in meaning to the underlined part in each statement.

1. Is America stuck in a rut of low growth, <u>feeble</u> inflation and rock-bottom interest rates?

    A. weak   B. long-run   C. temporary   D. strong

2. A country in the grip of secular stagnation cannot find enough good investments to <u>soak up</u> available savings.

    A. absorb   B. submerge   C. consume   D. swallow

3. The <u>drain</u> on demand from these underused savings leads to weak growth.

    A. drip   B. exhaustion   C. loss   D. drought

4. Worse, in the process of trying, they may end up inflating financial bubbles, which lead to unsustainable growth and grisly <u>busts</u>.

    A. vigor   B. attacks   C. wishes   D. depression

5. The authors of the Chicago paper <u>dispute</u> this interpretation of events.

    A. refute   B. discuss   C. prove   D. disagree

6. After the Second World War, for example, government controls on rates ("financial <u>repression</u>") prevented the market from having its say.

    A. impression   B. distress   C. suppression   D. mistress

7. The authors note that such stormy periods are usually short-lived, and that when the headwinds <u>abate</u>, the equilibrium rate tends to pop back up.

    A. allay   B. reverse   C. accumulate   D. stop

8. Growth in the 1990s was not <u>illusory</u>, they argue.

    A. credible   B. illusive   C. real   D. faraway

9. Yet the behavior of the economy in this period looks more like a product of <u>distortion</u> than stagnation.

    A. divergence   B. derivation   C. disturbance   D. deformation

10. Baby-boomers approaching retirement may be <u>stashing</u> more money away.

    A. slashing   B. withdrawing   C. depositing   D. dashing

II. Comprehension

Decide whether the following statements are true (T) or false (F) according to the information given in the press clipping. Mark T or F for each statement.

1. Ageing population, bright long-run growth prospects and rock-bottom interest rates are the evidence for the idea of "secular stagnation" in the American economy.

2. Judging from the news, not all of American economists believe that secular stagnation is quite the right diagnosis for America's ills.

3. If the real "equilibrium" interest rate has been negative for a long time, central banks will fall into a bind.

4. As many economic models assume, low real rates imply that future growth will be weak.

5. The authors from the University of Chicago's Booth School of Business note that stormy periods like "50-miles-per-hour headwinds" are usually short-lived.

6. "The 2000s" in the news refers to the bad economic situation in the year of 2000.

7. Expensive oil and rising Chinese exports worked together to place a drag on the growth of American domestic economy.

8. Deleveraging is the key to turning household finances into better shape.

9. A consumer-driven recovery in America will eventually lead to higher interest rates.

10. The increase in life expectancy has raised the desired stock of savings.

11. American stagnationists believe that a lower equilibrium rate implies a sign that growth will secularly fall below past averages.

12. The authors of the Chicago paper believe that the Fed will soon raise rates for the risk of secular stagnation is overdone.

III. Topics for Discussion

1. Today, even the U.S., the world's only superpower, suffers from economic woes at times. What do you think are the possible reasons that lead to this phenomenon?

2. What do you learn about the international financial situation in the 2000s?

3. In America, there are two opposing attitudes towards whether the economy will be "secularly stagnant" or not. Could you provide evidence for the different ideas respectively?

4. If you were the next chairman of the Federal Reserve, how would you promote economic growth of America?

5. Have you heard of "baby boomers"? What do you know about this generation?

6. On today's world stage, China is rising as a new power. What role do you think China should play for a healthier world economic situation in the future? Please illustrate your ideas.

《华盛顿邮报》简介

　　《华盛顿邮报》（*The Washington Post*），1877 年由斯蒂尔森·哈钦斯（Stilson Hutchins）创办，1880 年成为首家在华盛顿哥伦比亚特区每日出版的报纸，是该地区发行规模最大、历史最悠久的报纸。

20 世纪 60 年代以来，《华盛顿邮报》在前总编本·布莱德利（Ben Bradlee）的带领下，开发了新闻调查的新思路，创立了新闻报道的新模式。20 世纪 70 年代初，该报通过揭露"水门事件"，迫使时任美国总统理查德·尼克松辞职下台，获得了国际威望。此后，在关于"五角大楼事件"的报道中，面对政府高压，该报不卑不亢地回应，最终促成了越南战争的结束，影响了美国的历史进程。

由于位于美国首都地区，《华盛顿邮报》尤其擅长报道美国国内政治动态，注重报道国会消息，号称"美国国会议员与政府官员早餐桌上少不了的一份报纸"。在鼎盛时期，华盛顿邮报公司旗下拥有《华盛顿邮报》《新闻周刊》等新闻企业、斯坦利·卡普兰教育服务中心、六家电视台、一个有线电视网和电子媒体、健康保险等宽领域、多层次的业务，员工近两万名。

2013 年 8 月，华盛顿邮报公司宣布将旗下包括《华盛顿邮报》在内的报纸业务及资产以 2.5 亿美元售予美国亚马逊公司 CEO 杰夫·贝索斯（Jeff Bezos）。2013 年 11 月，华盛顿邮报公司更名为格雷厄姆公司（Graham Holdings Company）。

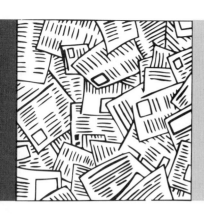

Unit 3
Technology

英语报刊文章标题的特点

标题是新闻最基本的部分之一（姚正萍，2020），好的标题能够以新颖的创意、精练的语言和独特的形式吸引读者去进一步选择相关内容阅读，发掘文章内涵，领悟报道主题。然而，有时标新立异、凝练浓缩的标题会给读者的理解造成一定困难，因此认识和学习英语报刊文章标题的特点，将有助于读者准确理解新闻重点、提高报刊阅读水平。

第二单元已经就标题的特点做过简要说明，本单元将从词汇、句法和修辞的角度对英语报刊文章标题的文体特征进行概述和分析，从而进一步增强读者的英语理解能力，同时更加了解欧美社会文化。

一、词汇特点

限于篇幅，英语报刊文章标题力求短小精悍、简明扼要，通常采用省略、缩略语、简单词、短词等词形，这些已经在第二单元有所提及，本节将主要从外来词和新词两个方面进行概述。

（一）外来词

随着世界各国间的交往日益频繁，英语作为世界语言，不断从各国语言中借用独具特色的词语，展现了新闻英语的时代性、趣味性和可读性。新闻英语标题中经常使用外来词，凸显其异域特色，其中有些词语保留了源语的格式和特征，如 tsunami [日] 海啸、attaché [法] 使馆随员、maskirovka [俄] 军事欺骗、*yin yang* [中] 阴阳等。而有些外来词经常使用，已经完全英语化，如 percent [拉丁] 百分比、tea [中] 茶、visa [法] 签证等。

（二）新词

时代发展与进步使新闻英语中的新词源源不断地出现。由于新鲜事物层出不穷，英语报刊中经常出现临时拼造的新词，并逐渐为人们所接受，如 netizen（网民）、test-tube baby（试管婴儿）、e-Post Project（电子邮政项目）等。

一个典型的例子是 Megxit，入选英国权威《柯林斯词典》2020 十大年度热词，由 Meghan（梅根）和 exit（退出）拼缀而成，指的是哈里和梅根退出王室公职的事件。国内外知名媒体针对这一事件均使用了 Megxit 进行报道。例如：

- Megxit one year on: Was it a success story for the Sussexes?（*The Telegraph*, Jan. 8, 2021）

此外，政治、经济、社会的发展也使新词不断涌现。例如，Watergate（水门事件）是在 1974 年美国总统尼克松丑闻事件发生时出现的，之后"-gate"就用来表达有关丑闻的词语，如克林顿任美国总统时的 Zippergate（拉链门事件），以及 2016 年希拉里竞选美国总统时的 Emailgate（邮件门事件）。在经济领域中有 Euro（欧元）、dehiring（裁员）、soft-landing economy（软着陆经济）等新词；社会领域有 outplacement（转岗）、home schools（家庭学校）等新词。再比如，世界卫生组织总干事谭德塞于 2020 年 2 月 11 日宣布，将新型冠状病毒病命名为 COVID-19（Coronavirus Disease 2019）。

所有这些外来词及新词都使新闻英语标题富有时代气息并新颖独到，构成了报刊英语标题特有的表达方式。只有熟悉并掌握这些特点，读者才能读懂标题、了解新闻内容，从而提高报刊英语阅读能力。

二、句法特点

（一）省略

新闻标题为了节省篇幅、突出重点，经常会省略诸如冠词、介词、连词、助动词、代词等具有语法功能的虚词，以强调名词、形容词和动词等关键性词语，使标题内容紧凑、言简意赅，在尽可能精简的版面中提供最大量的信息（陈明瑶等，2006）。其中省略最多的是冠词和系动词。例如：

- Boxer Marvelous Marvin Hagler dead at 66, wife says (Boxer Marvelous Marvin Hagler **was** dead at 66, **his** wife says)(*New York Daily News*, Mar. 14, 2021)
- Wandering bulldog rescued by LIRR crew (A wandering bulldog **was** rescued by **the** LIRR crew)(*Washington News*, Mar. 14, 2021)

（二）一般现在时

一般现在时主要用来表示现在或与现在相关的动作或状态。英语报刊中的新闻报道一般都是新近发生的事实，如果使用过去时态会给读者一种陈旧感，因此为保持新鲜感与现实感，英语报刊文章标题常常会使用一般现在时。另外，一般现在时还可以替代进行时或将来时表示目前正在进行或将要发生的事情。例如：

- Former student **sues** St. Mary's high school over 1980s sex abuse (= sued) (*Washington News*, Mar. 14, 2021)
- Maskless, urinating flyer **faces** possible prison, $250K fine (= will face) (*USA Today*, Mar. 14, 2021)
- China's worst sandstorm in a decade **clouds** Beijing skyline, **cancels** hundreds flights (= clouded; cancelled) (*Chicago Tribune*, Mar. 15, 2021)
- Pandemic **prompts** state to offer break on overdue traffic fines and other fees for low-income residents (= is prompting) (*Chicago Tribune*, Mar. 15, 2021)

（三）动词的非谓语形式

不定式、现在分词、过去分词等动词的非谓语形式也常常出现在英语报刊的文章标题中，分别用来表示即将发生的动作、正在进行的动作，以及被动语态，这样可以使标题简单明了、主题突出。例如：

- FEMA **to help** manage unaccompanied minors at the border (= will help / is to help) (*Los Angeles Times*, Mar. 13, 2021)
- GOP House Leader **to call** for Swalwell's removal from Intel Committee (= will call / is to call) (*USA Today*, Mar. 13, 2021)
- COVID **still preying** on nursing home (= is still preying) (*Washington News*, Mar. 13, 2021)
- Michigan hospital system **investigating** after photos from operating room posted on Instagram (= is investigating) (*Chicago Tribune*, Mar. 14, 2021)
- Chicago River **dyed** green for St. Patrick's Day weekend, prompting selfies and cheering: 'It's a little bit of normalcy' (= was dyed) (*Chicago Tribune*, Mar. 13, 2021)
- 1M-plus COVID-19 vaccine doses **given** in NY in past week (= have been given) (*Washington News*, Mar. 14, 2021)
- 4 people, including 13-year-old, **shot** during South Shore attack, police say (= were shot) (*Chicago Tribune*, Mar. 15, 2021)

三、修辞特点

英语报刊文章标题除在词汇和句法方面求新求简，通常还会使用修辞手法，使标题简明洗练、形象生动。本节主要介绍较为常用的三种修辞手段：比喻（metaphor）、双关（pun）和引用（quotation）。

（一）比喻

比喻这一修辞手法在英语报刊中被广泛使用，旨在使报道更加生动活泼、韵味无穷。例如，在标题"American states are now Petri dishes of polarisation"中，Petri dish 本意是指用于培养细菌的皮氏培养皿，而此处比喻美国各州现在已经成为政治极化的培养皿。又如，标题"Swimming with Bigger Fish"将商界大小企业比喻成大鱼和小鱼，将企业间的激烈竞争描述成大小鱼之间的生存之战，显得形象生动、幽默风趣（肖小月，2013）。

（二）双关

双关是指同音 / 近音异义或一词二义的诙谐用法，可分为谐音双关和语义双关两种。英语报刊的文章标题中常会巧妙地利用双关语，来同时表达深浅两层不同的含义。谐音双关的例子如"Damon Is Bourne Again"这一标题，其中 Bourne（伯恩）读作 [bɔn]，发音与 born（[bɔːn]，出生）接近。事实上，该报道讲述的是伯恩的扮演者马特·达蒙（Matt Damon）重返环球影业拍摄《谍影重重5》的经历过程。该标题包含两层意义：一是说明马特·达蒙再次出演伯恩这个角色；二是说明马特·达蒙回归伯恩系列影片的拍摄犹如再生一般，经历了痛苦和煎熬，寓意深刻。再如，在"Yao Ming: NBA Giant Is Big in U.S., Bigger in China"这个标题里，big 就是一个双关词。在口语中，big 可以表示"受欢迎的"（popular）意思，既指姚明在美国篮球界取得的巨大成功，同时暗示姚明 2.26 米的"巨人"身高，这一用法使整个标题形象鲜明、活泼有趣。

（三）引用

英语标题常常引用典故谚语、名著名篇或名人名言，以增强语言的趣味性，从而引人注目。例如，"Farewell to Arms"一文直接引用美国著名作家海明威的小说题目《永别了，武器》（A Farewell to Arms），报道了美国 20 世纪 90 年代的枪支回收运动，由此可见标题和内容十分贴切。再如，"In Rome, Using 'Roman Holiday' as a Guide"一文介绍了意大利首都罗马的游览路线，标题引用美国著名影片《罗马假日》（Roman Holiday）的片名，文章则按照影片中奥黛丽·赫本（Audrey Hepburn）饰演的安妮公主在罗马一天中所到访过的地方安排行程、介绍景点，以期勾起读者的美好回忆，激发其浓厚的阅读兴趣。

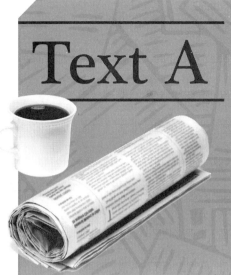

导读

在现代生活中，汽车为人们提供了极大的便利，汽车公司对汽车技术的研发也是日新月异。新能源汽车和无人驾驶汽车可以减少能源消耗，降低环境污染，避免人为失误，提高出行安全，因此越来越受到人们的欢迎。

美国特斯拉汽车公司生产纯电动汽车，并推出了自动辅助驾驶模式，使无人驾驶技术真正进入了人们的生活。但是，一起因特斯拉 Model 5 使用 Autopilot 致命的事故引发了人们对无人驾驶汽车安全性的质疑。本文就这起事故进行分析，从不同角度对无人驾驶汽车的发展和应用提出了意见和看法。

What Tesla Autopilot crash means for self-driving cars

By Greg Gardner

This summer, autonomous cars collided with reality.

All those sensors and cameras and spinning cylinders of laser beams don't know as much as we thought they did. At least not yet.

Sure, Tesla Motors[1] is taking the brunt of the public relations and political damage. To be fair, we don't yet know whether and to what extent the upstart electric vehicle maker's Autopilot[2] feature contributed to a series of recent crashes, including one fatality.

But Karl Benz[3] (the Benz in Mercedes-Benz) and Henry Ford[4] (of well...you know) had setbacks too. Billy Durant, who assembled what would become the empire of General Motors[5], was ousted from the company twice before winding up running a bowling alley.

Don't expect development to stop driver-assist technologies or the search for the holy grail[6] of full self-driving autonomy.

But still, it's time to ask what we can learn from recent events. Here are a few lessons to draw from Tesla's recent stumbles:

• **Roads.** In a country that has neglected its roadways so badly for so long, our infrastructure makes autonomous driving riskier.

• **Communication Tech.** Autonomous vehicles will depend on a much more extensive network of what is called vehicle-to-vehicle communication. Southeast Michigan is lucky to be the

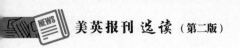

nation's first test-bed for this type of technology, but extending it to the rest of the country could take decades and major public spending.

• **Man vs. machine.** We must get over the notion that sensors and cameras can replace humans as vehicle operators, at least for the foreseeable future. Humans are imperfect drivers who make mistakes. Technology and humans together can save lives.

• **Tuning out.** The more we see autonomous vehicles as a way to "free" us to work, entertain ourselves or tune out, the longer this evolution will take.

"Everyone in the autonomous vehicle industry understands consumer over-trust is a significant problem," said John Maddox, CEO[7] of the American Center for Mobility[8], the proposed proving ground for connected and automated vehicles under development on 335 acres at Willow Run, where the U.S. produced B-24 bombers during World War II. "No one has an answer to that problem yet, to be perfectly blunt."

At the heart of the recent Tesla crashes is the question of how engaged or disengaged the driver was when things went wrong. Josh Brown, the 40-year-old who died in Williston, Fla., on May 7 when his Tesla Model S ran into a tractor-trailer turning left in front of him, was playing a Harry Potter DVD when the crash occurred.

"It's a human nature that when we're bored with a given task we find something else to occupy our minds. There are ways the industry can look at to maintain driver interest," Maddox said.

Later this summer, the National Highway Traffic Safety Administration[9] is expected to release its federal guidelines for autonomous vehicles.

Though Michigan is known for being home to the nation's traditional auto industry, it could play an outsized role in development of self-driving cars. Michigan wants to be a leader in the research and development of self-driving vehicles. That goal must be balanced against MDOT's[10] mission to maximize traffic safety.

"These technologies will be significantly better when the vehicles can 'talk' to each other and to signals in traffic lights and elsewhere," says Kirk Steudle, director of the Michigan Department of Transportation.

MDOT is working with General Motors, Ford and the University of Michigan to deploy vehicle-to-infrastructure communication technology on more than 120 miles of metro Detroit roadway.

The technology uses a Wi-Fi derivative called "dedicated short-range communication". The system can configure stoplights or alert drivers to adjust speeds in order to smooth traffic flows during rush hours.

To be effective in the long term, projects like this depend on a much higher penetration of technology within the vehicle population. In the shorter term, automakers, suppliers and technology companies are making important strides on their own.

Yet with every step forward there is a growing awareness of autonomous driving's limits.

Steudle said the owner of a Tesla with Autopilot offered him a test drive recently.

"We came up to a busy intersection with a traffic light and there were one or two cars ahead of me, and the car stopped on its own," Steudle said. "But if there had been no other car ahead of us, I would have had to pump the brakes myself at the traffic light."

Michigan alone has 122,000 miles of public roads, Steudle said. Half of those will never have a paint line on them because they are either dirt or subdivision streets. Paint lines are part of the language that sensors, cameras, and LiDAR[11], an acronym for Light Detection and Ranging, can interpret in such a way that lets them guide the vehicle.

Self-driving advocates contend that when this technology is perfected, we can save 35,200 lives a year—the number of auto-related traffic deaths last year in the U.S.—because many of us are bad drivers.

"The argument goes that human error causes 90% of all accidents, so let's get rid of the human driver," said Maddox of the American Center for Mobility. "But that overlooks that we drive 100 million miles between fatal accidents. We overestimate the shortcomings of human drivers."

Early next year General Motors will launch its Super Cruise[12] feature on the Cadillac CT6. As described by GM executives, it is similar to Tesla's Autopilot, but the company declined to comment on what it has learned from Tesla's recent incidents.

Google[13] also declined to comment. Most of the pod-like self-driving cars Google tests on public roads in northern California operate at speeds of under 35 miles per hour. Often a Google employee is on board and knows how to respond if something out of the ordinary happens.

Consumers also have much to learn. Tesla's owners manuals make clear that drivers must be prepared to take the steering wheel if Autopilot acts unpredictably or can't process a traffic situation. But not all Tesla owners, like customers of every other automaker, read their manuals.

"An informed consumer is the best consumer," MDOT's Steudle said. "They really need to understand the limitations of what the technology can do currently. There's a lot of information out there about where it can take us. But it's not there yet."

（From *USA Today*, Jul. 17, 2016）

NOTES

1. **Tesla Motors**：特斯拉汽车公司，美国一家生产和销售纯电动汽车的公司，于 2003 年在加利福尼亚州硅谷成立。2008 年，特斯拉推出第一款纯电动汽车 Tesla Roadster，使用锂离子电池提供动力。2023 年，根据特斯拉发布的第一季度全球生产及交付报告，交付量超过 42.2 万，打破了特斯拉单季度的交付纪录，继续领跑电动车行业。现在所有车型均配备具有全自动驾驶功能的硬件，并可以随技术发展提供系统升级服务，从而提高驾驶安全性。

2. **Autopilot**：自动辅助驾驶模式。根据美国国家公路交通安全管理局的分类，特斯拉汽车的自动驾驶功能属于第二级半自动驾驶，驾驶员的双手应该放在方向盘上，以便于必要时操控汽车。特斯拉增强版自动辅助驾驶的软件将使特斯拉汽车能够根据交通状况调整车速、保持在车道内行驶、自动变换车道、在接近目的地时驶出高速、在接近停车场时自动泊车、在车库内听候车主的"召唤"等。

3. **Karl Benz**：卡尔・本茨（1844—1929），德国著名汽车公司梅赛德斯 – 奔驰汽车公司（Mercedes – Benz）的创始人之一，被认为是现代汽车工业的先驱者。他于 1984 年入选美国汽车名人纪念堂（The Automotive Hall of Fame），以表彰其在汽车制造领域的突出贡献。

4. **Henry Ford**：亨利・福特（1863—1947），美国汽车工程师与企业家，福特汽车公司（Ford Motor Company）的创始人。他是世界上第一位使用流水线进行汽车批量生产的汽车制造者。1999 年，福特被《财富》（*Fortune*）杂志评为"20 世纪最伟大的企业家"，以表彰他以及福特汽车公司对人类发展做出的贡献。2005 年，《福布斯》（*Forbes*）杂志公布了有史以来最有影响力的 20 位企业家，亨利・福特位居榜首。

5. **General Motors**：美国通用汽车公司（GM），由威廉・杜兰特（William Durant）于 1908 年创建，全球总部设在美国底特律，旗下拥有雪佛兰（Chevrolet）、别克（Buick）、GMC 商用车、凯迪拉克（Cadillac）、霍顿（Holden）等品牌。

6. **holy grail**：也作 Holy Grail，圣杯，据说是耶稣基督在最后的晚餐时饮用葡萄酒的酒杯，后来不知所踪，为此引出许多以寻找圣杯为题材的故事。现在常用来指"可望而不可即的东西或事物"；"努力追求但不可能实现的目标或理想"。

7. **CEO**：全称是 Chief Executive Officer，指首席执行官、总裁，是企业中负责日常事务的最高行政官员，主管企业行政事务。该词起源于亚历山大・汉密尔顿（Alexander Hamilton），他成立美国纽约银行后，找了专业经理人管理，因美国《宪法》称总统为 Chief Executive，于是他就把专业经理人称为 Chief Executive Officer。

8. **The American Center for Mobility**：美国行驶车辆中心。它是密歇根大学交通研究学院的一个非营利机构，致力于促进先进的行驶车辆安全发展，同时为密歇根东南部及美国带来经济发展机会。

9. **National Highway Traffic Safety Administration**：美国国家公路交通安全管理局。它隶属于美国交通部，是根据 1970 年《道路交通法案》设立的有关机动车辆和道路安全的机构，致力于通过教育、研究、安全标准制定与实施来拯救生命、防止受伤并减少由道路交通事故造成的经济损失。

10. **MDOT**：全称为 Michigan Department of Transportation，密歇根州交通部。它负责管理密歇根州公路系统，同时负责管理其他州和联邦的航空运输方案、城际客运服务、铁路运输、当地公共交通服务、交通运输经济发展基金，以及其他服务等。

11. **LiDAR**：激光雷达。本文是指一种安装在汽车上的激光探测和测距系统，通过激光的反射波来测量汽车和其周围物体的距离，它是自动驾驶模式的重要组成部分。

12. **Super Cruise**：超级巡航系统。它是指美国通用汽车公司将搭载于凯迪拉克 CT6 上的自动驾驶系统，能够让车辆在高速公路上保持安全速度与行驶在既定车道。

13. **Google**：谷歌公司，1998 年由拉里·佩奇（Larry Page）和谢尔盖·布林（Sergey Brin）创建，总部设在美国加利福尼亚州山景城，提供互联网搜索、电邮、博客等网络信息服务。谷歌也涉足无人驾驶领域，现已推出全自动驾驶汽车——不设方向盘和刹车，但能够自行启动、行驶以及停止，现处于测试阶段。

USEFUL WORDS

advocate	['ædvəkət]	*n.*	a person who supports or speaks in favor of sb. or of a public plan or action 拥护者，支持者；提倡者
autonomous	[ɔːˈtɒnəməs]	*adj.*	(of a person) able to do things and make decisions without help from anyone else （人）自主的；有自主权的
brunt	[brʌnt]	*n.*	the main force of sth. unpleasant 主要力量；撞击，冲击
configure	[kənˈfɪɡə]	*v.*	to set up for a particular purpose 配置；设定
deploy	[dɪˈplɔɪ]	*v.*	(formal) to use sth. effectively 有效地利用
engaged	[ɪnˈɡeɪdʒd]	*adj.*	(formal) busy doing sth. 忙于；从事于
evolution	[ˌiːvəˈluːʃn]	*n.*	the gradual development of sth. 演变；发展；渐进
fatality	[fəˈtæləti]	*n.*	an occurrence of death by accident, in war, or from disease （事故、战争、疾病等导致的）死亡
infrastructure	[ˈɪnfrəstrʌktʃə(r)]	*n.*	the basic systems and services that are necessary for a country or an organization to run smoothly, such as buildings, transport and water and power supplies （国家或机构的）基础设施，基础建设
manual	[ˈmænjuəl]	*n.*	a book that tells you how to do or operate sth., especially one that comes with a machine, etc. when you buy it 使用手册，

说明书；指南

oust	[aʊst]	*v.*	~ *sb. (from sth./as sth.)* to force sb. out of a job or position of power, especially in order to take their place 剥夺；罢免，革职
outsized	['aʊtsaɪzd]	*adj.*	larger than normal for its kind 特大的；特大号的
overestimate	[ˌəʊvər'estɪmeɪt]	*v.*	to estimate sth. to be larger, better, more important, etc. than it really is 高估
penetration	[ˌpenə'treɪʃn]	*n.*	the act or process of making a way into or through sth. 穿透；渗透；进入
setback	['setbæk]	*n.*	a difficulty or problem that delays or prevents sth., or makes a situation worse 挫折；阻碍
stride	[straɪd]	*n.*	an improvement in the way sth. is developing 进展，进步；发展
stumble	['stʌmbl]	*n.*	an unintentional but embarrassing blunder 差错；失误，过失
upstart	['ʌpstɑːt]	*adj.*	characteristic of sb. who has risen economically or socially but lacks the social skills appropriate for this new position 自命不凡的；狂妄自大的

EXERCISES

I. Vocabulary

Choose among the four alternatives one word or phrase that is closest in meaning to the underlined part in each statement.

1. This summer, autonomous cars collide with reality.

A. crash into   B. cross into   C. conflict with   D. converse with

2. Sure, Tesla Motors is taking the brunt of the public relations and political damage.

A. suffering from   B. dealing with   C. worried about   D. concerned about

3. The more we see autonomous vehicles as a way to "free" us to work, entertain ourselves or tune out, the longer this evolution will take.

A. turn out   B. turn off   C. shut off   D. zone out

4. At the heart of the recent Tesla crashes is the question of how engaged or disengaged the driver was when things went wrong.

A. free   B. distracted   C. isolated   D. indifferent

5. Later this summer, the National Highway Traffic Safety Administration is expected to release its federal guidelines for autonomous vehicles.

A. issue   B. deliver   C. express   D. relieve

6. The system can <u>configure</u> stoplights or alert drivers to adjust speeds in order to smooth traffic flows during rush hours.

    A. assemble   B. form   C. arrange   D. design

7. To be effective in the long term, projects like this depend on a much higher <u>penetration</u> of technology within the vehicle population.

    A. attack   B. perception   C. intrusion   D. breakthrough

8. "We came up to a busy <u>intersection</u> with a traffic light and there were one or two cars ahead of me, and the car stopped on its own," Steudle said.

    A. mixture   B. crossroad   C. juncture   D. connection

9. Self-driving advocates <u>contend</u> that when this technology is perfected, we can save 35,200 lives a year—the number of auto-related traffic deaths last year in the U.S.—because many of us are bad drivers.

    A. compete   B. fight   C. maintain   D. debate

10. "An <u>informed</u> consumer is the best consumer," MDOT's Steudle said.

    A. wise   B. resourceful   C. reliable   D. knowledgeable

II. Comprehension

Decide whether the following statements are true (T) or false (F) according to the information given in the press clipping. Mark T or F for each statement.

1. We know clearly how Tesla's Autopilot feature results in the recent accidents.

2. In spite of the car crashes, the research of self-driving technology will continue.

3. Since humans are imperfect drivers, sensors and cameras can replace human as vehicle operators, at least for the foreseeable future.

4. Consumer over-trust in technology is a significant problem, which does not have a solution yet.

5. In the research and development of self-driving vehicles, traffic safety should be the most important mission to fulfil.

6. Michigan, as the home to American traditional auto industry, plays a leading role in developing self-driving technology.

7. With Autopilot feature, the driver would not have to brake the car at the traffic light.

8. In Michigan, most of the public roads have paint lines to provide signals for sensors, cameras and LiDAR to guide the cars.

9. According to the text, General Motors has learned much from Tesla's recent incidents.

10. Tesla's owner manuals clearly state what the drivers ought to do if Autopilot does not act properly, but not all Tesla owners read their manuals.

III. Topics for Discussion

1. According to the analysis of Tesla's fatal crash, there are four aspects to consider: roads, communication technology, relation between man and machine, and tuning out. Are there any

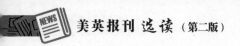

other aspects to consider? Please discuss with your partners.

2. With the improvement of technology, do you believe that self-driving devices can replace human drivers in the future? Why or why not?

3. In face of all the setbacks and accidents in autonomous vehicles, why do the major automobile manufacturers keep on the research of self-driving technology?

4. "An informed consumer is the best consumer." How do you interpret this statement?

5. Suppose you are a driver, which one will you choose, a traditional car or a self-driving car?

源于美国的第三次科技革命

美国经济趋势基金会主席、经济社会评论家杰里米·里夫金（Jeremy Rifkin）认为第三次工业革命的标志是互联网和可再生能源的结合，提出互联网、绿色能源和3D打印技术将开启第三次工业革命的大门。但是，关于第三次工业革命的起讫时间众说纷纭，为避免混淆，本文采用"第三次科技革命"的说法。第三次科技革命是在第二次世界大战后起源于美国科技领域的重大革命，是人类文明史上继蒸汽技术革命和电力技术革命之后取得的又一次重大飞跃。它以原子能、电子计算机、空间技术和生物工程的研发应用为主要标志，涉及信息技术、新能源技术、新材料技术、生物技术、空间技术和海洋技术等诸多领域（邓友平，2014），产生了大批新型工业，开辟了信息时代，催生了知识经济，出现了一大批科技新成果。

第一，空间技术的利用和发展。继苏联于1957年成功发射第一颗人造地球卫星以后，美、苏展开了长达数十年的太空竞赛。为此，美国于20世纪60年代就制订了登月计划，并于1969年成功登月。20世纪70年代后，空间技术领域从近地空间发展为超越太阳系的技术研发。

第二，原子能技术的利用和发展。美国于1945年成功试制原子弹之后，又于1952年成功试制氢弹。在1949年至1964年期间，苏、英、法、中四国相继成功研制核武器。除军事领域以外，原子能技术在其他工业领域的和平利用也有了较大发展。

第三，电子计算机技术的利用和发展。1946年，世界上第一台现代电子计算机在美国诞生。20世纪50年代，贝尔实验室成功研制出晶体管计算机，运算速度每秒在100万次以上。60年代至70年代，相继出现了小规模、中规模、大规模和超大规模的集成电路（英文简称分别为SSI、MSI、LSI、VLSI），极大地提高了计算机的性能。1978年，计算机的运算速度可达1.5亿次每秒。80年代出现了智能计算机（intelligent computer），微机（microcomputer）得到了迅速发展。90年代出现了光子计算机（photon computer）、生物计算机（biological computer）等。计算机在速度提高、体积减小、成本降低方面发展迅速。电子计算机技术以及互联网技术在世界范围内的广泛应用，极大提高了生产生活的自动化和现代化水平，使人们之间的物理距离不再成为障碍。

科技革命和科技创新是国际竞争的决定性实力，加剧了各国发展的不平衡，使国家之间的国际地位发生了新变化（王长勤等，2015）。同时，第三次科技革命对现行经济带来了较大影响。

第一，科技成果转化得到重视。在发达国家，企业具有较高的科技成果研发的自觉意识和责任意识，是科技研发的投资主体，所投资金占科技研发经费总投入的 60%~70%，特别是在高新技术产业方面投入巨大（李孔岳，2006）。根据经济合作与发展组织等机构在 2021 年公布的数据，从各国具体研发支出来看，美国持续位居全球第一，2019 年为 6,127 亿美元；从全球研发强度（国内研发支出占 GDP 的比重）来看，大多数经济合作与发展组织成员国的研发强度普遍有所增长，其中美国首次突破 3%；从全球研发投入 TOP 2500 家企业行业分布来看，全球前四大行业对总研发投入的贡献约占 77%，其中信息与通信技术（ICT）生产占 23%，健康产业占 20.5%，ICT 服务占 16.9%，汽车业占 16.3%。各国研发增长模式有所不同，欧盟由汽车领域主导；美国由 ICT 领域和以生物技术为主的健康领域主导，中国由以软件和互联网为主的 ICT 领域主导。

第二，科技进步因素占国民生产总值的比例增大。在两次世界大战期间，西方国家工业生产的年均增长率为 1.7%，在 1950 年至 1972 年增为 6.1%。在世界范围内，1953 年至 1973 年的工业产量，与 1800 年以后 150 年的工业产量总和大致相当。发达国家科技进步因素带来的产值占国民生产总值比重由最初的 5%~10%，增至 70 年代的 60%，21 世纪以来已增至 80%。

第三，学科日趋融合。从单一技术到高科技群，自然科学已成为多层次、综合性的学科统一体，学科之间的交叉与融合不断加深，联系日益密切，各学科之间的空隙得到了有效弥补。随着社会进步和科技发展，研究一些复杂的问题需要多个学科的知识，传统经典学科间的界限被不断打破，一些交叉学科（如物理化学、分子生物学）和多学科的研究领域（如城市研究、脑科学研究）大量出现。

第四，发达国家的经济结构变化较大。随着新一轮科技革命的推进，西方发达国家的不同部门经济结构发生了新的变化。首先，第一、第二产业的 GDP 占值以及从业人数比重均有所下降。美国的农业人口在 1970 年占总人口的 5%，1979 年降为 3%；制造业从业人口在 1970 年占 30%，1979 年降为 13%。其次，新旧工业发生了分化。由劳动和资本密集的传统工业转为技术与知识密集的新兴工业，如电子科技、激光技术、合成材料、遗传工程等主导的工业部门长足发展，钢铁、纺织、采矿等工业部门缓慢发展，占比逐渐下降。

第三次科技革命将促使健康的绿色能源和新型能源系统的形成，以改变社会发展的动力，同时将促使计算机技术、互联网技术和新型的通讯系统的形成，以改良整个社会生产过程和生活方式（刘燕华等，2013）。可以说，科技革命不仅极大地推动了人类社会经济、政治、文化领域的变革，而且影响了人类的生活方式和思维方式。随着科技的不断进步，人类的衣、食、住、行、用等日常生活的各个方面必将发生重大变革。

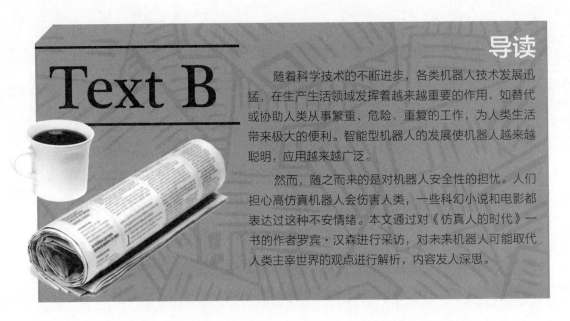

导读

随着科学技术的不断进步，各类机器人技术发展迅猛，在生产生活领域发挥着越来越重要的作用，如替代或协助人类从事繁重、危险、重复的工作，为人类生活带来极大的便利。智能型机器人的发展使机器人越来越聪明，应用越来越广泛。

然而，随之而来的是对机器人安全性的担忧。人们担心高仿真机器人会伤害人类，一些科幻小说和电影都表达过这种不安情绪。本文通过对《仿真人的时代》一书的作者罗宾·汉森进行采访，对未来机器人可能取代人类主宰世界的观点进行解析，内容发人深思。

If robots are the future of work, where do humans fit in?

We need to rethink our view of jobs and leisure—

and quickly, if we are to avoid becoming obsolete

By Zoe Williams

Robin Hanson thinks the robot takeover, when it comes, will be in the form of emulations. In his new book, *The Age of Em*[1], the economist explains: You take the best and brightest 200 human beings on the planet, you scan their brains and you get robots that to all intents and purposes are indivisible from the humans on which they are based, except a thousand times faster and better.

For some reason, conversationally, Hanson repeatedly calls these 200 human prototypes "the billionaires", even though having a billion in any currency would be strong evidence against your being the brightest, since you have no sense of how much is enough. But that's just a natural difference of opinion between an economist and a mediocre person who is now afraid of the future.

These Ems, being superior at everything and having no material needs that couldn't be satisfied virtually, will undercut humans in the labour market, and render us totally unnecessary. We will all effectively be retired. Whether or not we are put out to a pleasant pasture or brutally exterminated will depend upon how we behave towards the Ems at their incipience.

When Hanson presents his forecast in public, one question always comes up: What's to stop the Ems killing us off? "Well, why don't we exterminate retirees at the moment?" he asks, rhetorically, before answering: Some combination of gratitude, empathy and affection between individuals, which the Ems are modelled on us precisely, will share (unless we use real billionaires for the model).

Opinion on the precise shape of the robot future remains divided: The historian Yuval Noah Harari argues, in *Homo Deus: A Brief History of Tomorrow*[2], that artificial intelligence robots will be the first to achieve world domination. This future is bleaker than Hanson's—lacking empathy, those robots wouldn't have a sentimental affection for us as their progenitors—but essentially the same. Harari predicts the rise of the useless class: humans who don't know what to study because they have no idea what skills will be needed by the time they finish, who can't work because there's always a cheaper and better robot, and who spend their time taking drugs and staring at screens.

These intricacies, AI[3] versus Ems, AI versus IA (intelligence amplification, where humans aren't superseded by our technological advances but enhanced by them), fascinate futurologists. Hanson argues that AI is moving too slowly, while only three technologies need coincide to make an Em possible: faster and cheaper computers, which the world has in hand; brain scanning, which is being worked on by a much smaller but active biological community; and the modelling of the human mind, "which is harder to predict".

But all the predictions lead to the same place: the obsolescence of human labour. Even if a robot takeover is some way away, this idea has already become pressing in specific sectors. Driverless cars are forecast to make up 75% of all traffic by 2040, raising the spectre not just of leagues of unemployed drivers, but also of the transformation of all the infrastructure around the job, from training to petrol stations.

There is always a voice in the debate saying: we don't have to surrender to our own innovation, we don't have to automate everything just because we can. Yet history teaches us that we will, and teaches us, furthermore, that resisting invention is its own kind of failure. Fundamentally, if the big idea of a progressive future is to cling on to work for the avoidance of worklessness, we could dream up jobs that were bolder and much more fulfilling than driving.

There are two big threats posed by an automated future. The first—that we will irritate the robots and they will dominate and swiftly obliterate us—is for Hollywood[4] to worry about. There

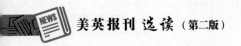

is not much apparatus we can build in advance to make ourselves less annoying. There will undoubtedly be those who believe our obliteration is so inevitable that every other anxiety is a sideshow.

If you can hold your nerve against that, the critical question becomes: In a world without work, how do we distribute resources? It is a question articulated precisely by Stephen Hawking[5] last year, when he noted: "Everyone can enjoy a life of luxurious leisure if the machine-produced wealth is shared, or most people can end up miserably poor if the machine owners successfully lobby against wealth redistribution."

Like so many things, from debt cancellation to climate change, the reality of the situation is easily understood by scientists, academics, philosophers from the left and right, activists from within and without the establishment; and the only people who staunchly resist it are the self-styled political "realists".

The question of how to distribute wealth in the future curves back round to meet a conundrum raised by the past: How do we remake the social safety net so that it embodies solidarity, generosity and trust, rather than the welfare state of the present, rickety with the woodworm of mutual suspicion.

The idea of a universal basic income is generally framed as a way to "shift from the Beveridge principle of national insurance[6] based on contributions and the sharing of risk, to a system of income as of right" (as described in a Compass paper by Howard Reed and Stewart Lansley[7]). In its simplest iteration, all citizens receive the same income. There is work to be done on the numbers—whether this income needs to be supplemented for housing, in what form it has its most progressive effect, whether and how it is taxed back in the higher deciles, how it can be affordable at the same time as genuinely livable.

There is also work to be done on the surrounding incentives, whether a basic income would capsize the work ethic and leave the world understaffed while we await the robot takeover (a pilot scheme in Canada concluded the only groups who worked less with an income were mothers of young babies and teenagers still in education; other pilots are under way in Kenya and across Europe).

Enter the future, with its possibility that many vocations will be unnecessary, and we face more existential questions: How do we find meaning without work? How do we find fellowship without status? How do we fill leisure intelligently? These mysteries possessed Bertrand Russell[8] and John Maynard Keynes[9], then fell out of currency as we realised we could consume our way out of futility, and ignite our urge to earn by spending it before it arrived.

Even absenting the constraints of the globe, that plan has failed. Consumption may have lent necessity to work, but it didn't confer meaning upon it. And perhaps the most profound accommodation we have to make with the future isn't whether or not we are capable of sharing, but where we will find our impetus.

"Can you just write," Hanson asked at the end of our conversation, "that even though I'm talking about dire and dramatic things, I'm a friendly guy who smiles a lot?" I'm not sure how much this helps. Some of his predictions are only bearable if you assume that you'll have died before they come to pass.

Hanson doesn't insist that his is the only possible outcome. Rather, "you should expect that, whatever change is going to happen, it's going to happen pretty fast. Like, five years from nothing different that you'd notice to a completely different world. What I want is to have people understand how urgent it is, when this thing shows up, to have made a plan."

（From *The Guardian*, May 24, 2016）

NOTES

1. ***The Age of Em***：《仿真人的时代》，由美国乔治梅森大学（George Mason University）经济学教授罗宾·汉森（Robin Hanson）创作，2016 年 5 月由牛津大学出版社出版。该书描述了模拟人脑形成的机器人在未来会取代人类，并对世界产生巨大影响。

2. ***Homo Deus: A Brief History of Tomorrow***：《超人：人类未来简史》，由以色列希伯来大学（The Hebrew University of Jerusalem）历史系教授尤瓦尔·赫拉利（Yuval Harari）创作，描述了未来人类的生存状态。该书是作者继畅销书《人类简史：从动物到上帝》（*Sapiens: A Brief History of Humankind*，2014）之后的又一力作。

3. **AI**：全称为 artificial intelligence，人工智能，一种新型的科学技术。它是指通过对模仿和扩展人类智能的理论、方法、技术及应用的研究，包括机器人制造、语言和图像识别、自然语言处理等领域的开发应用。

4. **Hollywood**：好莱坞，位于美国加利福尼亚州洛杉矶市西北郊，世界影业的中心，聚集着美国六百多家影视公司，如梦工厂、迪士尼、20 世纪福克斯、索尼公司、环球公司、华纳兄弟、派拉蒙等电影巨头。好莱坞制作过不少关于机器人的科幻大片，如《人工智能》（*AI*，2001）、《我，机器人》（*I, Robot*，2004）、《机器人启示录》（*Robopocalypse*，2015）等，传达了其关于未来机器人对人类生活影响的一些思考。

5. **Stephen Hawking**：史蒂芬·霍金（1942—2018），英国著名物理学家和宇宙学家。他患有肌肉萎缩性侧索硬化症（也称"渐冻症"），全身瘫痪，不能发音。霍金教授主要研究宇宙理论和黑洞理论，主要科普作品包括《时间简史》（*A Brief History of Time*，1988）、《果壳中的宇宙》（*The Universe in a Nutshell*，2001）等。本文提到的霍金教授关于资源分配的说法源于他通过 Reddit AMA 对人工智能领域问题的回答（详见《连线》网络版）。

6. **Beveridge principle of national insurance**：指英国经济学家威廉·贝弗里奇爵士（Sir William Beveridge）1942 年提交的《社会保险和相关服务》[*Social Insurance and Allied Services*，也称作 *The Beveridge Report*（《贝弗里奇报告》）] 中的社会保障原则和计划。这份报告对全世界社会保障制度的发展产生了深远影响，是社会保障发展史上具有划时代意义的著作。

7. **a Compass paper by Howard Reed and Stewart Lansley**：指由英国指南针出版社于 2016 年 5 月出版的由霍华德·里德和斯图尔特·兰斯利撰写的论文 "Universal Basic Income: An idea Whose Time Has Come?"。该文章主要对全民基本收入计划（universal basic income）的可行性及实施进行分析论证。

8. **Bertrand Russell**：伯特兰·罗素（1872—1970），20 世纪英国著名哲学家、数学家、逻辑学家、历史学家、无神论（或者不可知论者），也是 20 世纪西方最著名、影响力最大的学者及和平主义社会活动家之一。1950 年，伯特兰·罗素被授予诺贝尔文学奖。他的代表作品有《数学原理》（*Principia Mathematica*，1910—1913）、《物的分析》（*The Analysis of Matter*，1927）、《幸福之路》（*The Conquest of Happiness*，1930）、《西方哲学史》（*A History of Western Philosophy*，1945）等。

9. **John Maynard Keynes**：约翰·梅纳德·凯恩斯（1883—1946），英国经济学家。他创立了宏观经济学，是现代西方最有影响力的经济学家之一。其代表作品为《就业、利息和货币通论》（*The General Theory of Employment, Interest and Money*，1936）。书中第一次提出国家政府可以干预经济，强调贸易顺差利于提高投资水平和扩大就业，使国家经济走向繁荣昌盛。该书为宏观经济学的确立和发展做出了突出贡献。

USEFUL WORDS

capsize	[kæp'saɪz]	*v.* (a boat) to turn over in the water （船）翻；倾覆
conundrum	[kə'nʌndrəm]	*n.* a confusing problem or question that is very difficult to solve 令人迷惑的难题；复杂难解的问题
empathy	['empəθi]	*n.* the ability to understand another person's feelings, experience, etc. 同感；共鸣；同情
emulation	[ˌemjʊ'leɪʃn]	*n.* the act of a computer or computer program working in the same way as another computer or program and performing the same tasks 仿真；模仿
exterminate	[ɪk'stɜːmɪneɪt]	*v.* to kill all the members of a group of people or animals 灭绝，根除；消灭，毁灭
futility	[fjuː'tɪlətɪ]	*n.* uselessness as a consequence of having no practical result 无益，无用；徒劳，白费
impetus	['ɪmpɪtəs]	*n.* sth. that encourages a process or activity to develop more

quickly 动力；推动，促进；刺激

incipience	[ɪnˈsɪpɪəns]	*n.*	beginning to exist or to be apparent 开始；早期
iteration	[ˌɪtəˈreɪʃn]	*n.*	doing or saying again; a repeated performance 反复；重述
mediocre	[ˌmiːdiˈəʊkə(r)]	*adj.*	(disapproving) not very good; of only average standard 平庸的；普通的
obliterate	[əˈblɪtəreɪt]	*v.*	to remove all signs of sth., either by destroying or covering it completely 毁掉；覆盖；清除
obsolescence	[ˌɒbsəˈlesns]	*n.*	(formal) the state of becoming old-fashioned and no longer useful 过时；陈旧；淘汰
progenitor	[prəʊˈdʒenɪtə(r)]	*n.*	(formal) a person or thing from the past that a person, animal or plant that is alive now is related to（人或动、植物等的）祖先；祖代
rickety	[ˈrɪkəti]	*adj.*	not strong or well made; likely to break 不结实的；不稳固的；易折断的
solidarity	[ˌsɒlɪˈdærəti]	*n.*	support by one person or a group of people for another because they share feelings, opinions, aims, etc. 团结，齐心协力；同心同德；相互支持
spectre	[ˈspektə(r)]	*n.*	sth. unpleasant that people are afraid might happen in the future 恐惧；恐慌；忧虑
staunchly	[ˈstɔːntʃli]	*adv.*	in a way that shows strong support 坚定地；忠实地
supersede	[ˌsuːpəˈsiːd]	*v.*	to take the place of sth./sb. that is considered to be old-fashioned or no longer the best available 取代，替代（已非最佳选择或已过时的事物）
undercut	[ˌʌndəˈkʌt]	*v.*	to sell goods or services at a lower price than your competitors 削（价）竞争；以低于（竞争对手）的价格做生意
understaffed	[ˌʌndəˈstɑːft]	*adj.*	not having enough people working and therefore not able to function well 人员不足，人手太少

EXERCISES

I. Vocabulary

Choose among the four alternatives one word or phrase that is closest in meaning to the underlined part in each statement.

1. But that's just a natural difference of opinion between an economist and a mediocre person who is now afraid of the future.

    A. inferior   B. poor   C. average   D. timid

2. These Ems, being superior at everything and having no material needs that couldn't be satisfied

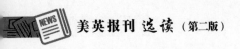

virtually, will <u>undercut</u> humans in the labour market, and render us totally unnecessary.

    A. prevent   B. beat   C. defeat   D. be cheaper than

3. Whether or not we are <u>put out to a pleasant pasture</u> or brutally exterminated will depend upon how we behave towards the Ems at their incipience.

    A. retired   B. sent to a good place C. troubled   D. defeated

4. Even if a robot takeover is some way away, this idea has already become <u>pressing</u> in specific sectors.

    A. important   B. urgent   C. critical   D. necessary

5. There is always a voice in the debate saying: we don't have to <u>surrender</u> to our own innovation, We don't have to automate everything just because we can.

    A. yield   B. abandon   C. show   D. relinquish

6. There will undoubtedly be those who believe our obliteration is so inevitable that every other anxiety is <u>a sideshow</u>.

    A. unpleasant   B. additional   C. accompanying   D. less important

7. If you can <u>hold your nerve against that</u>, the critical question becomes: In a world without work, how do we distribute resources?

    A. become nervous   B. feel frightened   C. keep calm   D. feel worried

8. There is also work to be done on the surrounding <u>incentives</u>, whether a basic income would capsize the work ethic and leave the world understaffed while we await the robot takeover (a pilot scheme in Canada concluded the only groups who worked less with an income were mothers of young babies and teenagers still in education; other pilots are under way in Kenya and across Europe).

    A. rewards   B. stimuli   C. occasions   D. payments

9. Consumption may have lent necessity to work, but it didn't <u>confer</u> meaning upon it.

    A. consult   B. give   C. discuss   D. exchange

10. Some of his predictions are only <u>bearable</u> if you assume that you'll have died before they come to pass.

    A. disposable   B. lasting   C. passable   D. tolerable

II. Comprehension

Decide whether the following statements are true (T) or false (F) according to the information given in the press clipping. Mark T or F for each statement.

1. In *The Age of Em*, the robots are based on humans and faster and better than humans.

2. Hanson calls the 200 human prototypes "the billionaires" because they are wealthy men.

3. The Ems not only imitate the human brains, but also share the human emotions.

4. In the future, it is predicted that humans do not need to work for there is no work to do.

5. Humans will automate everything in the future.

6. According to Stephen Hawking, everyone can enjoy a life of luxurious leisure on the basis of wealth distribution.

7. At present, our social safety net embodies solidarity, generosity and trust.

8. The idea of universal basic income advocates that all citizens receive the same income.

9. In the future when many vocations disappear, the ability of sharing will become the most profound accommodation we have to make.

10. Robin Hanson attempts to remind people to make full preparations as soon as possible for the future described in his book *The Age of Em*.

III. Topics for Discussion

1. Robin Hanson thinks that in the future, robots will dominate the world in place of human beings. Do you agree with him? Why or why not?

2. Robin Hanson calls the human prototypes "the billionaires" for the Ems, but he makes the Ems share human emotions of gratitude, empathy and affection "unless we use real billionaires for the model". How do you understand "real billionaires"?

3. The historian Yuval Noah Harari predicts in his book that humans will turn into "a useless class who don't know what to study because they have no idea what skills will be needed by the time they finish, who can't work because there's always a cheaper and better robot, and who spend their time taking drugs and staring at screens". What does the author try to tell us about human beings in the future?

4. In order to avoid worklessness in the automated future, this text makes a suggestion that "we could dream up jobs that were bolder and much more fulfilling than driving". What kind of jobs could meet such a need?

5. Work is of great significance in human life, without which life may become meaningless. Do you agree with this statement? Please elaborate your opinion with examples.

《今日美国》简介

　　《今日美国》（*USA Today*）是美国唯一一份全国性综合日报，由美国最大的报刊集团甘尼特报业集团（Gannett Co., Inc.）总裁艾伦·纽哈斯（Al Neuharth）于 1982 年 9 月创办，总部设在弗吉尼亚州的罗斯林。该报创办之初，并未被寄予厚望。经过多年的努力，作为美国大报中最年轻的一份报纸，《今日美国》的发行量已经连续多年名列前茅，如今已与百年老报《华尔街日报》和《纽约时报》并驾齐驱。截至 2023 年，《今日美国》已经成为美国最受欢迎的全国性日报之一，每天有数百万人阅读，移动端下载量超过 2,100 万次。

该报利用彩色的版面、快速密集的消息、丰富的图表、大量的体育报道等特色来吸引读者。报纸设有两个版面——国内版和国际版，分别在国内和国外多个印刷点印刷发行，以满足美国各地及亚欧等地人们的阅读需求。2012 年，《今日美国》重新设计报标和版面，用一个蓝色圆圈替代原来的蓝色地球标识，而且圆圈会根据版面内容变换颜色和版面名称。

《今日美国》虽然办报时间不长，但特色鲜明。首先，报纸版面固定清晰、内容丰富，读这一份报纸即可了解美国各地及全世界的重大新闻。其次，语言简洁明快，报道突出新闻内容，整体篇幅较短以便刊登更多信息，适应人们快节奏、忙碌的生活方式。再次，图片色彩鲜艳、图表数据丰富，使报纸版面图文并茂、生动活泼、形象醒目，迎合了读者通过图像方式获取信息的习惯。该报还有整版的色彩绚丽的气象地图、股市行情和各州体育赛事成绩等。最后，报纸内容积极正面。该报奉行"希望新闻"的原则，注重"新闻平衡"，让读者看到希望和光明（端木义万，2005：26）。

Unit 4
Lifestyle

报刊英语的构词特点

　　作为大众媒体，新闻报刊写作内容需要适合广大读者的水平，语言也需要通俗易懂，所以报刊用词往往简单而具体。同时新闻传播十分强调时效性，以体现特有的新闻价值。新闻报道在提供最新消息的同时也传播了相关的新词（端木义万，2005）。记者们不断创造出新式词语，以反映社会生活日新月异的变化，并增加文章的新鲜感和吸引力，达到出奇制胜的效果。如此，就不难理解为何新词往往首先出现在报纸、杂志等新闻媒体上了。

　　新词的产生方式包括词类转化、派生、拼缀、复合、省略等构词法，旧词赋予新义，以及临时更换词素仿造等。本章将从词类转化、派生词、拼缀词、缩略词、截短词和复合词六个方面探讨报刊英语的构词特点。

一、词类转化

　　词类转化（conversion）是指不需要改变形态就可以从一种词类转化为另一种词类的构词法，无需借助词缀即可实现词类转化，使其产生新的意义和作用，成为新词。在报刊英语中，词类转化的方法经常使用，这不仅可以节约篇幅，也使句子变得生动有力。常见的词类转化类型有名词转动词、动词转名词、形容词转动词或名词等（端木义万，2005）。

1. 名词转化成动词

- He **mouthed** fine words about friendship.（他满口是友谊。）

2. 动词转化成名词

- Like today's **haves** and **havenots**, we will have a society of the **knows** and **knownots**.（就像今天社会上有富人和穷人一样，将来社会上会出现有知识的人和无知识的人。）

3. 形容词转化成动词或名词

● The leaders, who exchanged views without aids for an hour today, will **brief** newsmen after a second round of talks tomorrow.（今天，领导人在没有助手出席的情况下交换了一个小时意见，并准备在明天第二轮谈判后向新闻记者做简要的介绍。）

形容词修饰语用作名词的例子也有不少，如 undesirables（不受欢迎的人）、the young marrieds（新婚的年轻人）等。

二、派生词

派生词（derivation）是用词根加上词缀组合后形成的新词。派生法是现代英语中使用最多的构词法，所构成的词占新词总数的 30%~34%（端木义万，2005）。英语词缀可分为三类：前缀、中缀和后缀。其中主要以前缀和后缀为主，通常前缀改变词义，后缀改变词性。在报刊英语中，通过添加前后词缀合成新词的方式比较常见，以便快捷地发布消息，使语言更加生动形象。

新闻中比较活跃的前缀有 anti-、eco-、inter-、mini-、non-、out-、over-、pro- 等，如 anti-tank weapons（反坦克武器）、anticlimax（扫兴的结局）、eco-friendly（环保的）、eco-tourism（生态旅游）、intercity（市际的）、Internet（互联网）、minicam（微型照相机）、miniboom（短暂繁荣）、non-governmental organization（NGO，非政府间组织）、non-interference（不干涉）、outnumber（数量上压倒）、outpatient（门诊病人）、overproduction（生产过剩）、overload（超载）、pro-European（亲欧的）、pro-democracy（拥护民主）等。

另外，比较常见的后缀有名词后缀 -in、-ism、-speak、-wise 等，如 sit-in（静坐抗议）、phone-in（电话抗议）、ageism（年龄歧视）、sexism（性别歧视）、bizspeak（商业语言）、White-House-speak（按白宫的说法）、educationwise（在教育方面）、securitywise（在安全方面）等；形容词后缀 -friendly 等，如 environment-friendly（利于环保的）、user-friendly（用户友好的）等；还有动词后缀 -ize 等，如 modernize（现代化）、computerize（计算机化）等。

此外，科学技术的发展也催生了不少派生词。例如，信息技术革命促生了许多与前缀 cyber-（网络的）相关的词汇或短语，如 cybercafé（网吧）、Cyber Monday（网购星期一，指感恩节后第一个星期一的疯狂网购现象）、cyber love/romance（网恋）等。

三、拼缀词

拼缀词（blending）是将两个词语进行剪裁之后复合而成的新词，如 motel（motor + hotel，汽车旅馆）。在现代英语中，这类拼缀词越来越多。拼缀词可以使文字新颖活泼，又节省空间，符合报刊英语简洁性的需求。根据端木义万（2005），就混合的方式而言，拼缀词大体可分为以下四类：

- 前词首部 + 后词尾部：stagflation（stagnation + inflation，滞涨）、medicide（medical + suicide，医助安乐死）等；
- 前词全部 + 后词尾部：screenager（screen + teenager，屏幕青少年，即从小就看电视、玩电脑的青少年）、Obamacare（Obama + medicare，奥巴马医改计划）等；
- 前词首部 + 后词全部：exerhead（exercise + head，运动狂）、e-journal（electronic + journal，电子刊物）等；
- 前词首部 + 后词首部：interpol（international + police，国际警察）、hi-tech（high + technology，高科技）等。

四、缩略词

缩略词（abbreviation）是可以使新闻报道经济、简洁的有效办法，因此新闻报道使用缩略词的频率很高。缩略词的形式主要有首字母缩略词（alphabetism）和首字母缩拼词（acronym）。

- 首字母缩略词：由词组中每个词的首字母组成并按字母发音，如 GM（genetically modified，转基因的）、WTO（World Trade Organization，世贸组织）等。
- 首字母缩拼词：由词组中每个词的首字母组成并拼读为一个词，如 APEC（Asia-Pacific Economic Cooperation，亚洲和太平洋经济合作组织）、FAST（Five-hundred-meter Aperture Spherical Telescope，500 米口径球面射电望远镜）等。

五、截短词

截短词（clipping）是指把原词的某一部分或某些部分截除之后形成的新词，如 TV（television，电视）。这类词在英语报刊中较为常见，可以节约篇幅、精练语言。截短词可分为以下五类：

- 截去后面部分，只留词头：pop（popular，流行的）、celeb（celebrity，名流）等；
- 截去前面部分，只留词尾：copter（helicopter，直升机）、Net（Internet，因特网）等；
- 截去首尾部分，只留中间：flu（influenza，流行性感冒）、tec（detective，侦探）等；
- 截去中部，保留头尾：int'l（international，国际的）、Cwealth（Commonwealth，英联邦）等；
- 截去词组中的一个词，只留一个词：seniors（senior citizens，老年人）、tabloids（tabloid newspapers，小报）等。

六、复合词

复合词（compound）是指把两个或两个以上的词结合在一起构成的新词。在英语的发展过程中，复合法在构词方面起着积极作用，所构成的新词数量仅次于派生法（端木义万，

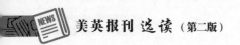
2005）。复合词可以使意图表达得简洁有效，使读者根据旧词或背景猜出词义。数量较多的复合词有复合名词、复合形容词和复合动词。

- 复合名词：letter bomb（书信炸弹）、moonwalk（月亮上行走）、Watergate（水门事件）等；
- 复合形容词：freezing-cold（冰冷的）、top-heavy（头重脚轻的）、war-weary（厌倦战争的）等；
- 复合动词：fast-talk（用花言巧语来企图说服）、green wash（绿刷洗，指塑造关于环境保护的形象）、wallet X-ray（钱袋透视，指收治病人前对其经济能力的审查）等。

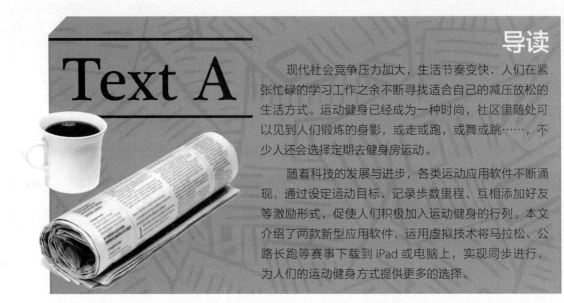

导读

现代社会竞争压力加大，生活节奏变快，人们在紧张忙碌的学习工作之余不断寻找适合自己的减压放松的生活方式。运动健身已经成为一种时尚，社区里随处可以见到人们锻炼的身影，或走或跑，或舞或跳……，不少人还会选择定期去健身房运动。

随着科技的发展与进步，各类运动应用软件不断涌现，通过设定运动目标、记录步数里程、互相添加好友等激励形式，促使人们积极加入运动健身的行列。本文介绍了两款新型应用软件，运用虚拟技术将马拉松、公路长跑等赛事下载到 iPad 或电脑上，实现同步进行，为人们的运动健身方式提供更多的选择。

New running apps blur the line between virtual reality and real life

By Mike Plunkett

During the extreme winter of 2009–2010, Gary McNamee relied on his treadmill to train for the Boston Marathon[1]. McNamee lives in Hopkinton, where the race starts, but the weather stymied his attempts to go out for a long run.

"I'm in my basement thinking, 'Jeez, the course is right up the road. I can go out there and film it and watch it while I was on the treadmill,' " McNamee said.

So he did—and realized that he could market a video simulation of the famed course to other runners.

Thus he began Outside Interactive[2], a company that, along with others, is merging fitness with high-definition virtual technology.

Runners log in to the Outside Interactive app and pay for videos of routes, which they watch on their iPad or Android tablet or on an HD television. While running, they can manually select the pace or sync their tracking device to the app. The video will speed up and slow down as the runners change speed. In a bit of surreality, the crowds and fellow racers in the video will run and cheer in proportion to the speed of the real runners.

Taking it a stride further, RunSocial[3], a company based in Singapore that launched its running app last year, uses augmented reality technology[4], where the app overlays the runner's virtual presence via an avatar with a video of a real-world route (a la *Pokémon Go*[5]). The avatar's speed is determined by the company's TreadTracker foot pod[6] or can be set manually.

"We had this idea of a mixed-reality concept, where basically we wanted to run real-world routes but didn't want computer graphics, but also would love to see others in these routes while we run," said Marc Hardy, RunSocial's co-founder and chief executive.

Hardy, who describes himself as a regular runner, saw an opportunity for treadmill users who struggle with boredom and motivation to enhance their running experience.

Although RunSocial's main products are virtual running apps for indoors, Hardy said the company is focusing more on the sociability factor. Both the virtual running app and RunSocial GPS, an outdoor tracking system that the company just launched, feature ways for participants to race one another, complete with a countdown clock and a leader board.

"Everybody, everywhere can run together, virtually," Hardy said.

Both Outside Interactive and RunSocial offer what McNamee calls the "holy grail"—the ability to sync with smart treadmills to adjust the incline levels to match the flat and hilly sections of each of the recorded courses.

Real Collaborations

Some real-life races are working with Outside Interactive and RunSocial to expand and enhance their own efforts.

Earlier this year, RunSocial launched a digital version of the Prague Marathon[7] and also offered a digital version of the Virgin Money London Marathon[8] for a second year. The digital London Marathon featured astronaut Tim Peake[9], who ran the course on a treadmill aboard the International Space Station. Hardy said RunSocial is looking to make inroads in the U.S. market with future partnerships and more U.S.-based video routes.

In 2015, Outside Interactive collaborated with the New Balance Falmouth Road Race[10], a seven-mile course on Cape Cod, Mass. Jennifer Edwards, Falmouth's general manager, said the race organizers were hesitant at first when they heard McNamee's pitch but saw the opportunity to give those who couldn't run the live race—because of scheduling or geography—a chance to participate.

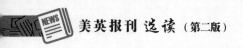

Edwards said Falmouth's goal was "not to add to the race day experience but add another opportunity to be a part of the experience".

Edwards said 40 finishers completed the virtual race, which was held at the same time as the actual race. Each was given a bib and a finisher's certificate, as well as guaranteed entry to the 2016 Falmouth. Edwards said the field included competitors from as far away as California, Florida, Texas and Oregon.

It also included Kara Salvagno, a longtime Connecticut resident who relocated to Scottsdale, Ariz., last year. She has competed in the Falmouth Road Race almost every year since 1993.

"I thought, this is fabulous! I have so many friends who still run the race, but I can't do it this year," she said.

Salvagno said she made the virtual run a full event. She asked her home gym to open at 6 a.m. so she could start racing at the same time the race began on Cape Cod.

She also FaceTimed[11] with a friend who was running seven miles at their favorite running spot in Connecticut at the same time Salvagno ran the virtual Falmouth.

"It was a waltz down memory lane, really," Salvagno said. "We just laughed the entire time. It didn't feel like we were running."

The Peachtree Road Race[12] in Atlanta, the world's biggest 10km race with more than 60,000 participants, allowed Outside Interactive to film its course this past Fourth of July before the actual race.

Rich Kenah, the president of the Atlanta Track Club, which operates the race, said the success of the Falmouth led his team to use the app as a way to promote the Peachtree Race. That event usually draws 90 percent of its participants from Georgia.

"As we look toward the future of the race, we want to attract more people from out of state. So this partnership gives us the opportunity to showcase the race to those unfamiliar with Atlanta, Peachtree Road and what the race looks like and feels like," Kenah said.

Virtual Racing's Future

Outside Interactive and RunSocial hope that interest eventually will match the opportunity, especially in generating revenue.

"Can you imagine in the future a million people literally running, walking or crawling the virtual Boston Marathon on a global scale? I mean, it's kind of a mind-blower," McNamee said.

For now, McNamee and Hardy said their goal is to find pioneers who are technologically savvy and receptive to the concept. Although questions remain about the value of virtual racing,

McNamee said that the app isn't meant to replace an actual race. He added that some experience of racing is better than no experience at all.

Hardy said that although he is invested in what the next level of virtual technology will bring, he is more intrigued by the shifting definitions of shared experiences.

"When you're doing an event, you're not having a chat with everyone, right? But you are sharing an experience together, and that's more motivating than a regular run on your own. That doesn't mean you want to talk to everyone, but you're still sharing an experience together, and that's interesting."

Both apps are free, and users pay per video, starting at $3.99. Real-life races such as Falmouth incorporate the price of the video route into the overall race package, which can include a bib, swag and a finisher's certificate. Visit official websites for more information.

（From *The Washington Post*, Jul. 19, 2016）

NOTES

1. **The Boston Marathon**：波士顿马拉松赛，作为全球首个城市马拉松比赛于 1897 年开始举办。迄今为止，波士顿马拉松赛通常在每年 4 月中旬进行。整个路线的起伏较大，有超过一万人参加。

2. **Outside Interactive**：由美国人加里·麦克纳米（Gary McNamee）于 2011 年创办的一家公司。该公司开发出以著名公路长跑赛事为基础的虚拟视频路线应用软件 Virtual Runner，在跑步机上实现与真实比赛同步进行。

3. **RunSocial**：总部设在新加坡的一家公司。该公司使用增强现实技术开发出跑步应用软件，实现在跑步机上与著名马拉松赛事同步比赛。

4. **augmented reality technology**：简称 AR，增强现实技术。该技术利用计算机生成一种逼真的虚拟环境，通过各种传感设备让用户的视、听、触、动等感觉都沉浸到这个虚拟环境中，实现用户和环境直接进行自然交互，是一项能"把现实带入虚拟，让虚拟增强现实"的应用技术。

5. ***Pokémon Go***：《口袋妖怪 Go》，由宝可梦公司（Pokémon）、任天堂（Nintendo）和谷歌的 Niantic Labs 公司在 2016 年合作开发的一款现实增强手机游戏。它属于饲养宠物精灵进行对战的游戏，可以将虚拟世界和现实世界联系起来，玩家可以通过智能手机在现实世界里寻找发现精灵，进行抓捕和战斗。

6. **foot pod**：计步器 / 步感器，指具有测量速度、步幅、距离等功能的传感器。它一般固定在鞋上，可以记录跑步者的脚部运动，供跑步者分析其跑步特性以改进表现等。

7. **The Prague Marathon**：布拉格马拉松赛，始于 1995 年，每年 5 月在捷克首都布拉格举行，属于国际田联路跑金标赛事，根据报道，它是世界上沿途风景最美丽的马拉松比赛之一。

8. **The Virgin Money London Marathon**：伦敦马拉松赛，始于 1981 年，每年 4 月下旬举行。该比赛

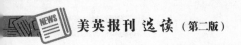

的出发点在伦敦西南的布莱克希思格林尼治公园，途经议会大厦和白金汉宫，终点靠近圣琼斯公园，沿途可以欣赏到伦敦许多历史名胜古迹。

9. **Tim Peake**：蒂姆·皮克（1972—），英国陆军航空队少校，欧洲航天局宇航员，于 2015 年 12 月至 2016 年 6 月作为首位英籍宇航员进入国际空间站（International Space Station）执行任务。2016 年 4 月，蒂姆·皮克在国际空间站跑步机上通过 RunSocial 虚拟视频软件完成了伦敦马拉松比赛。

10. **The New Balance Falmouth Road Race**：马萨诸塞州法尔茅斯公路赛，始于 1973 年，2011 年由纽柏伦公司（New Balance）冠名赞助，每年举办一次，全程 11.26 公里。

11. **FaceTime**：苹果手机自带的一款免费视频聊天软件。通过接入互联网，装有 FaceTime 软件的设备之间可进行视频通话。该词在本文作动词使用，表示视频聊天、视频通话。

12. **The Peachtree Road Race**：佐治亚州亚特兰大桃树公路赛，始于 1970 年 7 月，每年举办一次，全程 10 公里。

USEFUL WORDS

augment	[ɔːgˈment]	v.	(formal) to increase the amount, value, size, etc. of sth. 增加；提高
avatar	[ˈævətɑː(r)]	n.	a picture of a person or an animal which represents a person, on a computer screen, especially in a computer game or chat room（尤指电脑游戏或聊天室中代表使用者的）头像；化身
bib	[bɪb]	n.	(especially British English) a piece of cloth or plastic with a number or special colors on it that people wear on their chests and backs when they are taking part in a sport, so that people know who they are （运动员佩戴的）号码
blur	[blɜː(r)]	v.	to become or make sth. become difficult to distinguish clearly （使）难以区分
enhance	[ɪnˈhɑːns]	v.	to increase or further improve the good quality, value or status of sb./sth. 提高；增强
fabulous	[ˈfæbjələs]	adj.	(informal) extremely good 极好的
high-definition	[ˌhaɪ defɪˈnɪʃn]	adj.	(technical) using or produced by a system that gives very clear detailed images 高清晰度的
incline	[ɪnˈklaɪn]	n.	(formal) a slope 斜坡
intrigue	[ɪnˈtriːg]	v.	to make sb. very interested and want to know more about sth. 激起……的兴趣
proportion	[prəˈpɔːʃn]	n.	the relationship of one thing to another in size, amount, etc. 比例
revenue	[ˈrevənjuː]	n.	the money that a government receives from taxes or that an

organization, etc. receives from its business 税收收入；收益

savvy	['sævi]	*adj.*	(informal, especially North American English) having practical knowledge and understanding of sth.; having common sense 有见识的；通情达理的
showcase	['ʃəʊkeɪs]	*v.*	to display or present to the best advantage 展示
surreal	[sə'riːəl]	*adj.*	very strange; more like a dream than reality, with ideas and images mixed together in a strange way 离奇的；超现实的
surreality	[ˌsəri'æliti]	*n.*	noun form of *surreal* 离奇；超现实主义
sync	[sɪŋk]	*v.*	to make synchronous or adjust in time or manner 同时；同步
treadmill	['tredmɪl]	*n.*	an exercise machine that has a moving surface that you can walk or run on while remaining in the same place （锻炼身体的）跑步机；走步机
virtual	['vɜːtʃuəl]	*adj.*	made to appear to exist by the use of computer software, for example on the Internet （通过计算机软件，如在互联网上）模拟的；虚拟的

EXERCISES

I. Vocabulary

Choose among the four alternatives one word or phrase that is closest in meaning to the underlined part in each statement.

1. Thus he began Outside Interactive, a company that, along with others, is <u>merging</u> fitness <u>with</u> high-definition virtual technology.

   A. combining...with   B. changing...into   C. turning...into   D. separating...with

2. In a bit of surreality, the crowds and fellow racers in the video will run and cheer <u>in proportion to</u> the speed of the real runners.

   A. in spite of   B. due to   C. in line with   D. in relation to

3. Both the virtual running app and RunSocial GPS, an outdoor tracking system that the company just launched, <u>feature</u> ways for participants to race one another, complete with a countdown clock and a leader board.

   A. include   B. display   C. find   D. explain

4. Hardy said RunSocial is looking to <u>make inroads in</u> the U.S. market with future partnerships and more U.S.-based video routes.

   A. enter into   B. invade into   C. march towards   D. head for

5. Jennifer Edwards, Falmouth's general manager, said the race organizers were hesitant at first

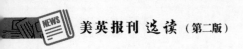

when they heard McNamee's <u>pitch</u> but saw the opportunity to give those who couldn't run the live race—because of scheduling or geography—a chance to participate.

    A. sound   B. strength   C. promotion   D. degree

6. It also included Kara Salvagno, a longtime Connecticut <u>resident</u> who relocated to Scottsdale, Ariz., last year.

    A. physician   B. immigrant   C. guest   D. inhabitant

7. That event usually <u>draws</u> 90 percent of its participants from Georgia.

    A. moves   B. attracts   C. pulls   D. takes

8. Outside Interactive and RunSocial hope that <u>interest</u> eventually will match the opportunity, especially in generating revenue.

    A. attraction   B. hobby   C. concern   D. benefit

9. "Can you imagine in the future a million people literally running, walking or crawling the virtual Boston Marathon on a global scale? I mean, it's kind of <u>a mind-blower</u>," McNamee said.

    A. a drug   B. a shock   C. an excitement   D. a surprise

10. Hardy said that although he is invested in what the next level of virtual technology will bring, he is more <u>intrigued by</u> the shifting definitions of shared experiences.

    A. interested in   B. affected by   C. startled by   D. amazed by

II. Comprehension

Decide whether the following statements are true (T) or false (F) according to the information given in the press clipping. Mark T or F for each statement.

1. Gary McNamee did not take part in the Boston Marathon in 2010 due to the extreme cold weather.

2. Runners can log in the Outside Interactive app and watch the videos of routes free of charge.

3. Using running apps, the runners cannot select their speed on their own.

4. The routes in the Outside Interactive or RunSocial apps are from real-world races.

5. RunSocial's virtual running apps cover the race routes both indoors and outdoors.

6. Both RunSocial and Outside Interactive have collaborated with the real-life long-distance races in the United States.

7. Virtual running apps can provide those who cannot run the actual race with an opportunity to participate.

8. The Peachtree Road Race is the world's biggest 10km race with more than 60,000 participants mainly from Atlanta.

9. Both Outside Interactive and RunSocial have obtained great benefits from the virtual running apps.

10. According to Marc Hardy, it is interesting to share experience with others through virtual races.

III. Topics for Discussion

1. What do you think are the advantages of virtual running apps developed by Outside Interactive and RunSocial?

2. Suppose you are a regular runner, would you like to try a virtual race when you are unable to take part in the real-life race? Please state your reasons.

3. Both RunSocial and Outside Interactive offer free apps, but you need to pay for the videos of virtual routes. How would you comment on this charging policy?

4. According to Gary McNamee, the virtual running app is not meant to replace an actual race. Do you agree with him? What do you think is the relationship between the virtual race and the actual one?

5. Both Outside Interactive and RunSocial hope they will generate profit on their virtual apps and find investors to support their projects. What do you think of the future of the virtual races?

美英两国的饮食文化简介

　　运动与饮食同人们的生活方式密切相关。在人们的生活中，饮食是不可或缺的部分，不同国家和地区拥有不同的饮食文化。所谓饮食文化，是指附着在饮食上并在饮食过程中体现出来的文化意义（隗静秋，2010）。美英两国的饮食文化体现着美英两国的生活方式、价值观以及文化传统。因此，在美英报刊中，通常会有关于美食的专栏。比如，《华盛顿邮报》中的 Lifestyle 栏目开辟了 Food 专栏，分成 Voraciously、Recipe Finder、Going Out Guide、Tom Sietsema、Tim Carman、Nourish、Dinner in Minutes、Wine、Spirits 等主题版块。

一、日常饮食

　　和我们一样，美英两国的人们在正常情况下每天有三顿饭——早餐、午餐和晚餐。早上七点半至八点半通常是早餐时间，中午十二点至两点为午餐时间，晚上七点至九点为晚餐时间。除此之外，下午四五点钟是英国人的下午茶时间。他们会喝热茶或咖啡，还会配上蛋糕、饼干等点心。下午茶起源于 19 世纪英国上层社会，最初是由于晚餐时间要等到晚上八点之后，午餐后至下午四五点钟，人们会感觉饥肠辘辘，于是就会准备些面包、松饼等点心，同时配上上等红茶。这渐渐演变成一种礼仪，形成英国独有的下午茶文化。

　　传统的英式早餐比较丰盛，包括煎培根、香肠、炒蛋、烤番茄、茄汁黄豆、烤面包等主食，还有麦片粥或麦片、玉米片搭配牛奶或酸奶，并可以加入干果或水果；饮料包括红茶、咖啡或果汁。传统美式早餐基本上汇集了英式早餐和欧洲大陆各国的早餐内容，营养齐全、种类丰富，涵盖燕麦、玉米片等谷类，煎蛋、水煮蛋、炒蛋等蛋类，吐司、法式牛角面包、丹麦甜面包等面包，水果或果汁，以及红茶、咖啡、牛奶等饮料。

午餐通常比较简单，多数人选择三明治、汉堡、烤马铃薯或炸薯条，基本以快餐为主。

晚餐则是一天中最重要的一餐，也称正餐，一般饭前先喝汤，饭后吃水果。正餐的顺序大致包括开胃饮料或酒，汤（浓汤为主，有时会配有面包），主菜（牛排、火腿等肉类或鱼类、蔬菜沙拉、土豆等），餐后甜品（点心、水果、冰激凌等），最后是咖啡。在英国，人们在喝咖啡之前还会吃饼干和乳酪。

从上述日常饮食中可以看出，美英人士的饮食主要以丰富的肉类食品和奶制食品为主，以蔬菜为辅。这主要与美英两国以畜牧业为主的农业产业结构有关。他们采用简单的烹饪方式，主要以煎、煮、炖、炸、拌为主，讲求食物的营养和搭配，注重选取新鲜的食材和原料，讲究菜肴的原汁原味，强调在烹调过程中保持食物原有的营养成分和味道。美国人追求食物的营养，讲求食物的营养成分，会考虑蛋白质、脂肪、碳水化合物等元素的组成是否能为人们所吸收（赵敬，2010）。

二、就餐礼仪

以美英两国饮食为代表的西餐非常讲究礼仪，主要包括入座方式、餐具使用、用餐规矩等。

首先，从左侧入座是最得体的入座方式。在西餐厅，就座前先靠近桌子站直，等餐厅领位者把椅子拉出后再站进去，椅子会被再推进来，直至腿弯碰到椅子时，就可以坐下。就座时需要端正坐好，双手自然下垂放在腿上，双腿平放，与餐桌的距离以便于使用餐具为佳。之后将餐巾对折放在膝上准备用餐，注意不宜随意摆弄餐桌上已摆好的餐具。

其次，西餐中餐具的布置和摆放十分讲究。通常是有几道菜就摆放几副刀叉，吃一道菜就换一副刀叉，如吃主菜用主餐刀和主刀叉，饭后甜品也配有专门的刀叉。使用刀叉进餐时，按照摆放顺序从外侧往内侧取用，左手持叉、右手持刀。切东西时左手拿叉按住食物，右手执刀将其切成小块，用叉子送入口中。使用刀时，刀刃向内。进餐中放下刀叉时，应将刀叉顶端靠拢，摆放在餐盘边上。刀刃朝向自身，表示还要继续使用。每吃完一道菜，则要将刀叉并拢放在盘中。用餐过程中如果要谈话，可以拿着刀叉，无需放下。不用刀时，可用右手持叉。但若需要做手势时，就应放下刀叉，不要手执刀叉在空中挥舞摇晃，也不要一手拿刀或叉，而另一只手拿餐巾擦嘴，也不可一手拿酒杯，另一只手拿叉取菜。

最后，在西餐用餐过程中有很多规矩要遵守。用餐时不要弄出声响，喝汤时不要吸啜，吃东西时要闭嘴咀嚼。如果汤菜过热，可待稍凉后再吃，不要用嘴吹。喝汤时，用汤勺从里向外舀，当汤盘中的汤快喝完时，用左手将汤盘的外侧稍稍翘起，用汤勺舀净即可。吃完汤菜时，可以将汤匙留在汤盘（碗）中，匙把指向自己。吃鱼、肉等带刺或带骨头的菜肴时，不要直接外吐，可用餐巾捂嘴轻轻吐在叉上再放入盘内。吃牛排、鸡肉、鱼肉等大块食物时，要切一块吃一块，不能切得过大，或一次将肉都切成块。注意嘴里有食物时一般不要开口说话。就餐时宜低声交谈，切勿大声喧哗。另外，使用餐巾也有讲究：要用餐巾轻轻地沾擦留在脸上的残渣；不要抖开餐巾再去折叠，也不要在空中挥动餐巾；餐巾应放在大腿上，如果中途离开餐桌，要将餐巾放在椅子上，并把椅子推近餐桌；用餐结束后不要折叠餐巾，否则不了解情况的服务生可能会再给别的客人使用；用餐结束后要将餐巾从中间拿起，轻轻地放在餐桌上盘子的左侧。

　　餐桌礼仪是随着社会进步与社会交往而逐步形成的规范和礼节，体现着对他人的尊重，是人类文明的表现，从中可以感受美英饮食文化的独特魅力，也是了解和学习西方文化的一种真实体验。

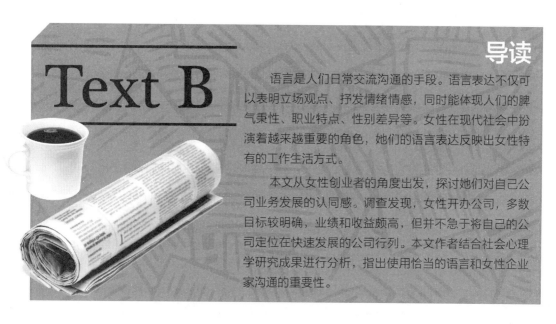

Text B

导读

　　语言是人们日常交流沟通的手段。语言表达不仅可以表明立场观点、抒发情绪情感，同时能体现人们的脾气秉性、职业特点、性别差异等。女性在现代社会中扮演着越来越重要的角色，她们的语言表达反映出女性特有的工作生活方式。

　　本文从女性创业者的角度出发，探讨她们对自己公司业务发展的认同感。调查发现，女性开办公司，多数目标较明确，业绩和收益颇高，但并不急于将自己的公司定位在快速发展的公司行列。本文作者结合社会心理学研究成果进行分析，指出使用恰当的语言和女性企业家沟通的重要性。

Women's talk: Why language matters to female entrepreneurs

When Sue Stockdale set out to find women business-owners with fast-growth companies, she found the language we use to offer opportunities to women is key

By Sue Stockdale

"Wanted—successful women entrepreneurs running fast-growing companies." You would think that an advert like this would have hordes of women making contact, wouldn't you? Well, that's not the case.

A few years ago I was involved in an initiative whose target market was women entrepreneurs running fast-growth companies. My role was to find these businesses to see how they could be

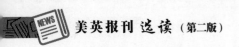

supported in raising capital, and gaining access to mentors to help them during their growth journey. However, the problem was that we could not find many women who identified with this description. The traditional advertising routes were not working, so I set out to check if the lack of interest meant that they actually didn't exist.

What I discovered surprised me. There were many women who had ambitious growth plans and whose businesses were generating annual revenues well in excess of £250,000—but they did not categorise themselves as a "fast growth company". In fact, it took a little time during the conversations for them to recognise how successful they actually were. I would begin with getting to know them as individuals and find out what their passions were, why they started up their business and what progress they had made to date. Then I would enquire what their future plans were, and what they hoped to gain as a result of that success. In other words, I started with where they were now, and slowly uncovered what they were moving towards.

As a result of these conversations I realised that in every case, the businesses did qualify as fast growth, and the business owner was focused and driven to achieve further success. What I had uncovered was that the women did not identify with the label used and had not come forward as a result. So the language seemed to matter.

More recently I have been delivering a series of talks on the subject of risk, and using the risk type compass[1] as a way to help leaders to appreciate that risk-taking can look quite different depending on your risk disposition. For those that are warier and prudent, or more risk averse, stating ambitious growth aspirations for their company may seem highly uncomfortable. While they are perfectly capable of getting that outcome, how they express their ambitions may be somewhat different to those who are more adventurous and carefree, and more comfortable with risk-taking.

I describe these differences using the story of climbing a mountain. If I was to ask the more risk-averse woman to climb a mountain, their immediate reaction is likely to be, "No, that's too difficult; I can't do that—you should ask my friend Jo; she likes adventures."

However, if I said, "Let's go out for a walk, and enjoy the fresh air; we can have a chat along the way—it might get a bit uneven under foot, so come prepared," they are likely to turn up with enthusiasm and the correct footwear; then before they know it we have walked half way up the mountain! Two ways to achieve a similar outcome, but different languages used to motivate the individual depending on what words resonate with them.

TED[2] talk superstar, Amy Cuddy[3] also talks about how language can have an impact on action in her recent book, *Presence*. She recalls her desire to become a runner and that she repeatedly failed in her New Year resolution[4] because in every run she did, she felt like a failure against her ideal of someone who was self-disciplined, fast and able to complete marathons. Eventually she took a different approach. She just resolved to run once. She dropped the long-term, aspirational goals, and just set out to make running a positive experience. Rather than focusing on what she believed she could not do, she focused on what she could do and linked it to something she enjoys, which is travel. So now when she travels for work, so goes for a short run to experience a little more of her new environment in a different way.

Cuddy uses the term "self-nudging" to describe this approach. Along with her Harvard colleague Alison Wood Brooks, they arranged a seminar on the topic, aiming to discover more about the psychological hurdles that stop people from performing well. What they learned was that when we reframe anxiety as excitement, the better we are likely to do.

Brooks carried out experiments with people using three different stressful situations and found that those who took a moment to reframe their anxiety as excitement outperformed the others. Self-nudging, is about focusing on each moment in front of you, rather than the end outcome, to slowly nudge yourself towards being bolder.

So what does this mean for those who are working in the field of women's enterprise support? I think it means that language matters. We are so used to talking about aspirational end goals— start-up to IPO[5], fast growth to exit, making a million, that maybe some thought should be given to "being the best you can be in your business today" mantra. Reflect on "what is" as well as "what could be" using real-time feedback as a means of motivating oneself without being pressurised into defining what the end outcome should be.

The UK government formed a behavioural insights team focused on implementing changes in processes and systems to nudge people. They have had successes in the areas of car tax and income tax, so perhaps they should now turn their attention to developing some nudges to encourage more women to start up and grow their businesses, or encourage more diversity in the workplace. We can all think about how to encourage people to make different choices based on how options are presented, so maybe a little more thought about the words you are using can make a big difference.

(From *The Guardian*, Jun. 29, 2016)

NOTES

1. **risk type compass**: 风险承担类型罗盘，一种心理学测试工具，用来分析个人承受风险的倾向类型。

2. **TED**："Technology, Entertainment, Design" 的缩写，即技术、娱乐、设计，美国一家非营利机构。该机构以其组织的 TED 大会著称，大会宗旨是 "值得传播的创意"（ideas worth spreading）。TED 诞生于 1984 年，其发起人是理查德·沃曼（Richard S. Wurman）；2001 年起，克里斯·安德森（Chris Anderson）接管 TED，创立了种子基金会（The Sapling Foundation），并运营 TED 大会。TED 大会每年举行一次，邀请世界各领域的杰出代表出席大会，进行演讲。演讲内容涉及科学、设计、文学、音乐、宗教、慈善等方方面面，受邀代表同与会者一同思考和探索有关技术、社会和人的关系。TED 大会将演讲做成视频上传到互联网上，供全球观众免费观看。

3. **Amy Cuddy**：艾米·卡迪，美国社会心理学者，哈佛大学商学院副教授。2012 年 6 月，艾米·卡迪在 TED 大会上做了题为 "肢体语言塑造你自己"（Your Body Language Shapes Who You Are）的演讲，全球观看人数达到 3,500 万人，受到广泛好评。这次演讲内容后编入 2015 年出版的《风度》（Presence）一书中，该书荣登美国《纽约时报》畅销书排行榜，在同类图书中排名第三。

4. **New Year resolution**：新年愿望，通常是指人们在 1 月 1 日新年时许下的心愿清单，希望在新的一年里能够完成，这是英美人士的一种惯行做法。

5. **IPO**：全称为 Initial Public Offering，指首次公开募股或首次公开发行。它是指一家企业或公司（股份有限公司）第一次将其股份向公众出售，或首次向社会公众公开招股的发行方式。

USEFUL WORDS

advert	['ædvɜːt]	*n.*	(British English) (= advertisement) an announcement in a newspaper, on television, or on a poster about sth. like a product, event, or job 广告
ambitious	[æmˈbɪʃəs]	*adj.*	needing a lot of effort, money or time to succeed 规模宏大的；艰巨的；耗资的
aspiration	[ˌæspəˈreɪʃn]	*n.*	~ for sth. / ~ to do sth. a strong desire to have or do sth. 渴望；抱负，志向
averse	[əˈvɜːs]	*adj.*	(formal) not liking sth. or wanting to do sth.; opposed to doing sth. 不乐意的；反对的
disposition	[ˌdɪspəˈzɪʃn]	*n.*	(formal) a tendency to behave in a particular way 倾向；意向
enthusiasm	[ɪnˈθjuːziæzəm]	*n.*	a strong feeling of excitement and interest in sth. and a desire to become involved in it 热情；热心，热忱
entrepreneur	[ˌɒntrəprəˈnɜː(r)]	*n.*	a person who makes money by starting or running businesses, especially when this involves taking financial risks 创业者；企业家（尤指涉及财务风险的）

horde	[hɔːd]	*n.*	(sometimes disapproving) a large crowd of people 一大群人
hurdle	['hɜːdl]	*n.*	a problem or difficulty that must be solved or dealt with before you can achieve sth. 难关；障碍
implement	['ɪmplɪment]	*v.*	to make sth. that has been officially decided start to happen or be used 使生效；贯彻，执行，实施
initiative	[ɪ'nɪʃətɪv]	*n.*	a new plan for dealing with a particular problem or for achieving a particular purpose 倡议；新方案
mantra	['mæntrə]	*n.*	a statement or a principle that people repeat very often because they think it is true, especially when you think that it is not true or is only part of the truth （尤指认为并不正确或只是部分正确的）准则；原则；圭臬
mentor	['mentɔː(r)]	*n.*	an experienced person who advises and helps sb. with less experience over a period of time 导师；顾问
nudge	[nʌdʒ]	*v.*	to push sb./sth. gently or gradually in a particular direction （朝某方向）轻推；渐渐推动
outperform	[ˌaʊtpə'fɔːm]	*v.*	to achieve better results than sb./sth. （效益上）超过；胜过
prudent	['pruːdnt]	*adj.*	sensible and careful when you make judgments and decisions; avoiding unnecessary risks 谨慎的；慎重的；精明的
resolution	[ˌrezə'luːʃn]	*n.*	a firm decision to do or not to do sth. 决心；决定
resonate	['rezəneɪt]	*v.*	to remind sb. of sth.; to be similar to what sb. thinks or believes 使产生联想；引起共鸣；和……的想法（或观念）类似
wary	['weəri]	*adj.*	careful when dealing with sb./sth. because you think that there may be a danger or problem （对待人或事物时）小心的，谨慎的；留神的

✒EXERCISES

I. Vocabulary

Choose among the four alternatives one word or phrase that is closest in meaning to the underlined part in each statement.

1. A few years ago I was involved in <u>an initiative</u> whose target market was women entrepreneurs running fast-growth companies.

    A. a process   B. a plan   C. an action   D. a decision

2. The traditional advertising routes were not working, so I <u>set out</u> to check if the lack of interest meant that they actually didn't exist.

    A. started   B. left   C. arranged   D. explained

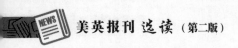
3. There were many women who had ambitious growth plans and whose businesses were generating annual revenues well in excess of £250,000—but they did not <u>categorise</u> themselves as a "fast growth company".

A. place   B. display   C. suggest   D. classify

4. What I had uncovered was that the women did not identify with the label used and had not <u>come forward</u> as a result.

A. offered help   B. taken action   C. stood out   D. turned up

5. More recently I have been delivering a series of talks on the subject of risk, and using the risk type compass as a way to help leaders to appreciate that risk-taking can look quite different depending on your risk <u>disposition</u>.

A. temperament   B. property   C. tendency   D. arrangement

6. While they are perfectly capable of getting that outcome, how they express their ambitions may be somewhat different to those who are more adventurous and <u>carefree</u>, and more comfortable with risk-taking.

A. thoughtless   B. irresponsible   C. trouble-free   D. cheerful

7. Two ways to achieve a similar outcome, but different languages used to motivate the individual depending on what words <u>resonate</u> with them.

A. identify   B. resound   C. repeat   D. echo

8. What they learned was that when we <u>reframe</u> anxiety as excitement, the better we are likely to do.

A. rearrange   B. reorganize   C. redefine   D. reset

9. <u>Reflect on</u> "what is" as well as "what could be" using real-time feedback as a means of motivating oneself without being pressurised into defining what the end outcome should be.

A. Remember   B. Consider   C. Reverberate   D. Indicate

10. We can all think about how to encourage people to make different choices based on how options are presented, so maybe a little more thought about the words you are using can <u>make a big difference</u>.

A. become quite different   B. draw a clear distinction

C. turn into a different state   D. have an important effect

II. Comprehension

Decide whether the following statements are true (T) or false (F) according to the information given in the press clipping. Mark T or F for each statement.

1. With the advert for successful women entrepreneurs running fast-growing companies, many women came to apply for it.

2. In fact, many successful women did not recognize themselves as running a fast-growth company.

3. One's risk disposition decides what kind of risk one would like to take.

4. The women who are risk-averse seem uncomfortable to state their ambition for they are unable to achieve fast-growth in their company.

5. The story of mountain-climbing indicates the effect of language used to motivate the

individuals to accomplish their goals.

6. Amy Cuddy failed to become a runner because she did not find the right way to practice.

7. Self-nudging refers to the approach to focusing on what one can do for the moment, rather than for the final outcome.

8. The experiment discovered that those who treated anxiety as excitement performed better than others.

9. Proper language has an important influence on helping women entrepreneurs with their aspirational end goals.

10. It is suggested that the words can make a difference if we think about the way we present options for others to choose.

III. Topics for Discussion

1. What was the purpose of the initiative Sue Stockdale participated in a few years ago, that found women entrepreneurs running fast-growth companies?

2. Many women entrepreneurs have made great success in their business, but they do not regard their companies as fast-growing ones. How do you explain this phenomenon?

3. As to the subject of risk, one's risk disposition can decide the degree of risk-taking. Those who are warier and prudent may seem different in expressing their ambitions from those who are more adventurous and carefree. What category do you belong to in terms of risk-taking? Would you like to share your risk-taking experience with your classmates?

4. Amy Cuddy and her colleague have found that self-nudging, focusing on each moment in front rather than the end goal, can push one person towards being braver. What is the significance of this finding to the women entrepreneurs?

5. In this article, it is concluded that language plays an important role in encouraging women to start up and grow their businesses. What do you think are the functions of language?

《华尔街日报》简介

　　《华尔街日报》（*The Wall Street Journal*）于 1889 年在纽约创刊，归美国道·琼斯公司（Dow Jones & Company）所有，后被新闻集团（News Corp）收购，是侧重商业和经济新闻的英语国际日报。《华尔街日报》具有广泛的国际影响力，日发行量达 200 万份，是美国发行量最大的财经类报纸。该报同时还出版了亚洲版、欧洲版、网络版，每天大概有 2,000

多万人阅读纸质或电子版报纸。《华尔街日报》系列的目标是为高层管理人员、政府官员以及商界决策者提供公正、准确、独立的财经新闻。

作为一家享誉全球一百多年的财经类报纸，保证质量是关键，《华尔街日报》始终不遗余力地追求高质量新闻。该报擅长进行深度报道，谨慎选择适合题材，选题周期较长，通常为一月有余。该报对新闻写作手法历来要求非常严格，逐渐形成了独特的文体——"华尔街日报体"，强调严谨文风、表达明了清晰。在报道抽象、枯燥的新闻时，开头通常以与新闻主题有关的感性人物故事入手，层层递进，不断深化主题。透过富于人情味的报道，非事件性新闻因人物的介入变得鲜明突出、引人注目。

《华尔街日报》的内容主要涵盖美国经济、国际话题以及财经新闻。高度可信的信息源是保证新闻质量的关键因素之一，《华尔街日报》的信息主要来源于世界著名的证券交易机构、权威的政府发布部门或著名的信息发布部门，言论分析则来自权威人士。

《华尔街日报》的报道风格严肃，较少使用新闻图片，报纸主要以文字报道为主。经过改版，报纸与网络形成了更好的融合：纸质报纸精简记录昨日之报道，网络版则更为详尽。另外，《华尔街日报》还在网上推出了一系列免费博客。

《华尔街日报》的读者定位较高，绝大多数属于高收入、高学历、高职位人群。为了培养市场、抓住未来的读者，自 1991 年起，该报设立了《华尔街日报》教室版（*The Wall Street Journal* Classroom Edition），每月一期，专门刊登学生感兴趣的文章。同时，美国有些重点商学院会建议学生在校期间每人订阅一份《华尔街日报》，作为课外阅读的材料。

Unit 5
Sports

报刊英语中动词的应用

　　报刊内容的经济性要求新闻工作者在有限的篇幅内要传达尽量多的信息，以满足读者的阅读需求。就动词的使用而言，报刊英语往往以短小的动词来替换含字母较多的长词。这种趋势在英语报刊的标题中表现得尤为明显。

一、短动词

　　报刊英语中选用短小的动词既可节约版面，又能节省读者的阅读时间。表 5.1 列举的便是常见的英语短动词以及语义对应的长动词，这些短动词词汇经常在新闻报道中使用，因此在一定程度上成了新闻报道中的惯用词汇。

表 5.1　报刊英语中的常用短动词

常用短动词	对应长动词	汉语释义	常用短动词	对应长动词	汉语释义
aid	assist	帮助	sack	dismiss	解雇
allege	declare	宣布		search thoroughly and rob	劫掠；洗劫
begin	commence	开始	shun	keep away from	回避
bid	attempt	努力	slay	murder	谋杀
bilk	cheat	欺骗	snub	pay no attention to	冷落；拒绝
blast	explode	爆炸	soar	skyrocket	急剧上升
	criticise strongly	严厉抨击	spur	encourage	激励，鞭策
claim	cause the death of...	夺去……的生命	stem	prevent	制止；阻挡
	declare to be true	声称；断言	swap	exchange	交流，交换
clash	disagree strong1y	发生分歧；争议	sway	influence	影响
grill	investigate	调查	thwart	prevent from being successful	阻挠

续表

常用短动词	对应长动词	汉语释义	常用短动词	对应长动词	汉语释义
laud	praise	赞扬	trim	reduce	削减
lop	diminish	下降；减少	vie	compete	竞争
map	work out	制订	vow	determine	决心；发誓
mark	celebrate	庆祝	voice	express	表达
net	tak possession of	捕获，抓获	void	determine to be invalid	使无效
prompt	cause	引起	wed	marry	结婚
quiz	question	询问；审问	weigh	consider	考虑
rule	decide	裁决；裁定	woo	seek to win	争取；追求

二、"说"意动词

在新闻报道中，为了使内容具有真实感和生动性，显示客观与公正，新闻工作者需要适当引用有关人士的话语。引语分直接引语与间接引语：直接引语需要将新闻人物所说的话真实准确、一字不差地记录下来，并用引号标识；间接引语则是对新闻人物所说的话进行转述，无须引号，但转述的内容须与新闻人物所说的话保持一致。无论是转述还是直接引用，都有必要用"某人说"加以交代，以便读者能分辨出该部分内容是文章作者自己的观点还是他人的观点。

（一）标识直接引语的"说"意动词

英语中有大量表示"说"意的动词可用于标识直接引语，如表5.2所示：

表5.2 英语中标识直接引语的"说"意动词

"说"意动词	汉语释义	"说"意动词	汉语释义
acknowledge	承认	contend	声称；主张；认为
add	又说	contradict	反驳
admit	承认	croak	用低沉而沙哑的声音说
affirm	肯定；确认	declare	声明，声称
agree	同意	depict	描绘，描述
air	使公开	deny	否认；拒绝相信
allege	断言	denounce	谴责；宣布
analyze	分析	disagree	不同意
announce	宣布	disclose	透露
argue	争辩；主张	dispute	争论，辩论；反对，辩驳

续表

"说"意动词	汉语释义	"说"意动词	汉语释义
assert	断言	doubt	怀疑
believe	相信；认为	inquire	询问
blame	责备	emphasize	强调
boast	夸口说	exclaim	大声说
cackle	叽叽呱呱地讲；咯咯笑着表示	find	发现
call	大声说（或读）出，喊，叫	fuss	抱怨
challenge	质疑	emphasize	强调
caution	告诫	explain	解释
cheer	喝彩	elaborate	详细叙说
claim	声称	gurgle	以咯咯声表示
complain	抱怨	go on	继续说
commend	表示赞同，称赞	hasten	急急忙忙地说
comment	进行评论；发表意见	hypothesize	假设，假定
conclude	断定；下结论	insist	坚称
concede	承认	infer	推测
concur	同意，赞同	hold	认为；想；相信
confess	承认	imply	暗指，暗示
illustrate	（用图或例子）说明，阐明	shriek	尖声发出，尖声叫喊
indicate	简要地陈述；暗示	shrug	耸了耸肩不满地说
ignore	不理，忽视	sing out	（大声清晰地）喊出，唱出
joke	开玩笑说	speculate	推测，推断；怀疑；设想
maintain	坚持；断言；主张	sputter	（因激动、愤怒）唾沫飞溅地说
mistrust	对……有预感；猜测	state	声明，声称
note	谈及，表明	stress	着重说
object	反驳	scream	尖声地说，尖叫着发出
observe	说；评论，评述	shrug	以耸肩表示
persist	坚称；坚持问，追问	sputter	气急败坏地说
pledge	保证给予，许诺，保证发誓	stammer	结结巴巴地说
point out	指出	suggest	建议
proclaim	宣告	suspect	怀疑
propose	提出；提议，建议	suppose	假定，猜想；认为
protest	抗议	summarize	概括，总结

续表

"说"意动词	汉语释义	"说"意动词	汉语释义
predict	预测	suggest	建议
question	疑问	tweet	啾啾地说
quote	引用	urge	敦促
reaffirm	重申	warn	警告
remark	议论	whisper	小声说
reply	回应	write	写到
report	报道	validate	使生效；批准
reveal	透露，泄露	verify	证明，证实
retort	反诘	vow	郑重地宣告，声明
refute	反驳	voice	说；表达

具体实例如下：

● He **noted**, however, that "we've been working hand in glove with the CDC—or face to mask with the CDC—for some time". (*Los Angeles Times*, Jul. 27, 2021)

● "I'm grateful that starting out my career in broadcasting, he was the one by my side. I learned so much from him," Lipinski **said**. Weir **added**: "I'm proud of him covering the marquis sport at both the Summer and Winter Games. Gymnastics is in the best hands with Terry, but I admit I get jealous when there isn't ice behind him for his on-cameras!" (*USA Today*, Jul. 26, 2021)

● "Silence is the enemy," he **tweeted** Sunday to his 139,000 followers. (*The Washington Post*, Jun. 7, 2021)

● "Can you imagine if I was singing about texting?" She **cackles**. "You would never get me singing about having a drink in the club." (*Time*, Jan. 4, 2016)

● "We are doing a full review of the updated recommendations released by the U.S. Centers for Disease Control and Prevention today and will evaluate existing guidance to determine the best path forward to protect Californians from the spread of COVID-19 and the highly contagious Delta variant," the California Department of Public Health **wrote** Tuesday afternoon in response to an e-mail inquiry from *The Times*. (*Los Angeles Times*, Jul. 27, 2021)

在上述例子中，noted、said、added、tweeted、cackles、wrote 都是用来表达直接引语的动词。"说"意动词除与有明确消息来源的信息结合在一起以外，还常与模糊的消息来源一起用于新闻报道之中，如 sources said（消息人士说）、authorities said（权威人士说）、

witnesses said（目击者称）、top White House aides revealed（白宫高级助手披露）、a senior official in the British Foreign Office announced（英国外交部一位高级官员宣布）等。

（二）标识间接引语的"说"意动词

间接引语是指文章作者转述新闻人物所说的话，这种转述必须客观、真实。文章作者在转述过程中不能曲解原话的本意，不能随意增加或减少原话导致意思有变，这是新闻报道记者应该遵守的职业道德，也是新闻做到客观公正的底线。用于标识直接引语的动词也都常用于标识间接引语。例如：

- But Mr. Donney **said** he's still open to voting for Trump. "It depends on how he acts," he **said**. That was before Thursday night's debate. (*The Christian Science Monitor*, Mar. 4, 2016)

前一个句子"But Mr. Donney said he's still open to voting for Trump."本身是间接引语，是文章作者根据 Mr. Donney 的话做出的一种合理推论，这种推论当然不可避免地会包含其对原话的评判，当然这种判断在动词 said 一词上的体现是很弱的。随后的直接引语 It depends on how he acts 便是文章作者做出前面推论的依据。更多例子如下：

- Emergency responders **said** there were at least three water rescues at the intersection of West Dupont and Kinsman roads. "At least three vehicles stuck in the flooded roadway," an agency told the weather service. (*Chicago Tribune*, Jul. 13, 2021)
- In the book, Dawkins **contends** that a supernatural creator almost certainly does not exist and that religious faith is a delusion—"a fixed false belief"...In the book, Dawkins **argues** against the watchmaker analogy made famous by the eighteenth-century English theologian William Paley via his book *Natural Theology*. (From Wikipedia website, Apr. 20, 2022)
- Wang also **explained** that the Chinese see this talent pool as the key to moving from a "made in China" orientation to a "created in China" capability. China's future growth, **continued** Wang, will rely more on the new talent strategy, even as its past successes were built mainly on its population dividend and investment. (*The Washington Post*, Nov. 16, 2011)
- Maltese **alleges** that several high-ranking Giants officials have not taken sufficient action to remove offenders from the organization over the years. (*Daily News*, Jul. 27, 2021)

在上述例子中，said、contends、argues、explained、continued、alleges 都是用于间接转述他人观点或看法的"说"意动词。

由此可以看出，某些动词的选用会不可避免地传达出引述者的主观色彩，体现出其主观判断。当新闻报道者选用某个动词或某些动词表达"说"时，实际上已经加入了自身对被引用者或被转述者语气、态度、情态乃至举止方式等的判断，比如下列动词：admit（承认）、assert（断言）、believe（相信；认为）、boast（夸口说）、caution（告诫）、complain（抱怨）、concede（承认）、confess（承认）、contend（争辩）、contradict（反驳）、concur（同意，赞同）、claim（声称）、commend（赞同；称赞）、doubt（怀疑）、hold（怀有[见解]）、insist（坚持，坚决认为）、imply（暗含）、maintain（坚持，断言）、object（反驳）、protest（抗议）、pledge（承诺）、question（怀疑，对……提出疑问）、warn（警告）等。例如：

- A top federal pandemic official **warned** last June that Emergent BioSolutions, the government contractor that last month threw out millions of doses of COVID-19 vaccines because of contamination, lacked enough trained staff and had a record of problems with quality control. (*The New York Times*, Jul. 29, 2021)

warned 一词的使用体现了文章作者对说话者目的的把握与解读，他把新闻人物所说的话解读为一种警告。实际上，读者应该对文章作者的这种解读进行积极的思考，并做出自己的解读。又如：

- In light of all of her accomplishments, Twitter users **reminded** the world she will always be "the GOAT", or greatest of all time. (*USA Today*, Jul. 27, 2021)

在上例中，文章作者是在转述别人的话，用的标识间接引语的动词是 reminded，这是他对被引用话语的一种判断和归类。又如：

- Ken Livingstone also offered a critical assessment. He **blamed** Thatcher for causing unemployment and leaving people dependent on welfare: "She decided when she wrote off our manufacturing industry that she could live with two or three million unemployment," he **said**. (*The Guardian*, Apr. 8, 2013)

在上例中，文章作者使用的标识间接引语的动词是 blamed，这是他对被引用话语的一种"定性"，即把后面的话语"定性"为一种"责备"。又如：

- "All of these liars will be sued when the election is over": Donald Trump **denounces** accusers. (*Los Angeles Times*, Oct. 23, 2016)

在上例中，选用 denounces（谴责、公开抨击）一词当然是文章作者对特朗普的说话内容与态度的一种判断。

Text A

导读

2020 年 2 月 2 日晚，第 54 届美国国家橄榄球联盟年度冠军赛在佛罗里达州举行。对阵双方是堪萨斯城酋长队和旧金山 49 人队。这是酋长队时隔 50 年重回超级碗。酋长队在 1967 年第 1 届超级碗比赛时败给绿湾包装工队，在 1970 年再度杀入超级碗，并最终夺冠，但在随后近半个世纪，酋长队都没有再进入超级碗。而旧金山 49 人队战绩辉煌，此前曾 6 进超级碗并夺冠 5 次。此次比赛扣人心弦、精彩纷呈，双方多次逆袭反超，酋长队在第 4 节 10：20 落后的情况下大逆转，最终以比分 31：20 获得冠军，喜提隆巴迪杯。酋长队四分卫帕特里克·马霍姆斯在本场比赛中表现出色，获得本届超级碗最有价值球员称号。堪萨斯城酋长队 61 岁的主教练安迪·里德也是首次带领队伍获得超级碗冠军。在此之前，他虽然从未赢得过超级碗冠军头衔，却备受尊重，一直被业内视作最佳主帅。

本文主要评述酋长队主教练及队员们在职业生涯中的拼搏精神，虽然多次失败但永不言败，他们在逆境中始终努力拼搏，坚持不懈，最终反败为胜。他们的人生经历和职业精神令人钦佩。文章同时引用政治界、科学界、学术界等对失败和成功关系的评论和观点，充分论证了失败对于成功的重要意义。

The lasting lesson of this Super Bowl: Failure is necessary

By Sally Jenkins

There were failures all over the Super Bowl[1] field. They were everywhere you looked, the losers, drifters and discards. There were the guys who went undrafted, the guys who had been cut, or traded, or lowballed. There were the coaches who knew how it felt to be fired. What that should tell you is to never underestimate the virtues of failing.

Winning coated it all with such a false patina, the shine on the sterling of the Lombardi Trophy[2] covering all that came before, which was a sort of shame, because underneath the spectacularity of the Kansas City Chiefs'[3] 31：20 victory over the San Francisco 49ers[4] there was a dull yet invaluable truth to be found, something of use to any ordinary person trudging through a long day: namely, how to manage defeat and turn that demon around. They did it not with dazzlement but by being what Coach Andy Reid[5] called "dirty tough-minded".

If "success is the ability to go from one failure to another with no loss of enthusiasm", as Winston Churchill[6] once said, then surely the 61-year-old Reid qualifies as a success, with his first championship in 21 years of trying. But then so does the hard-yarder Damien Williams[7], whose journey to Super Bowl champion included clawing through junior college, getting kicked out of Oklahoma, going undrafted and an unappreciated stint with the Miami Dolphins[8]. "I'm not going to be stopped," he told the Chiefs in the huddle just before he tore outside for his second touchdown to ensure the victory. Williams had talked all week about the value of his old failures. "I've had a long, long road," he said.

Williams was one of 28 undrafted free agents in the game. Think about that for a second. More than a quarter of the players on the field were considered unworthy at one point in their careers. Even within the game, critical players at times looked like terrible blunderers, only to rebound. For three quarters, Chiefs quarterback Patrick Mahomes[9] was headed towards the most ignominious failure of his young career. With his team down by 10 early in the fourth quarter, he was just 18 for 31 with two interceptions and, "It looked rocky, man," defensive end Frank Clark[10] said. Mahomes admitted, "It was a bad situation." But Reid steadied his quarterback with a fascinating piece of advice. He told him: "Keep firing. Keep believing what your eyes are seeing." What he meant was to trust your experiences, even if it means we go down.

What these people demonstrate is that to win, you have to be willing to lose—badly. Even hurtfully. Reid entered the Super Bowl with a 14 : 14 playoff record. He had finished every single postseason as a head coach with a loss, left wanting. Time after time, he came back for more, willing to experience the radiological exposure of failure.

So many people, at the early stage of disappointment, flinch. We want to know just enough about ourselves and no more. We don't want to think the worst—that we're failures—and that means we never get close to our best, either. If there is one characteristic that any day laborer can draw from a pro coach or athlete, if there is any way in which an ordinary person can emulate them, it's in the ability to lose without losing heart.

Failure is a seriously under-analyzed experience. There are shelves upon shelves of books about how to succeed, but precious few of them make the vital connection that failure is an essential precondition for success. Nor do they acknowledge that reversal, a negative experience, a frustration, an obstacle, is the far, far more common work experience. About 3 million Americans lost a job for one reason or another between 2015 and 2017, according to the Bureau of Labor Statistics[11]. Their plant closed or their company moved, their shift was cut, their position was abolished or their boss simply wanted someone fresh. Running back Raheem Mostert[12] has that in common with them. He was laid off by six different teams before he landed with the 49ers. "I finally have a place to call home," he said.

One reason why coaches and athletes deal so resiliently with setback is that they understand something most people don't: You can't improve something until you've stressed it. You have to probe for your own weaknesses to correct them. If NFL[13] coaches have anything in common with any other profession, it might be with engineers. As Kevin Kelly[14], founding editor of *Wired* magazine has observed: "Great engineers have a respect for breaking things that sometimes surprises non-engineers, just as scientists have a patience with failures that often perplexes outsiders. But the habit of embracing negative results is one of the most essential tricks to gaining success."

Renowned research chemist Richard N. Zare[15] put it similarly: His lab failures can be comedies of errors, he says, but "failures are nature's way of guiding us to what really works". But maybe nobody put it more simply than Thomas Edison[16]. "I can never find the thing that does the job best until I find the ones that don't," he said.

Reversing failure takes more than just sheer resilience, of course. Everyone perseveres. What separates headbanging from an actual change in your circumstances is the ability to patiently diagnose and learn. According to an interesting 2019 study titled "Quantifying the Dynamics of Failure Across Science, Startups and Security" that appeared in *Nature*[17] magazine, it's not just the ability to keep trying that matters, but the ability to keep trying in an organized, well-directed way. The study, which looked at failure data in a variety of fields, including 46 years of venture-capital start-ups, concluded that the eventual succeeders made "critical refinements to systematically advance towards success", whereas others who encountered repeated failure reacted in a more disjointed way, especially making rash changes, tearing things up prematurely.

A lot of NFL teams could learn something from that observation.

If the Chiefs had a signature quality this season, it was their ability to deal with failure in an organized way. This was undoubtedly the leadership of Reid, the veteran of so many playoff years with the Philadelphia Eagles[18] when he was "so close" before he was fired in 2012. Last year, after the Chiefs suffered their bitter overtime loss to the New England Patriots[19] in the AFC[20] championship game, Reid went back to work without surrendering to the self-doubts over his sub-500 career playoff record.

So many teams respond to a disheartening loss by regressing, but Reid told the Chiefs they were "just four inches off". Four inches was the distance of an offside penalty that negated the interception that could have won them the game. A single four-inch mistake. "We decided we could all do four inches better," Reid said. It was the difference between another failure and the ultimate success.

(From *The Washington Post*, Feb. 4, 2020)

NOTES

1. **Super Bowl**：超级碗，美国国家橄榄球联盟的年度总决赛，是美国的一种超级体育赛事。该球季的美联冠军以及国家橄榄球联合会冠军才有资格参赛，胜出的球队将获得"世界冠军"称号。超级碗的比赛时间一般是每年1月末最后一个周日或2月初第一个周日，俗称"超级碗星期天"（Super Bowl Sunday）。此处 Bowl 指大型体育馆或季后赛。

2. **Lombardi Trophy**：文斯·隆巴迪杯，全称为 Vince Lombardi Trophy，指美国国家橄榄球联盟年度总决赛超级碗比赛的纯银冠军奖杯，以美国橄榄球历史上著名教练文斯·隆巴迪（Vince Lombardi）的名字命名。他曾带领绿湾包装工队获得了第1届和第2届的超级碗冠军。

3. **Kansas City Chiefs**：堪萨斯城酋长队，美国国家橄榄球联盟球队，前身是创立于1960年的达拉斯得州佬队（Dallas Texans），1963年搬迁至密苏里州堪萨斯城并更为现名，现属于美国橄榄球联合会西区。

4. **San Francisco 49ers**：旧金山49人队，美国国家橄榄球联盟球队，成立于1944年，位于加利福尼亚州旧金山市，现属于美国橄榄球联合会西区。

5. **Andy Reid**：安迪·里德（1958—），美国橄榄球教练，曾被业内誉为"无冕之王"，曾是美国国家橄榄球联盟历史上未获得过超级碗但常规赛胜场数最高的主教练。2020年，他带领堪萨斯酋长队在第54届超级碗比赛中夺冠，终于在经历21年风雨之后第一次成为超级碗冠军教练。

6. **Winston Churchill**：温斯顿·丘吉尔（1874—1965），英国政治家、军事家和作家。他曾两度出任英国首相，在第二次世界大战中成功领导英国联合美国等同盟国对抗轴心国并取得胜利，被视为20世纪影响英国乃至世界的重要领袖之一。

7. **Damien Williams**：达米恩·威廉姆斯（1992—），美国职业橄榄球运动员，司职跑卫或跑锋（running back）。他在超级碗酋长队战胜49人队的比赛中触地得分，为球队锁定胜局。hard yards 指在橄榄球场上通过激烈对抗而获得的进展。

8. **Miami Dolphins**：迈阿密海豚队，美国国家橄榄球联盟球队，成立于1965年，位于佛罗里达州迈阿密市，现属于美国橄榄球联合会东区。

9. **Patrick Mahomes**：帕特里克·马霍姆斯（1995—），美国职业橄榄球运动员，司职四分卫（quarterback）。他在2020年效力于美国国家橄榄球联盟堪萨斯城酋长队，获得美国国家橄榄球联盟史上最年轻的超级碗"最有价值球员"称号。

10. **Frank Clark**：弗兰克·克拉克（1993—），美国职业橄榄球运动员，司职防守边锋（defensive end）。

11. **Bureau of Labor Statistics**：劳工统计局，美国联邦政府主管劳工经济的政府机构。

12. **Raheem Mostert**：拉希姆·莫斯特尔特（1992—），美国职业橄榄球运动员，司职跑锋，2020年效力于旧金山49人队。

13. **NFL**：全称为 National Football League，美国国家橄榄球联盟，世界上最大的职业美式橄榄球联盟，也是最具商业价值的体育联盟之一。

14. **Kevin Kelly**：凯文·凯利（1952—），科技类期刊《连线》（*Wired*）的创刊主编，被视作"网络文化"（cyberculture）的发言人和观察者。

15. **Richard N. Zare**：理查德·尼尔·扎尔（1961—），国际著名物理化学家，美国斯坦福大学化学系教授。

16. **Thomas Edison**：托马斯·爱迪生（1847—1931），美国著名发明家、物理学家，拥有电灯、留声机等众多重要的发明专利，对世界产生了深远影响。

17. *Nature*：《自然》，一份在英国发行的科学杂志周刊，其出版商为自然出版集团。

18. **Philadelphia Eagles**：费城老鹰队，美国国家橄榄球联盟球队，成立于 1933 年，位于宾夕法尼亚州费城，现属于美国橄榄球联合会东区。

19. **New England Patriots**：新英格兰爱国者队，美国国家橄榄球联盟球队，成立于 1959 年，位于马萨诸塞州大波士顿地区，现属于美国橄榄球联合会东区。

20. **AFC**：全称为 American Football Conference，美国橄榄球联合会，简称"美联"。它与国家橄榄球联合会（National Football Conference，NFC，简称"国联"）合并组成美国国家橄榄球联盟。

USEFUL WORDS

blunderer	['blʌndərə]	*n.*	a person who makes stupid or careless mistakes 犯愚蠢错误的人；粗心大意的人
disjointed	[dis'jointɪd]	*adj.*	lacking a coherent sequence or connection 脱节的；脱臼的；不连贯的
emulate	['emjʊleɪt]	*v.*	(formal) to try to do sth. as well as sb. else because you admire them 效法
flinch	[flɪntʃ]	*v.*	to make a quick, nervous movement as an instinctive reaction to fear, pain, or surprise 畏缩，畏首畏尾；退缩
huddle	['hʌdl]	*n.*	a brief gathering of players during a game to receive instructions, especially in American football 在美式橄榄球中指比赛间隙球员聚在一起讨论战术
ignominious	[ˌɪgnə'mɪniəs]	*adj.*	deserving or causing public disgrace or shame 可耻的；下流的
interception	[ˌɪntə'sepʃn]	*n.*	(in sport) an act of catching a pass made by an opposing player （体育比赛中）抓住对方传球；拦截，截击
lowball	['ləʊbɔːl]	*v.*	to give a markedly or unfairly low offer 有意压低(成本、价值等的)估价
negate	[nɪ'geɪt]	*v.*	to make ineffective; to nullify 否定；使无效；取消
offside	[ˌɔf'saɪd]	*n.*	usually *offsides* (American football) over the scrimmage line or otherwise ahead of the ball before the play has begun 越位（美式橄榄球术语中，越位指防守队员在攻方启球之前先越过启球线，并且未能在攻方启球前

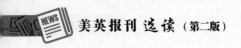

退回至启球线后）

patina	['pætɪnə]	*n.*	the impression or appearance of sth. 表面；外观
perplex	[pə'pleks]	*v.*	to make sb. feel completely baffled 使困惑；使费解
playoff	['pleɪˌɒf]	*n.*	an additional match played to decide the outcome of a contest 加时赛
pro	[prəʊ]	*n.*	a professional, especially in sport 专业人士，尤指体育运动中的专业人士
radiological	[ˌreɪdɪəʊ'lɑdʒɪkl]	*adj.*	relating to the science of X-rays and other high-energy radiation 放射学的；辐射学的
resiliently	[rɪ'zɪlɪəntlɪ]	*adv.*	(of a person or animal) able to withstand or recover quickly from difficult conditions 有恢复力地；富有活力地
sterling	['stɜːlɪŋ]	*n.*	*sterling silver* silver of a particular standard of purity 标准纯银；纯银制品
stint	[stɪnt]	*n.*	a person's fixed or allotted period of work 从事某项工作（或活动）的时间
touchdown	['tʌtʃˌdaʊn]	*n.*	an act of touching the ground with the ball behind the opponents' goal line, scoring a try 达阵（美式橄榄球中的"触地得分"，英式橄榄球用 try）
trudge	[trʌdʒ]	*v.*	to walk slowly and with heavy steps, typically because of exhaustion or harsh conditions 沉重地走；蹒跚地走
undrafted	[ʌn'drɑːftɪd]	*adj.*	(of a sports player) not selected for a team through a professional league's draft 没有球队问津的

EXERCISES

I. Vocabulary

Choose among the four alternatives one word or phrase that is closest in meaning to the underlined part in each statement.

1. What that should tell you is to never <u>underestimate</u> the virtues of failing.

    A. evaluate   B. investigate   C. stimulate   D. undervalue

2. ...because underneath the spectacularity of the Kansas City Chiefs' 31:20 victory over the San Francisco 49ers there was a dull yet <u>invaluable</u> truth to be found...

    A. priceless   B. valueless   C. evaluable   D. value

3. If "success is the ability to go from one failure to another with no loss of enthusiasm", as Winston Churchill once said, then surely the 61-year-old Reid <u>qualifies as</u> a success, with his first championship in 21 years of trying.

    A. is described as   B. is entitled to   C. feels like   D. just as

4. Even within the game, critical players at times looked like terrible blunderers, only to <u>rebound</u>.

　A. decrease　　　　B. respond　　　　C. bounce　　　　D. bound

5. You have to <u>probe for</u> your own weaknesses to correct them.

　A. know　　　　B. reach for　　　　C. search　　　　D. identify

6. <u>Renowned</u> research chemist Richard N. Zare put it similarly: His lab failures can be comedies of errors, he says, but "failures are nature's way of guiding us to what really works".

　A. Famous　　　　B. Notorious　　　　C. Particular　　　　D. Conscious

7. Reversing failure takes more than just sheer resilience, of course. Everyone <u>perseveres</u>.

　A. holds　　　　B. withdraws　　　　C. regresses　　　　D. persists

8. Last year, after the Chiefs suffered their bitter overtime loss to the New England Patriots in the AFC championship game, Reid went back to work without <u>surrendering to</u> the self-doubts over his sub-500 career playoff record.

　A. succumbing to　　　　B. leading to　　　　C. turning to　　　　D. giving in

9. So many teams respond to a disheartening loss by <u>regressing</u>, but Reid told the Chiefs they were "just four inches off".

　A. marching　　　　B. retreating　　　　C. reducing　　　　D. deducing

10. It was the difference between another failure and the <u>ultimate</u> success.

　A. end　　　　B. lasting　　　　C. finish　　　　D. final

II. Comprehension

Decide whether the following statements are true (T) or false (F) according to the information given in the press clipping. Mark T or F for each statement.

1. The sterling of the Lombardi Trophy covers all the success that came before.

2. The priceless truth we can find from Kansas City Chiefs is how to manage defeat and reverse the tide.

3. Damien Williams gave up because of so many old failures in the journey to Super Bowl champion.

4. Coach Reid encouraged the players to keep trying although they were in a disadvantage.

5. Many people give up at the early stage of disappointment. What they can learn from the professional coaches or athletes is the ability to lose without losing heart.

6. Many books about how to succeed explain that a frustration is the far more common work experience.

7. Both NFL coaches and engineers have the habit of embracing negative results in their pursuit of success.

8. An essay appeared in *Nature* magazine illustrates that the ability to keep trying is more important than the ability to keep trying in an organized, well-directed way.

9. The ability to deal with failure in an organized way is a signature quality of the Chiefs

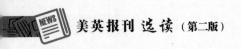

this season.

10. Coach Reid suffered a lot from the overtime loss and surrendered to the self-doubts over his sub-500 career playoff record.

III. Topics for Discussion

1. What do you know about Super Bowl? Surf the Internet, search for the information and exchange your ideas with your classmates.

2. What's your understanding of the title "Failure is necessary"? Could you give some examples of the failures in your life and the ways you tackled them?

3. According to this article, professional coaches, players and engineers have some characteristics in common. Do you agree? Please justify your idea.

4. Thomas Edison once said, "I can never find the thing that does the job best until I find the ones that don't." What do you think of his statement?

5. What is the value of failure, and how can you reverse it when you are faced with failures repeatedly?

美英两国的重要体育赛事

一、美国的重要体育赛事

（一）篮球

篮球发明于 1891 年，在美国是一项很普及的体育健身运动，国家篮球协会（National Basketball Association，NBA）被广泛赞誉为目前世界上最佳的男子篮球联盟，旗下拥有 30 支篮球队（美国 29 支，加拿大 1 支）。NBA 是美国和加拿大四大主要的职业运动联盟之一，其比赛分为季前赛（preseason）、常规赛（regular season）和季后赛（playoffs）三部分。

（二）美式橄榄球或美式足球

美式橄榄球或美式足球是在英式足球（association football）和英式橄榄球（rugby football，拉格比足球）的基础上逐渐发展起来的。在美国和加拿大，美式橄榄球或美式足球直接被称为足球（football）。自 2012 年起，每年约有 1,100 万高中生和 7 万大学生参与这一体育竞赛。沃尔特·坎普（Walter Camp）对美式橄榄球的规则加以改进，使其有别于英式足球，被称为"美式橄榄球之父"（Father of American Football）。美国国家橄榄球联盟是北美最大的美式橄榄球组织，成立于 1920 年，其组织的比赛有季前赛、常规赛和季后赛等。

（三）棒球

棒球是源于 19 世纪的一种儿童游戏，在美国非常普及，早在 1856 年，棒球就被称为美国的"民族消遣运动"（national pastime）。美国职业棒球大联盟（Major League Baseball，MLB）的赛季是每年的 4 月至 10 月，最后的冠军赛称为"世界大赛"（World Series）。

（四）冰球

冰球（ice hockey）是继棒球、橄榄球和篮球之后在美国特别是在美国北部最受欢迎的体育项目。冰球最重要的组织机构为国家冰球联盟（National Hockey League，NHL），是一个由北美冰球队伍组成的职业冰球运动联盟。队伍分成东、西两个大区，每个大区各有三个分区。最后产生的 16 支最强队通过淘汰赛的形式产生一个冠军，获得斯坦利杯（Stanley Cup）。

（五）足球

足球是继橄榄球、棒球、冰球、篮球之后在美国的第五大体育项目。在美国，英式足球被称为 soccer，而 football 一词指的是美式橄榄球或美式足球。全国性的足球组织有美国足球协会（United States Soccer Federation）等。美国职业足球大联盟（Major League Soccer）筹建于 1993 年，是美国及加拿大顶级足球赛事，1996 年起展开联赛，截至 2023 年，共有 29 支球队，而大联盟中不乏世界知名的足球运动员，如大卫·贝克汉姆（David Beckham）和蒂埃里·亨利（Thierry Henry）等。

二、英国的重要体育赛事

（一）网球

网球运动起源于 12 世纪的法国北方。同在法国一样，网球在英国也深受人们的喜爱。温布尔登网球锦标赛（The Championships, Wimbledon）始于 1877 年，是世界上著名的网球赛事之一，每年 6 月或 7 月在位于伦敦郊区的温布尔登举行。

（二）板球

板球运动（cricket）的规则确定于 1787 年，要求选手着装正式、穿白色裤子，比赛一般要持续数天。在 19 世纪，板球运动主要是上层阶级的运动，玩板球的群体限于在公学就读的男生。国际板球理事会（International Cricket Council）每四年举办一次的板球世界杯（Cricket World Cup）为一天单局板球比赛，该项比赛是世界上拥有观众最多的体育运动之一。板球被英国人看作是一项崇尚"体育精神"（sportsmanship）和"公平比赛"（fair play）的运动。

（三）高尔夫球

高尔夫球运动是苏格兰人发明的。截至 16 世纪，高尔夫在苏格兰已经很普及，皇室成员如苏格兰玛丽皇后都对高尔夫有浓厚的兴趣。英国高尔夫球公开赛（The Open Championship，常被称为 the British Open 或 The Open）始于 1860 年，是高尔夫球历史上最悠久、最负盛名的大赛之一，赛事由英国圣安德鲁斯皇家古典高尔夫俱乐部（Royal and Ancient Golf Club of St. Andrews）主办，在每年 7 月的第三个周末举行。

（四）赛马

赛马（horse racing）有平地赛（flat racing）、越野障碍赛（jump racing）、驾辕赛（harness racing）、耐力赛（endurance racing）等形式，在英国开展广泛的形式有平地赛和全国狩猎赛（National Hunt Racing）。赛马是英国第二大观赏性体育项目，比赛规则于 17 世纪至 19 世纪形成，有组织的国家级赛马在全英已有数百年历史。英国最大、最重要的赛马赛事是皇家阿斯科特赛马会（Royal Ascot），每年 6 月在英国伯克郡阿斯科特赛马场（Ascot Racecourse）举行，为期四天。阿斯科特赛马场 于 1711 年由安妮女王（Queen Anne）创办。看台设有皇家围场（Royal Enclosure）供国君（如伊丽莎白二世等）和家族成员使用。

Text B

导读

自行车比赛有三大类，分别是场地赛（track cycling）、公路赛（road race）和越野赛（cross country competition），场地赛在赛车场（velodrome）进行，包括冲刺赛（sprint）和耐力赛（endurance），冲刺赛有八段和十段赛程（lap）。自行车比赛的主要赛事有奥运会比赛（Olympic Games）、世界锦标赛（World Championship）、世界杯赛（World Cup）等。奥运会比赛项目有追逐赛（pursuit）、计时赛（time trial）、计分赛（points race）、争先赛（scratch race）、凯琳赛（Keirin）等，其中追逐赛又分个人（individual pursuit）和团体（team pursuit）项目。世界锦标赛指的是由国际自行车联盟（Union Cycliste Internationale，UCI）组织的世界自行车场地锦标赛（UCI Track Cycling World Championships），每年举办一次，通常在 3 月或 4 月。世界杯赛也是国际自行车联盟组织的赛事，英文全称为 UCI Track Cycling World Cup。

本文介绍的是英国自行车团队在 2016 年 8 月举办的里约热内卢奥运会上的表现，围绕英国职业自行车赛手布拉德利·威金斯爵士展开，披露了英国自行车团队内部的一些不和谐现象。

Team GB and Sir Bradley Wiggins[1] win Olympic gold in men's team pursuit

By Barry Glendenning

So what comes after a knighthood? Great Britain's perfect start to the Olympic track cycling continued as Sir Bradley Wiggins and his teammates Ed Clancy, Owain Doull and Steven Burke won the men's team pursuit[2] in thrilling style and world record time. They beat Australia in the showdown, reversing the outcome of the corresponding final at the World Championships in March. After that reverse, Wiggins advised anyone who'd listen to "put your house" on a British win here.

They were as good as his word, posting a time of 3 min. 50.265 sec. as they came from behind after 3,500 metres of the 4,000m trip. Even in defeat Wiggins would have become the most decorated Olympian in British history, assured as he was of a medal whatever the outcome. But having stated he had no interest in winning silver or bronze it would have been decidedly anticlimactic if he'd ascended to his new exalted status from anything other than the podium's top step. In a career incorporating five different Olympic Games not to mention assorted outdoor distractions, this was his fifth gold and takes his overall medal tally to eight. "I knew it would be close, so when we crossed the line it was more relief than anything," he said. "I'm just happy to be able to wake up on Monday and not have this. It is a burden. I wanted to go out like this, I wanted it to end like this and not with some crappy little race in the north of France, climbing off at the feed."

How Britain won gold and set a new world record in Olympics team pursuit

Great Britain did it the hard way. Australia led from the gun, with Alexander Edmondson, Jack Bobridge, Michael Hepburn and Sam Wellsford opening a gap of over half a second by halfway, but with eight laps of Siberian pine to negotiate, the eventual winners began to reel them in. Bobridge took a "death pull" for Australia and expended such effort that he left his team with just the three men required to post a time. It was a tactic that did not pay off, as the British closed the gap to less than one-hundredth of a second at the 3,000m mark and from then the outcome was never in doubt. "It was just about keeping your bottle; it wasn't easy," said Clancy. "We could sense by the crowd we weren't ahead. When we crossed that line a second ahead, I think it was the happiest moment in my life."

Asked about his short and long term plans, Wiggins was in typically forthright mood. "It's over in a flash and we'll all be hungover tomorrow," he said. "That wasn't my last race, but it was my last Olympic Games. My kids have never known anything other than me being an Olympic athlete and they need me now."

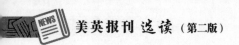

Unused in qualifying on Thursday, Mark Cavendish was once again fifth man but did not turn up at the velodrome[3] to warm up before the day's racing. *The Guardian* was told he had fallen out with British team pursuit coach Heiko Salzwedel, who Cavendish described as "very stubborn" during the team's training camp in Newport two weeks ago. British Cycling's head coach Iain Dyer described the claims that Cavendish had refused to attend the velodrome as "bollocks", while Wiggins said his teammate, who will contest the omnium "was hugging me yesterday and telling me he loved me".

On Cavendish's omission from the team, Wiggins said, "We gave Mark the opportunity in Newport to come into the squad and he didn't deliver. We saw how close it was and we couldn't afford, having been together for 18 months and it wasn't just me...I didn't freeze him out or anything like that and he knows that. Ask him about it after the omnium and he'll tell you a totally different story to the one he told Orla [Chennai, from Sky]."

Fresh from winning gold in the men's team sprint the previous day, both Jason Kenny and Callum Skinner followed up with fine performances in qualifying for the individual event. Skinner scorched up the track to set a new Olympic record of 9.703 sec. in his flying 200m time trial, beaten by Kenny's 9.551 soon after. Kenny went on to ease past Germany's Maximilian Levy in the last 16. Skinner subsequently led from the front to advance to quarter-finals, shutting the door on Australia's Patrick Constable after a two-lap game of cat and mouse. Both men will resume their respective assaults on the competition today [Saturday].

In the day's other final, China won the women's team sprint, beating Russia in the final while Germany bagged bronze in a contest where Great Britain were notable absentees. It was the failure of Jess Varnish and Katy Marchant to qualify that led to the former being dropped from the Team GB "podium programme" and the subsequent row that resulted in the resignation of the team Technical Director Shane Sutton amid allegations of discrimination and bullying, which he strenuously denies.

Two-times Olympic gold medallist Victoria Pendleton said it was "ridiculous" that Great Britain were not in the event, stating there is "no way" they are not among the five fastest teams in the world. It seemed something of a rum do that while two of Team GB's fastest women, Marchant and Becky James, were relaxing ahead of the individual competition on Sunday, the lady whose speed either has yet to match was actually in the velodrome providing informative if slightly wistful co-commentary for the BBC.

(From *The Guardian*, Aug. 13, 2016)

NOTES

1. **Sir Bradley Wiggins**：布拉德利·威金斯爵士（1980—），英国职业自行车赛手。他在 2000 年悉尼奥运会上夺得第一枚奥运铜牌。2001 年转为道路自行车专业赛手，2004 年在雅典奥运会上获得三枚奖牌，其中一枚为金牌，2008 年在北京奥运会上获得个人和团体两枚金牌，2009 年在环法自行车赛分段赛中获得第四名（后由于兰斯·阿姆斯特姆 [Lance Armstrong] 的成绩于 2012 年被宣布无效，排名被提到第三名），2014 年在道路自行车世界锦标赛计时赛中获得金牌，2016 年里约热内卢奥运会上，他所在的英国队击败澳大利亚队，他本人从而获得第八块奥运奖牌和第五块奥运金牌。

2. **team pursuit**：（自行车）团体追逐赛，每队由四名运动员组成，第三名运动员很关键，因为计算成绩是以第三名队员的前轮过终点线为准，每队必须有三名运动员到达终点方可计算成绩。现在奥运会比赛项目有男子 4,000 米个人追逐赛（1964 年列入）、4,000 米团体追逐赛（1920 年列入）和女子 3,000 米个人追逐赛（1992 年列入）。

3. **velodrome**: 场地自行车赛，包括争先赛、个人追逐赛、团体追逐赛、记分赛、团体竞速赛、凯琳赛、麦迪逊赛等男、女比赛十个项目。该比赛对于自行车的长度、宽度、重量等规格都有明确限制。

USEFUL WORDS

allegation	[ˌæləˈgeɪʃn]	*n.*	a public statement that is made without giving proof, accusing sb. of doing sth. that is wrong or illegal 指控；主张，宣称
assault	[əˈsɔːlt]	*n.*	a vigorous armed attack, especially a head-on charge 攻击；冲击
bollocks	[ˈbɒləks]	*n.*	nonsense 胡说，废话
crappy	[ˈkræpi]	*adj.*	of very bad quality 劣质的；蹩脚的
exalt	[ɪgˈzɔːlt]	*v.*	to raise up (in position or dignity) 使升高；提升，提拔
hungover	[ˈhʌŋˈəʊvə]	*adj.*	the headache and sick feeling that you have the day after drinking too much alcohol 因余醉未醒感到难受的；心里难受的
incorporate	[ɪnˈkɔːpəreɪt]	*v.*	to unite into a whole; to include 包含
lap	[læp]	*n.*	one journey from the beginning to the end of a track used for running, etc. （跑道等的）一圈
negotiate	[nɪˈgəʊʃieɪt]	*v.*	to successfully get over or past a difficult part on a path or route 顺利通过；成功越过
omnium	[ˈɒmnɪəm]	*n.*	a multiple race event in track cycling in which all contestants compete against each other in six different disciplines （自行车）全能赛

podium	['pəʊdiəm]	n.	a small platform that a person stands on when giving a speech or conducting an orchestra, etc. 领奖台；讲台；表演台
reel	[riːl]	v.	~ in to wind sth. on/off a reel 卷；绕
rum	[rʌm]	adj.	strange 古怪的；奇特的
scorch	[skɔː(r)tʃ]	v.	to burn and slightly damage the surface by making it too hot 烧焦，烤焦
showdown	['ʃəʊdaʊn]	n.	(usually sing.) an argument, a fight or a test that will settle a disagreement that has lasted for a long time 紧要关头；最后一决胜负
sprint	[sprint]	v.	to run for a short distance at the greatest speed of which one is capable 冲刺，用全速跑过
velodrome	['velədrəʊm]	n.	a track or building used for cycle racing （自行车等的）室内赛车场
wistful	['wɪstfl]	adj.	thinking sadly about sth. that you would like to have, especially sth. in the past that you can no longer have 伤感的；徒然神往的

EXERCISES

I. Vocabulary

Choose among the four alternatives one word or phrase that is closest in meaning to the underlined part in each statement.

1. But having stated he had no interest in winning silver or bronze it would have been decidedly anticlimactic if he'd ascended to his new underlined exalted status from anything other than the podium's top step.

   A. raised   B. excelled   C. obtained   D. excellent

2. Australia led from the gun, with Alexander Edmondson, Jack Bobridge, Michael Hepburn and Sam Wellsford opening a gap of over half a second by halfway, but with eight laps of Siberian pine to negotiate, the eventual winners began to reel them in.

   A. carry through (a transaction) by discussion   B. confer

   C. succeed in accomplishing   D. transfer (a cheque, etc.)

3. It was a tactic that did not pay off, as the British closed the gap to less than one-hundredth of a second at the 3,000m mark and from then the outcome was never in doubt.

   A. pay back   B. pay all the debts   C. work   D. fail

4. "It's over in a flash and we'll all be hungover tomorrow," he said.

   A. relaxed   B. upset   C. satisfied   D. happy

5. *The Guardian* was told he had <u>fallen out with</u> British team pursuit coach Heiko Salzwedel, who Cavendish described as "very stubborn" during the team's training camp in Newport two weeks ago.

    A. quarreled with   B. fallen behind

    C. dropped out the line   D. degenerated

6. ...I didn't <u>freeze him out</u> or anything like that and he knows that.

    A. take him out   B. force him to leave

    C. make him catch cold   D. pour cold water on him

7. Skinner <u>scorched up</u> the track to set a new Olympic record of 9.703 sec. in his flying 200m time trial, beaten by Kenny's 9.551 soon after.

    A. cycled extremely fast along the track   B. burned the track

    C. made the track very hot   D. sped up along the track

8. Both men will resume their respective <u>assaults on</u> the competition today [Saturday].

    A. vigorous armed attacks on   B. violent critical attacks on

    C. vigorous attacks by armed forces on   D. attempts on

9. ...and the subsequent <u>row</u> that resulted in the resignation of the team Technical Director Shane Sutton amid allegations of discrimination and bullying, which he strenuously denies.

    A. loud harsh noise   B. quarrel

    C. an orderly line of persons   D. a small street lined with houses

10. Two-times Olympic gold medallist Victoria Pendleton said it was "<u>ridiculous</u>" that Great Britain were not in the event, stating there is "no way" they are not among the five fastest teams in the world.

    A. humorous   B. rational   C. depressing   D. unreasonable

II. Comprehension

Decide whether the following statements are true (T) or false (F) according to the information given in the press clipping. Mark T or F for each statement.

1. After beating Australian in the showdown, Sir Bradley Wiggins became very arrogant.

2. Even if Sir Bradley Wiggins had not defeated Australian, he was the one who had taken part in Olympic Games and had won the most medals in British history.

3. It can be inferred from Sir Bradley Wiggins' words that he no longer had interest in taking part in cycling race in the north of France.

4. British team had an easy win over Australia.

5. Sir Bradley Wiggins, after the Olympic Games, will continue his career as a cyclist.

6. It can be inferred from Sir Bradley Wiggins' words that it was Mark Cavendish's fault not being with the team.

7. Because of his higher speed, Callum Skinner made it impossible for Australia's Patrick Constable to advance to quarter-finals.

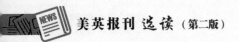

8. Jason Kenny defeated Germany's Maximilian Levy in the last 16.

9. Callum Skinner and Australia's Patrick Constable play a hide-and-seek game like the one played between a cat and a mouse in the racing.

10. According to Victora Pendleton, there is no possibility for Great Britain to be among the fastest teams in the world.

III. Topics for Discussion

1. What do you think of the very beginning of the news report "So what comes after a knighthood"? Is it a very good beginning to attract readers to go on reading?

2. Do you like cycling? And what benefits can a cyclist get from cycling?

3. What can you infer from Sir Bradley Wiggins' plan after the Olympic Games?

4. In the sentence "Both men will resume their respective assaults on the competition today", what does the phrase "both men" refer to?

5. What does Sir Bradley Wiggins think of Mark Cavendish? What do you think is the most important thing to a team?

《泰晤士报》简介

　　《泰晤士报》（*The Times*）由约翰·沃尔特（John Walter）于 1785 年在伦敦创刊，原名为《世鉴日报》（*Daily Universal Register*），1788 年起改用现名，是世界上第一份以 Times 命名的报纸。由于现在有《纽约时报》等众多以 Times 命名的时报，《泰晤士报》有时会被英语读者称为《伦敦时报》（*The London Times*）以示区别。

　　《泰晤士报》是一份在英国全面发行的综合性日报，在反映和塑造伦敦精英阶层对时事的观点和看法方面起着重要的作用，同时反映和影响着全世界的政治、经济与文化环境。1981 年，《泰晤士报》被属于鲁伯特·默多克（Rupert Murdoch）旗下的新闻集团收购，之后《泰晤士报》的风格渐趋保守。

　　《泰晤士报》有一份姊妹报《星期日泰晤士报》（*The Sunday Times*）（1812 年创刊），主要报道时事、政治、商业、体育、娱乐、金融及星期日新闻评论，是一份每周日出刊的英国报纸，由新闻国际公司（News International PLC）出版，该公司是新闻公司（News Corporation）的下属企业。该报创刊于 1821 年，于 1981 年被默多克的新闻公司收购。

Unit 6
Entertainment

 报刊英语的句式特征

　　新闻稿件具有一定的文学性和艺术性。但受版面和时效的限制，要在较短的时间内完成稿件、在有限的篇幅内融入较多的新闻事实和背景信息是非常不易的，这要求报刊英语的句型高度扩展、结构严谨，具体体现在报刊英语的省略句式、修饰语成分（如同位语、定语和状语等）以及被动语态结构等方面。

一、省略句式

　　省略是指省去一个或多个句子成分，以求表达简洁、节省篇幅、突出主要内容。省去的句子成分包括人称代词和部分非实义词，如冠词、介词、助动词等。例如：

- But as boss of a centre-left think-tank she had written tweets. (*The Economist*, Mar. 27, 2021) (= But as **the** boss of a centre-left think-tank she had written tweets.)（省略冠词）

- Prince William gets first dose of coronavirus vaccine. (*Fox News*, May 20, 2021) (= Prince William gets **his** first dose of coronavirus vaccine.)（省略代词）

- Worsening symptoms: Johnson in intensive care (*BBC*, Apr. 7, 2020) (= Worsening symptoms: Johnson **is** in intensive care)（省略连系动词）

- Contestants guessed a bit better after 2010, when GDP growth was weak and budgets tight. (*The Economist*, May 20, 2020) (= Contestants guessed a bit better after 2010, when GDP growth was weak and budgets **were** tight.)（省略连系动词）

- Cruise ship turned away from five countries allowed to dock in Cambodia. (*Reuters*, Feb. 12, 2020) (= Cruise ship turned away from five countries **was** allowed to dock in Cambodia.)（省略被动语态中的助动词）

- In 1968 the virus was flu and the space mission Apollo 8. (*The Economist*, Jun. 4,

2020) (= In 1968 the virus was flu and the space mission **was** Apollo 8.)（省略进行时态中的助动词）

- Pandemic business borrowing expected to hit £60 bn, says EY Item Club. (*The Times*, Feb. 8, 2021) (= Pandemic business borrowing **is** expected to hit £60 bn, says EY Item Club.)（省略被动语态中的助动词）

- India glacier burst: Rescue workers looking for 177 people feared dead in Uttarakhand (*CNN*, Feb. 8, 2021) (= India glacier burst: Rescue workers **are** looking for 177 people feared dead in Uttarakhand)（省略进行时态中的助动词）

- Pilot Andrew Buck and Lewis Stubbs killed when checking crashed plane (*BBC*, Apr. 21, 2021) (= Pilot Andrew Buck and Lewis Stubbs **were** killed when checking crashed plane)（省略被动语态中的助动词）

- China to ban single-use plastic in cities (*Forbes*, Jan. 20, 2020) (= China **is going to ban** single-use plastic in cities)（不定式表示未来动作）

- Queen's grandson Peter Phillips and wife Autumn to divorce (*CNN*, Feb. 12, 2020) (= Queen's grandson Peter Phillips and wife Autumn **are going to divorce**)（不定式表示未来动作）

二、同位语和解释性结构

同位语和解释性结构在报刊英语中的应用十分广泛。它们通常是指新闻中的背景信息，为读者提供新闻人物的职位、学历、社会背景或文化释义等信息，或为读者补充与新闻有关的其他信息。其中，同位语通常位于被限定的词之后。例如：

- That area, **roughly the size of Austria or Maine**, is home to masses of people and capital in booming sea-facing metropolises. (*The Economist*, Apr. 5, 2020)

本句主要对主语 That area 进行介绍。黑体部分作为同位语，补充说明了 That area 的面积大小，即这一区域"大概有奥地利或缅甸州大小"，让读者对其有了更为形象的认识。

- Mr. Niaz received help from the Responsible Business Initiative for Justice (RBIJ), **a transatlantic charity run by Celia Ouellette, a former death-row lawyer in America**. She points out that 2.2m Americans, **the population of a large metropolis**, are locked up. (*The Economist*, Apr. 5, 2020)

这一则新闻中包含了三个特殊信息，即 the Responsible Business Initiative for Justice (RBIJ)、Celia Ouellette 和 2.2m Americans，若不查找背景资料或许会影响读者对本段新闻内容的解读。从语法角度来分析，a transatlantic charity run by Celia Ouellette 作为同位语修饰 the Responsible Business Initiative for Justice (RBIJ)，说明了 RBIJ 是"由 Celia Ouellette 经营的一个跨大西洋

的慈善机构"；a former death-row lawyer in America 则作为同位语修饰 Celia Ouellette，解释了这一慈善机构的经营者"曾是一位为死囚犯工作的美国律师"；the population of a large metropolis 作为同位语更为形象地解释了 2.2m Americans 的意思，有助于加深读者对本段新闻内容的理解。

- On his previous spaceflight, **the Gemini 10 mission with John Young in 1966 to practice maneuvering in Earth orbit**, the two of them had squashed into a cabin the size of the front seat of a Volkswagen. (*The Economist*, May 8, 2021)

本句的黑体部分作为同位语，进一步解释了 his previous spaceflight，即"1966 年，他和约翰·杨（John Young）一起执行了地球轨道飞行的'双子座 10 号任务'"，为读者提供了背景信息。

解释性结构则大多出现在括号内或两个破折号之间，以便为读者提供额外的信息。例如：

- It was Premier Zhou Enlai's favorite tipple, shared with Richard Nixon in 1972. Its centuries-old craftsmanship—**it is distilled eight times and stored for years in earthenware jars**—is a source of national pride. (*The Economist*, Jan. 23, 2020)

本句主要介绍了中国名酒茅台的百年酿酒工艺。破折号之间的内容是对 centuries-old craftsmanship 的进一步补充描述，有利于读者更好地理解为何这一酿酒工艺是中国的民族骄傲。

- In the latest *Mulan* premiering Sept. 4 on Disney, the Chinese-American actress Yifei Liu stars in a tale that blends stunning battle sequences (**the film's $200 million budget included a portion for 80 trick riders from Kazakhstan and Mongolia**) with a story that makes much of the story's gender-bending subtexts. (*The New York Times*, Sept. 8, 2020)

本句主要介绍了迪士尼电影《花木兰》中融合了许多战争场景，括号里的内容补充说明了拍摄费用中有一部分用于电影特技支出，有利于读者更好地理解新闻的主要内容。

三、状语、状语从句、定语从句成分

报刊英语中多用状语和状语从句来修饰谓语、非谓语动词、定语或整个句子，明确描述新闻事件的时间、地点、条件、原因等要素。同时，报刊英语中也多用定语从句来修饰句子中的名词或代词，对新闻事件的信息进行详细描述。例如：

- Fiscal conservatives in Germany and elsewhere, **who grudgingly acceded to NGEU as a one-off, retain a visceral opposition to a permanent "transfer union" they fear would leave them on the hook for Europe's fiscally incontinent.** (*The*

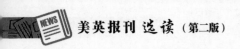

Economist, Apr. 3, 2021)

本句包括一个由 who 引导的非限制性定语从句，对 Fiscal conservatives 进行了补充说明。同时，transfer union 后还包含一个省略了引导词 that/which 的定语从句。这样的句法结构符合经济性原则且逻辑性强，往往被视为报刊英语中的典型句法特征之一。

- The practice of elevating a company's chief executive to chairman has come to be frowned upon, **if only because a new boss often struggles to break free if her predecessor is looking over her shoulder**. (*The Economist*, Apr. 24, 2021)

本句为现在完成时形式下的被动句，包括一个由 if only 引导的条件状语从句。其中，该状语从句中包含一个由 because 引导的原因状语从句和一个 if 引导的条件状语从句。这三个状语从句使本句句型变得复杂。

- This is long COVID, **which is becoming apparent in rich countries like America, Britain and Israel that have largely vaccinated their way out of the pandemic, but which will affect poor ones, too**. (*The Economist*, May 1, 2021)

本句包含两个由 which 引导的定语从句，第一个 which 引导的定语从句中套嵌了一个由 that 引导的定语从句，修饰 "America, Britain and Israel"，对这三个名词进行限定和解释。第二个 which 引导的定语从句同样限定先行词 COVID，但与第一个 which 引导的定语从句的内容为转折关系，故以 but 连接，属于从不同角度对先行词进行说明。

四、前置定语

报刊英语中经常将通常后置的名词修饰语移到名词前面，从而使句子结构变得紧凑严密，这是当代英语发展的一种趋势，在报刊英语里尤其明显。修饰语由后置变为前置常常需要借助于连字符号。例如：

- Great Britain's round-the-world yachtsmen (= the yachtsmen from Great Britain who plan to go round the world)
- the up-to-the-minute information (= the information up to the minute)

这种使英语句子高度浓缩的前置修饰语，可以分为带连字符的修饰语和不带连字符的修饰语。

（一）带连字符的前置修饰语

带连字符的前置修饰语有很多种表现形式，以下列举了 13 种。

1. 名词 + 名词

- billion-dollar deal：十亿美元的交易
- supply-demand imbalance：供求关系失衡
- north-south dialogue：北南对话
- Korea-Japan trade：朝日贸易
- shoulder-length hair：披肩发
- snail-pace progress：缓慢的进展
- world-class match：世界水准的比赛
- year-end report：年终报告
- stock-manipulation case：操控股票的案例

2. 名词 + 现在分词

- cancer-causing drugs：致癌药物
- peace-keeping force：维和部队
- oil-producing country：产油国
- policy-making body：决策机构
- breath-taking scenery：令人赞叹不已的景色
- energy-saving device：节能装置
- law-abiding resident：守法居民
- Pulitzer Prize-winning author：普利策奖获奖者
- time-consuming negotiation：耗时的谈判

3. 名词 + 形容词

- interest-free loan：无利息贷款
- vehicle-free promenade：无机动车场所
- hand-free phone：免手提电话
- capital-intensive country：资本密集的国家
- oil-poor country：贫油国家
- war-weary soldier：厌战的士兵
- energy-rich country：能源丰富的国家

4. 名词 + 过去分词

- poverty-stricken area：贫穷地区
- state-owned enterprise：国有企业
- bottle-necked road：瓶颈路段
- college-bred clerk：受过大学教育的职员
- crisis-ridden economy：危机四伏的经济
- disaster-hit area：灾区
- money-oriented politics：金钱政治
- tongue-tied spokesman：张口结舌的发言人
- standards-based test：基于标准的考试
- performance-oriented culture：以绩效为主的文化背景
- relationship-oriented culture：以人际关系或人情为主的文化氛围
- coin-operated washing machine：投币洗衣机
- U.S.-led Middle East conference：由美国主导的中东会议
- knowledge-based economy：知识经济

5. 名词 + 介词短语

- growth-at-all-cost 1970s：不惜一切代价达到经济目标的 20 世纪 70 年代
- stay-at-home mother：全职妈妈

6. 形容词 + 过去分词

- deep-rooted social and economic problem：根深蒂固的社会与经济问题
- quick-frozen food：速冻食品
- foreign-owned enterprise：外资企业
- clean-cut analysis：明晰的分析
- far-fetched explanation：牵强的解释
- long-faced job loser：愁眉苦脸的失业者
- short-lived coup：短暂的政变

7. 形容词 + 名词

- open-door policy：门户开放政策
- red-carpet welcome：隆重的欢迎
- private-eye industry：私家侦探业
- long-term low-interest loan：长期低利率贷款
- top-level talk：最高级别的会谈

8. 形容词 + 现在分词

- high-ranking official：高级官员
- long-standing issue：长期存在的问题
- wide-ranging report：内容广泛的报道
- wide-spreading AIDS：四处蔓延的艾滋病
- easy-going president：待人随和的总统
- far-seeing diplomat：卓有远见的外交官

9. 副词 + 过去分词

- dimly-lit room：光线昏暗的房间
- highly-polished table：擦得锃亮的桌子
- hard-won result：艰难赢得的结果
- highly-sophisticated technology：高度复杂的技术
- newly-found coal mine：新近发现的煤矿
- richly-paid job：薪水丰厚的工作
- sparsely-populated area：人口稀少的地区
- well-informed circle：消息灵通人士

10. 数词 + 名词

- 100-meter dash：100 米赛跑
- one-egg twins：单卵性双胎
- two-way street：双行道路
- one-shot criminal：初犯
- two-party system：两党制
- 4,000-plus lawsuits：四千件以上的诉讼案件

11. 名词 + to + 名词

- coast-to-coast protest：全国性的抗议
- dusk-to-dawn curfew：彻夜宵禁
- face-to-face talk：面晤
- hand-to-hand fighting：白刃战

12. 前后由 and 连接的词组

- hit-and-run driver：肇事逃逸司机
- touch-and-go affair：一触即发的局势
- wait-and-see policy：坐守观望的政策
- renewable-and-alternative-energy manufacturer：利用可再生和可替代能源的生产厂商

- up-and-down market：上下起伏的市场
- up-and-down relationship：时好时坏的关系
- off-and-on war：打打停停的战争
- life-and-death experiment：生死攸关的实验

13. 介词 + 名词

- on-site service：现场服务
- under-the-counter activity：隐蔽的活动

- around-the-clock bombing：昼夜不间断的轰炸

（二）不带连字符的前置修饰语

英语中同样存在无需连字符的前置修饰语的形式，用来为其后被修饰的名词提供解释。

- "out of the box" thinking：摆脱常规的思维
- a "made in China" orientation：中国的制造力

- a "created in China" capability：中国的创造力
- a study abroad experience：海外留学的经历

下列例句中体现了前置定语的用法：

- "I've found with all my books that they start with what is almost **an out-of-body experience** when I see myself in sharp relief from the side," he tells me. (*The Guardian*, Jan. 3, 2019)
- **The damage from COVID-19** means that, in the short term at least, universities will be more dependent on governments than ever. (*The Economist*, Aug. 8, 2020)
- Common causes of infant mortality are premature birth, low birth weight, maternal complications and **sudden infant death syndrome**, according to the Centers for Disease Control and Prevention. (*The Washington Post*, Jan. 8, 2021)

五、浓缩的后置名词修饰语

在有些情况下，报刊英语中会将定语从句压缩成由分词短语或不定式短语构成的后置定语。例如：

- Poor in-person lectures could be replaced by online ones from the best in the world, freeing up time for the small-group teaching which students value most. (*The Economist*, Apr. 10, 2021)

- These places now cover 100 acres across the city, **tended by a volunteer army of nearly 23,000 green-fingered New Yorkers**. (*The Economist*, Apr. 10, 2021)
- The idea, **promoted on social media by accounts with hundreds of thousands of followers**, is that vaccinated people might shed vaccine material, **affecting people around them as though it were secondhand smoke**. (*The New York Times*, Apr. 29, 2021)

在上述三例中，freeing、tended、promoted 和 affecting 分别是 which was freeing、which was tended、which was promoted 和 who will affect 的浓缩形式。

六、压缩的状语从句

在有些情况下，报刊英语中会将状语从句压缩成由从属连词加分词短语构成的状语结构，有时还会省略从属连词，以缩短句子长度，使信息得到最大限度的浓缩。从属连词主要包括 after、once、while、although、as、till、lest、if、since、when、whether 等。例如：

- The old are vital to the tourism industry because they spend much more, **when taking** a foreign holiday, than younger adults. (*The Economist*, Dec. 26, 2019)
- Among other allegations, the lawsuit alleges O'Bryant **once charged at** a different Black boyfriend of Rankin's with a broken bottle **while shouting** racial epithets. (*Seattle Times*, May 23, 2021)

在上述两例中，when taking、once charged at 和 while shouting 实际上分别是 when they take 状语从句、once he was charged at 状语从句和 while he was shouting 状语从句的压缩形式。

七、被动语态结构

在客观性要求很高的新闻领域，被动语态的使用非常广泛。为了显示公正和客观，或因文章的作者确实无法说出行为主体，美英报刊文章中常用以下固定的被动语态套语：

- It is alleged that...: 据称······
- It is argued that...: 有人争论······
- It was described that...: 据介绍······; 有人介绍······
- It is reported that...: 据报道······
- It is rumored that...: 谣传······; 听说······
- It is taken that...: 人们认为······; 有人认为······
- It is universally accepted that...: 普遍认为······

- It is asserted that...: 有人主张······
- It is claimed that...: 据称······
- It is generally recognized that...: 一般认为······, 普遍认为······
- It can be safely said that...: 可以有把握地说······
- It was first intended that...: 最初的打算是······
- Little was said about...: 关于······过去少有谈及

下列例句中体现了被动语态结构的用法:

- In the state of Gujarat **it was revealed that** factories making gas-storage tanks, which use oxygen in the manufacturing process, had halted production of the desperately needed containers because the government was allocating all oxygen to hospitals. (*The Economist*, May 8, 2021)

除上述常用的被动语态套语以外, 报刊英语中还有其他使用被动语态的场合和语境, 尤其在不方便透露受采访人物的身份时, 被动语态是一个非常有效的语言表达手段, 如以下例句中 was reported 的用法。

- In 2020, at least 20 known racist incidents **were reported** on North American construction sites, according to Construction Dive. (*The Washington Post*, May 21, 2021)

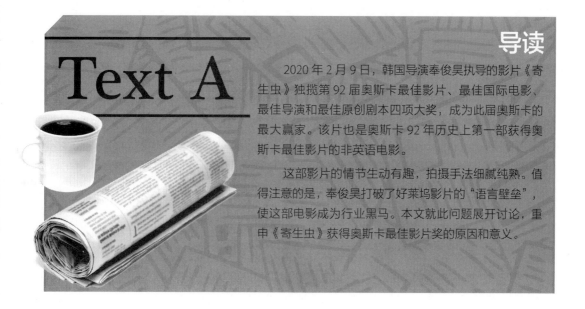

Text A

导读

2020 年 2 月 9 日, 韩国导演奉俊昊执导的影片《寄生虫》独揽第 92 届奥斯卡最佳影片、最佳国际电影、最佳导演和最佳原创剧本四项大奖, 成为此届奥斯卡的最大赢家。该片也是奥斯卡 92 年历史上第一部获得奥斯卡最佳影片的非英语电影。

这部影片的情节生动有趣, 拍摄手法细腻纯熟。值得注意的是, 奉俊昊打破了好莱坞影片的"语言壁垒", 使这部电影成为行业黑马。本文就此问题展开讨论, 重申《寄生虫》获得奥斯卡最佳影片奖的原因和意义。

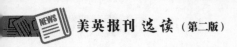

Hollywood barriers fall in milestone Oscars for *Parasite*

By Jake Coyle

LOS ANGELES—Before Bong Joon Ho's[1] *Parasite* made history as the first non-English best picture winner in Academy Awards[2] history, he made a modest plea to American moviegoers: Don't be afraid of subtitles.

Accepting the award for best foreign-language film at the Golden Globes[3] last month, the South Korean filmmaker, who has worked in both Seoul and Hollywood, said: "Once you overcome the 1-inch-tall barrier of subtitles, you will be introduced to so many more amazing films."

Reflecting on those words backstage at Sunday's Oscars while he clutched several of his statuettes, Bong wondered whether those boundaries were already breaking. He had good reason to. In a thrilling and raucously applauded upset, the revolutionary win for *Parasite* ended a more than nine-decade English-language monopoly on cinema's top prize.

"People were already overcoming these barriers through streaming services, YouTube[4], social media," said Bong through his translator. "In the environment that we currently live in, I think we're all connected. Naturally we will come to a day when a foreign language film or not, it doesn't really matter."

Hollywood's reach has long extended to all corners of the globe, but it has less frequently returned the favor. It's an exporter, not an importer. Even though the American film industry was built largely by immigrants, on Oscar night, its gaze has usually been turned inward.

But that's changing, and nothing showed it more than the weekend's incredible double-feature of winners. Before *Parasite* won over several Oscars, Chinese-American director Lulu Wang's[5] *The Farewell* triumphed at Saturday's Film Independent Spirit Awards[6]. Wang's family drama stars an all-Asian cast and was filmed in both Mandarin and English.

The Farewell, one of the most successful indie films at the box office last year, also won best supporting performance by a female actor, for Chinese actress Zhao Shuzhen[7]. Wang thanked Film Independent for "honoring a woman from China who a lot of people earlier in the year could barely pronounce her name".

Parasite was, in many ways, an extraordinary exception to the norm. The film, a ferocious tragicomedy about a family of grifters who leech onto a wealthy family, inspired nearly universal praise for its cunning construction and for the utter command of Bong, whose last two films (*Okja*, for Netflix; *Snowpiercer*, for The Weinstein Company's Radius label) were largely English. Its mastery was simply too much for voters to deny.

At a time when the national discourse often signals different attitudes about national borders, the Oscars have pushed in the other direction. On Monday, the Asia Society said of the win for *Parasite*: "Without question, this is a bridge-building moment." The film's victory resonated worldwide but especially in its native country. A headline in South Korea's biggest newspaper, *Chosun Ilbo*, blared: "Can you believe that *Parasite* won the Academy Best Picture? It rewrote the Academy's 92-year-old history."

Yet some were less enthusiastic about the Film Academy's newly global purview. A widely discussed post on *Mother Jones* on Monday lamented reading film subtitles. Conservative BlazeTV host Jon Miller on Twitter[8] criticized Bong's acceptance speech, spoken largely in Korean and translated by an interpreter. "These people are the destruction of America," wrote Miller.

But few films have inspired the kind of celebration that *Parasite* did at the Dolby Theatre, where the crowd greeted the film's best picture win with thunderous applause. For some, the film's win was a tremendous relief and a much-needed counterpoint to an Oscars field that was otherwise notably lacking in diversity. *Parasite* also followed the much-debated win last year for *Green Book*[9], a film many saw as racially retrograde.

"The world is big and it is beautiful and films from everywhere deserve to be on that stage winning the Academy's highest honor," said Ava DuVernay.

The lack of acting nominations for DuVernay's *Selma* led, in part, to the #OscarsSoWhite backlash of 2015. Since then, the Academy of Motion Pictures Arts and Sciences has worked to diversify its largely white and male ranks, a process that's led to the induction of many more international members.

"These awards should be global and that happens within the Academy," said Antonio Banderas, a best actor nominee for Pedro Almodóvar's Spanish language drama *Pain & Glory*, on the red carpet before Sunday's ceremony. "These past two years, joining the Academy have been 1,500 members. This is a very powerful injection of international members, which gives power to the Academy, which pretends to be global."

The movie business has never been more global. Overseas ticket sales last year exceeded $30 billion of the first time. Hollywood's largest productions are deliberately crafted to appeal to movie audiences worldwide. China is expected to surpass the U.S. at the world's top movie market this year.

With America's moviemaking supremacy increasingly on the wane, the Oscars are likely to only further expand their scope in the future. And not just because of international productions, but homegrown ones, too.

At last month's Sundance Film Festival[10], Korean-American filmmaker Lee Isaac Chung's tender autobiographical tale about his upbringing in rural Arkansas, *Minari*, took top honors. Chung said producers of his immigrant drama (made by Brad Pitt's Plan B production company) urged him to prize authenticity over what's typically commercial. "Make this as Korean as possible," Chung said he was advised. His movie is largely in Korean with subtitles.

Backstage at the Oscars, Bong was still staggered by his film's awards when he tried to articulate their significance.

"I don't think it's necessary to separate all the borders and divisions, whether it's Asia, Europe or the U.S.," said Bong. "If we pursue the beauty of cinema and focus on the individual charms that each piece has then, I think, we will naturally overcome these barriers."

（From *The Washington Post*, Feb. 11, 2020）

NOTES

1. **Bong Joon Ho**: 奉俊昊（1969—），韩国导演、编剧。2000 年至今，奉俊昊执导《汉江怪物》（*The Host*, 2006）、《雪国列车》（*Snowpiercer*, 2013）等多部影片，荣获多个韩国和国际电影奖项。其执导的影片《寄生虫》（*Parasite*）获得第 92 届奥斯卡金像奖、第 72 届戛纳国际电影节（Cannes International Festival）等多个奖项。

2. **Academy Awards**：学院奖，全名为"学院功绩奖"（Academy Award of Merit），通称"奥斯卡金像奖""金奖""奥斯卡奖"或"奥斯卡（the Oscars）"，举办方为美国电影艺术与科学学院（Academy of Motion and Picture Arts and Sciences）。自 1929 年后，此奖项每年在美国加利福尼亚州的洛杉矶举行颁奖礼。该奖项是目前最受世界瞩目的电影奖项之一。

3. **Golden Globe**：金球奖，英文全称为 Golden Globe Awards，美国年度电影与电视奖项，举办方为好莱坞国外记者协会（Hollywood Foreign Press Association）。自 1944 年起，金球奖每年颁发一次，包括最佳剧本、最佳导演、最佳外语片、最佳男女主角等奖项。

4. **YouTube**：油管，一个视频网站，注册于 2005 年 2 月 15 日，由美籍华人陈士骏（Steve Chen）等人创立，用户可通过该网站下载、观看及分享影片或短片，是当前行业内顶尖的在线视频网站。

5. **Lulu Wang**：王子逸（1983—），美籍华人导演、编剧、制片人，毕业于波士顿学院。2019 年，她自编自导的剧情电影《别告诉她》（*The Farewell*）入围第 29 届哥谭独立电影奖（29th Gotham Independent Film Awards）最佳剧本奖，并凭借该片入围第 3 届好莱坞影评人协会奖（3rd Annual Hollywood Critics Association Awards）最佳女导演奖，同时获得第 77 届美国电影电视金球奖最佳外语片奖提名。

6. **Film Independent Spirit Awards**：独立精神奖，好莱坞电影界为鼓励独立电影制片人创作的一个重要奖项，相当于独立电影界的奥斯卡。该奖项于 1984 年正式创办，机构成员包括美国八大电影公司以外的所有独立制片业者。

7. **Zhao Shuzhen**：赵淑珍（1944—），中国女演员。2019 年，她因出演影片《别告诉她》获得第 35 届独立精神奖最佳女配角，成为继章子怡后第二位获得该奖项的中国人。

8. **Twitter**：推特，一家美国社交网络服务网站，注册于 2006 年，致力于服务公众对话，于 2023 年 7 月 31 日正式更名为 X。

9. *Green Book*：《绿皮书》，一部由彼得·法雷利（Peter Farrelly）执导、维果·莫特森（Viggo Mortensen）和马赫沙拉·阿里（Mahershala Ali）主演的剧情片，于 2018 年 9 月 11 日在多伦多国际电影节首映。电影的主要内容为：1962 年，牙买加裔美国钢琴家唐纳德·雪利前往亚拉巴马州、佐治亚州等美国南部保守地区巡回演出，雇用了白人托尼·瓦勒隆加作为司机和保镖。一路上，两人迥异的性格使他们之间产生了很多的矛盾，而唐纳德在南方所遭受的种种不公平对待也让托尼对种族歧视感到深恶痛绝。旅程结束后，两人建立了深厚的友谊。《绿皮书》荣获第 76 届金球奖最佳音乐喜剧影片、最佳男配角和最佳剧本奖，以及第 91 届奥斯卡金像奖最佳影片、最佳男配角和最佳原创剧本奖等奖项。

10. **Sundance Film Festival**：圣丹斯电影节，即"日舞影展"，专门为独立电影制片人而设，是全世界首屈一指的独立电影节。该电影节由罗伯特·雷德福（Robert Redford）于 1984 年一手创办，每年 1 月 18 日至 28 日在美国犹他州的帕克城举行。

USEFUL WORDS

backlash	['bæklæʃ]	*n.* a strong and adverse reaction by a large number of people, especially to a social or political development 强烈反对
backstage	[ˌbæk'steɪdʒ]	*adv.* in or to the backstage area in a theater 在后台
blare	[bleə(r)]	*v.* to make or cause to make a loud, harsh sound 刺耳地鸣响；刺耳地发出
cast	[kɑːst]	*n.* the actors taking part in a play, film, or other production 全体演员
counterpoint	['kaʊntəpɔɪnt]	*n.* a pleasing or interesting contrast 惬意（或有趣）的对比
cunning	['kʌnɪŋ]	*adj.* having or showing skills in achieving one's ends by deceit or evasion 狡猾的
grifter	['grɪftə(r)]	*n.* a person who engages in petty or small-scale swindling 骗财的人
indie	['ɪndi]	*adj.* (of a pop group, record label, or film company) not belonging to or affiliated with a major record or film company 独立的

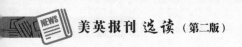

lamented	[lə'mentɪd]	*adj.*	a conventional way of describing sb. who has died or sth. that has been lost or that has ceased to exist 令人悼念（或怀念）的
monopoly	[mə'nɒpəli]	*n.*	the exclusive possession or control of the supply of or trade in a commodity or service 垄断
nomination	[ˌnɒmɪ'neɪʃn]	*n.*	the action of nominating or state of being nominated 提名
nominee	[nɒmɪ'niː]	*n.*	a person who is proposed or formally entered as a candidate for an office or as the recipient of a grant or award 被提名者
parasite	['pærəsaɪt]	*n.*	(derogatory) a person who habitually relies on or exploits others and gives nothing in return 寄生虫
purview	['pɜːvjuː]	*n.*	(formal) the scope of the influence or concerns of sth. 范围
retrograde	['retrəgreɪd]	*adj.*	reverting to an earlier and inferior condition 倒退的
streaming	['striːmɪŋ]	*adj.*	relating to or making use of a form of tape transport, used mainly to provide backup storage, in which data may be transferred in bulk while the tape is in motion 流播的
subtitle	['sʌbtaɪtl]	*n.*	captions displayed at the bottom of a movie or television screen that translate or transcribe the dialogue or narrative 字幕
supremacy	[su'preməsi]	*n.*	the state or condition of being superior to all others in authority, power, or status （权力）至高无上
tragicomedy	[ˌtrædʒi'kɒmədi]	*n.*	a play or novel containing elements of both comedy and tragedy 悲喜剧
triumph	['traɪʌmf]	*v.*	to achieve a victory 获胜

EXERCISES

I. Vocabulary

Choose among the four alternatives one word or phrase that is closest in meaning to the underlined part in each statement.

1. Before Bong Joon Ho's *Parasite* made history as the first non-English best picture winner in Academy Awards history, he made a modest <u>plea</u> to American moviegoers: Don't be afraid of subtitles.

    A. request   B. prayer   C. invocation   D. blame

2. Reflecting on those words backstage at Sunday's Oscars while he <u>clutched</u> several of his statuettes, Bong wondered whether those boundaries were already breaking.

    A. clung   B. grasped   C. adhered   D. hung

3. Hollywood's <u>reach</u> has long extended to all corners of the globe, but it has less frequently returned the favor.

    A. extent   B. influence   C. destination   D. distance

4. Even though the American film industry was built largely by immigrants, on Oscar night, its <u>gaze</u> has usually been turned inward.

   A. glance   B. peek   C. stare   D. direction

5. *Parasite* was, in many ways, an extraordinary exception to the <u>norm</u>.

   A. standard   B. principal   C. average   D. formal

6. The film, a ferocious tragicomedy about a family of grifters who <u>leech onto</u> a wealthy family, inspired nearly universal praise for its cunning construction and for the utter command of Bong, whose last two films (*Okja*, for Netflix; *Snowpiercer*, for The Weinstein Company's Radius label) were largely English.

   A. bum on   B. bludge off   C. loaf about   D. attach themselves to

7. The film's victory <u>resonated</u> worldwide but especially in its native country.

   A. recalled   B. oscillated   C. rang   D. echoed

8. For some, the film's win was a <u>tremendous</u> relief and a much-needed counterpoint to an Oscars field that was otherwise notably lacking in diversity.

   A. very great   B. monstrous   C. mighty   D. towering

9. China is expected to <u>surpass</u> the U.S. at the world's top movie market this year.

   A. excel   B. exceed   C. dwarf   D. stunt

10. Chung said producers of his immigrant drama (made by Brad Pitt's Plan B production company) urged him to prize <u>authenticity</u> over what's typically commercial.

   A. legitimacy   B. genuineness   C. rightfulness   D. certainty

II. Comprehension

Decide whether the following statements are true (T) or false (F) according to the information given in the press clipping. Mark T or F for each statement.

1. According to the text, the revolutionary win for *Parasite* contributed to proving that the 1-inch-tall barrier of subtitles was already breaking.

2. Bong Joon Ho agreed with American moviegoers on their remarks about the subtitles of foreign-language films.

3. There is excellent proficiency in the movie *Parasite* which received the voters' recognition.

4. Although the film industry in the U.S. was established mainly by filmmakers from all over the world regardless of the languages they speak, on Oscar night, it has usually tended to focus on English films, not foreign-language ones.

5. *The Farewell*, made by the Chinese-American director Lulu Wang, had also won great awards.

6. Though an actress from China may win a prize for her good performance in a movie, many people might not pronounce her name earlier in the year.

7. The victory of *Parasite* resonated worldwide, and everyone was enthusiastic about reading film subtitles.

8. Nowadays, the movie business has gained the most popularity ever in history.

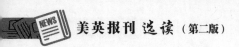
美英报刊 选读（第二版）

9. The Academy pretended to be global as the great injection of international members has given power to it.

10. Bong Joon Ho suggested that Hollywood's barriers should naturally be overcome if the Academy pursues authentically the beauty of cinema and the charms of films.

III. Topics for Discussion

1. Do you like seeing films? If so, what is your favorite one? And what is the most impressive scene in the film that you have watched?

2. Have you ever seen *Parasite*? What is your point on the theme of the story?

3. What is your understanding of the remarks in the text, i.e., "Hollywood's reach has long extended to all corners of the globe, but it has less frequently returned the favor"?

4. Why did the author of the text regard the victory of the film *Parasite* as a bridge-building moment?

5. What are the social and psychological causes that have led to the formation of Hollywood barriers?

美英两国的电影业

一、美国电影的发展历程

（一）美国电影业："从无声到有声"

1893 年，托马斯·阿尔瓦·爱迪生（Thomas Alva Edison）发明了电影视镜并创建了"囚车"摄影场，美国电影业由此诞生。早期，制片基地在纽约，制片公司主要为爱迪生公司（Edison Studios）、比沃格拉夫公司（Biograph Company）和维太格拉夫公司（American Vitagraph Company）。1903 年，导演埃德温·鲍特（Edwin S. Porter）在拍摄短片《一个美国消防员的生活》（*Life of an American Fireman*）时，首次运用了"交叉蒙太奇"的拍摄技巧，富有戏剧效果地展现了同时发生的事情，开启了电影史的新篇章。自此，电影发展成为一门独立的艺术。

1908 年，爱迪生成立了电影专利公司，在电影制作、发行和放映等环节进行垄断和控制，因此，独立制片人开始将拍摄基地转移至位于西海岸的好莱坞。其中，导演大卫·沃克·格里菲斯（David Wark Griffith）在好莱坞拍摄期间，将电影的拍摄基本单位由"场面"改为"镜头"（一个连续拍摄的画面），提出通过改变拍摄的距离和角度、镜头的长短以及组接的节奏，使影片能够有效地叙事和抒情，从而操纵观众的反应。同时，格里菲斯还规定了电影演员的表演规则，培养了以吉许姐妹（Lillian Gish & Dorothy Gish）为代表的优秀电影演员。由此，格里菲斯建立了电影艺术的完整体系，好莱坞开始成为美国电影的摄制大本营。

1915 年，爱迪生的电影专利公司解体，好莱坞正式成为美国电影的拍摄中心；美国各大公司开始实行的"明星制"（电影和广告均用明星招揽观众）极大地推动了电影的发展；1914 年至 1918 年，第一次世界大战爆发，欧洲电影业遭受重创，美国电影趁机抢占欧洲市场，建立霸权地位。因此，第一次世界大战前夕，美国电影获得蓬勃发展。

截至 1928 年，美国八大电影公司形成，五家较大的影片公司为派拉蒙（Paramount Pictures, Inc.，1914 年组建）、20 世纪福克斯（Twentieth Century Fox Corporation，1915 年组建，1935 年合并）、米高梅（Metro-Goldwyn-Mayer，1924 年合并）、华纳兄弟（Warner Bros. Entertainment, Inc.，1923 年成立）和雷电华（Radio-Keith-Orpheum Pictures，又称 RKO Productions，1928 年成立），三家较小的公司为环球（Universal Picture Co.，1912 年成立）、哥伦比亚（Columbia Pictures Corp.，1924 年成立）和联美（United Artists，简称 UA，1919 年成立）。

1926 年，由导演艾伦·克罗斯兰（Alan Crosland）执导、华纳兄弟影业公司拍摄的歌剧片《唐璜》（*Don Juan*）选用了唱片进行配唱，备受欢迎；1927 年，华纳兄弟影业公司在拍摄无声故事片《爵士歌王》（*The Jazz Singer*）时，加入了部分有声台词，首次放映就引起轰动；1928 年，华纳兄弟影业公司任命导演布莱恩·福尹（Bryan Foy）拍摄了有声片《纽约之光》（*Lights of New York*），电影的所有情节均通过演员的有声台词讲述，自此电影步入有声时代。

（二）美国类型片的发展与繁荣

20 世纪 30 年代至 40 年代，各种类型的影片（歌舞片、纪录片、恐怖片、侦探片、故事片等）获得繁荣发展，代表作品为《四十二街》（*42nd Street*，1933）。20 世纪 60 年代，歌舞片的代表作品主要为《窈窕淑女》（*My Fair Lady*，1964）、《音乐之声》（*The Sound of Music*，1965）等；浪漫喜剧作品主要为《一夜风流》（*It Happened One Night*，1934）、《摩登时代》（*Modern Times*，1936）等；反映历史的浪漫影片代表作品主要为《乱世佳人》（*Gone with the Wind*，1939）等；惊悚影片的代表作品主要为《蝴蝶梦》（*Rebecca*，1940）、《上海快车》（*Shanghai Express*，1932）和《呼啸山庄》（*Wuthering Heights*，1939）等。

动画片在类型片中占有重要的地位，最受欢迎的是迪士尼（Walt Disney Productions）及其模仿者拍摄的动画片。20 世纪 30 年代至 40 年代，美国动画短片进入最辉煌的时期，米老鼠（Mickey Mouse）、唐老鸭（Donald Duck）等一系列动画形象家喻户晓、人人喜爱，影响了整个世界。此外，迪士尼还创作摄制了《白雪公主和七个小矮人》（*Snow White and the Seven Dwarfs*，1937）、《木偶奇遇记》（*Pinocchio*，1940）、《幻想曲》（*Fantasia*，1940）、《小鹿斑比》（*Bambi II*，1942）等众多脍炙人口的动画长片。

这一时期，奥逊·威尔斯（Orson Welles）导演的影片《公民凯恩》（*Citizen Kane*，1941）在叙事方式、摄影技术和音乐制作等方面均有创新，对当代的电影理论研究和影片拍摄实践具有重要意义。同时，高质量的纪录片也在大量问世，其中，《开垦平原的犁》（*The Plow That Broke the Plains*，1936）、《中途岛战役》（*The Battle of Midway*，1942）和《我们为何而战》（*Why We Fight*，1942）三部影片堪称长纪录片的经典之作。

第二次世界大战期间和 20 世纪 50 年代初期，故事片为美国影坛做出了很大的贡献，代表作品为《卡萨布兰卡》（*Casablanca*，1942）、《费城的故事》（*The Philadelphia Story*，1940）、《破坏者》（*Saboteur*，1942）、《魂断蓝桥》（*Waterloo Bridge*，1940）、《守望莱茵河》（*Watch on the Rhine*，1943）、《战地钟声》（*For Whom the Bell Tolls*，1943）、《凡尔杜先生》（*Monsieur Verdoux*，1947）、《东京上空三十秒》（*Thirty Seconds Over Tokyo*，1944）、《当代奸雄》（*All the King's Men*，1949）、《欲望号街车》（*A Street Car Named Desire*，1951）、《罗马假日》（*Roman Holiday*，1953）等。

然而，至 20 世纪 50 年代中期，美国电影的发展遭受重重困难。首先，1948 年，美国最高法院根据反托拉斯法对"派拉蒙案"做出裁决，判定大公司的垄断为非法行为，要求制片公司放弃发行和经营电影院的业务，因此，影片数量大幅度减少。其次，从 1947 年开始，好莱坞一批进步人士受到"非美活动调查委员会"的政治迫害，美国电影业的创作元气大伤。再次，电视的迅速普及导致电影观众人数大减。在此时期，美国电影业发展艰难，但导演赫尔倍特·比伯曼（Herbert J. Biberman）克服困难，拍摄了描写锌矿工人罢工的重要影片《社会中坚》（*Salt of the Earth*，1954），至今仍受到电影研究人员的重视。

在这一背景下，《海斯法典》（The Motion Picture Production Code，俗称 Hays Code）被废止，微型影院（micro theatre）、艺术影院（art theatre）、汽车影院（drive-in theatre）、独立制片（independent filmmaking）及实验电影（experimental film）得以发展，传统的类型片在内容上渐渐有了新的变化。在这一时期，美国青年对社会现实和传统产生不满情绪，比如影片《无因的反抗》（*Rebel Without a Cause*，1955）和《毕业生》（*Graduate*，1967）均反映了当时年轻人反叛和不满的思想与行为。

同时期其他著名的影片还有《陆军野战医院》（*MASH*，1970）、《第二十二条军规》（*Catch-22*，1970）、《巴顿将军》（*Patton*，1970）、《热情似火》（*Some Like It Hot*，1959）、《后窗》（*Rear Window*，1954）、《玛尔妮》（*Marnie*，1964）等。

随着美国电影的发展，黑人演员在美国电影中逐渐开始扮演正面的角色。同时，刚大学毕业的年轻导演开始崭露头角，比如《教父》（*The Godfather*，1972）、《美国风情画》（*American Graffiti*，1973）等影片均体现了青年导演的创新精神。

（三）美国类型片的变化

美国电影业一直在不断创新与发展。早在 20 世纪 30 年代，"黑色电影"（film noir）

就已出现。该类型影片多采用黑白影片的形式，反映的主题通常与神秘或犯罪有关，代表作品有《吓呆了的森林》（*The Petrified Forest*，1936）和《加倍赔款》（*Double Indemnity*，1944）。

同时，西部片的变化较为突出。首先，西部片的人物形象发生了变化。在《搜索者》（*The Searchers*，1956）、《虎豹小霸王》（*Butch Cassidy and the Sundance Kid*，1969）等电影中，群体取代了单枪匹马的英雄，而《复仇者联盟》（*Marvel's The Avengers*，2012）中单打独斗的超级英雄也变成了一股力量；影片《断背山》（*Brokeback Mountain*，2005）的主人公不再是惩恶扬善的英雄，而是在对社会准则采取抵制态度的人物。其次，西部电影涉及的范围也发生了变化，已延伸到太空与外星人。譬如，影片《火星人玩转地球》（*Mars Attacks*，1996）就是其中一部代表作。

到20世纪末，美国电影在形式和内容上变得更为标新立异。首先，科幻片、灾难片、冒险片更贴近现实，更直面未来，更令人震撼，如《弗兰肯斯坦》（*Frankenstein*，1931）、《第三类接触》（*Close Encounters of the Third Kind*，1977）、《外星人》（*E.T. the Extra-Terrestrial*，1982）、《侏罗纪公园》（*Jurassic Park*，1993）和《2012》（2009）等影片。其次，科幻片也有了反类型的电影，譬如影片《超能失控》（*Chronicle*，2012）是以纪录片的方式拍摄的科幻片，其叙事方式颠覆了科幻电影的叙事方式。

当代动画电影中的动画形象也发生了变化，部分形象由传统动画中积极而明朗变为恐怖而阴暗，吸血鬼、幽灵、僵尸、亡魂、女巫、狼人等已成为当代动画电影里的重要角色。《圣诞夜惊魂》（*The Nightmare Before Christmas*，1993）、《精灵旅社》（*Hotel Transylvania*，2012）和《科学怪狗》（*Frankenweenie*，2012）等影片均为当代动画电影的代表作品。

（四）美国电影的学术研究与奖励

20世纪60年代至70年代，美国设立电影学术研究机构，在电影学术研究方面取得巨大发展。1967年，华盛顿和洛杉矶两地的美国电影研究院建成；1969年，近300所美国的学院和高校开始提供电影专业课程，其中68所提供电影研究的本科学位，如南加利福尼亚大学设立电影艺术专业（Cinematic Arts），纽约大学设立电影制作、电影理论、影剧剧作等多个电影相关专业；20世纪70年代中期，随着录像带的普及，人们可以通过录像带接触到老电影，让仔细分析和解读电影变成可能。这些都对电影资料的收集、分类、整理和研究发挥着重要的作用。

另外，各种电影理论研究机构和学会开始发展，创办多种电影学术性刊物，为美国电影研究提供了条件，如《好莱坞记者报》（*Hollywood Reporter*）、《电影季刊》（*Film*

Quarterly）、《电影评论》（*Film Comment*）等。

此外，美国电影业开设奥斯卡金像奖、美国影评人学会奖（National Society of Film Critics，创办于 1996 年）等奖项，奖励优秀的电影作品和杰出的电影从业者。同时，业界还举办有影响的国际电影节来加强国际交流，如芝加哥国际电影节（Chicago International Film Festival）、洛杉矶国际文化电影节（Los Angeles International Culture Film Festival，LAICFF）、纽约国际儿童电影节（New York International Children's Film Festival，NYICFF）、旧金山国际电影节（San Francisco International Film Festival，SFIFF）等。

凭借雄厚的资金支持，强大的科技力量，专业且对社会生活有深刻洞察力的导演，以及数量庞大、演技非凡的演员和卓有成效的营销策划与商业运作，美国电影业给美国带来了巨大利润，也向世界展示了美国的社会文化。

二、英国电影的发展历程

（一）英国电影的起步

英国是电影业起步较早的国家，早在 1889 年就制造出了摄影机、转动架等。罗伯特·保罗（Robert W. Paul）于 1896 年 3 月 26 日放映了由他自己拍摄的《多佛海的狂浪》（*Rough Sea at Dover*），这是电影在世界范围内的首次商业性放映。

英国人不仅参与了早期电影器材的发明创造，而且英国的电影艺术家和技术革新家对电影的拍摄技巧做出了多方面的研究和探索。例如，乔治·阿尔伯特·史密斯（George Albert Smith）采用特大特写镜头拍摄《祖母的放大镜》（*Grandma's Reading Glass*，1900）；希塞尔·海普华斯（Cecil Hepworth）撰写的《活动照相术——或电影摄影入门》（*Animated Photography：The ABC of the Cinematography*，1897）是世界上最早的电影论著之一。

但自 1909 年起，美、法两国影片占领了英国市场，加上第一次世界大战的爆发和国内加征娱乐税的政策颁布，这些使英国电影业的发展变得十分糟糕。1927 年，英国正式颁布了利于电影产业发展的《电影法》（*Cinematograph Films Act*），之后英国影片的上映率逐年好转，英国电影业开始出现转机。

（二）英国电影的发展与繁荣

20 世纪 20 年代末，由英国导演摄制的一批影片使英国电影业出现了一番繁荣景象，安东尼·阿斯奎斯（Anthony Asquith）摄制的《地下》（*Underground*，1928）、E. A. 杜邦（E. A. Dupont）摄制的《皮卡迪利大街》（*Piccadilly*，1929）便是其中的两部。

1929 年，有声影片问世。由阿尔弗雷德·希区柯克（Alfred Hitchcock）导演的《讹诈》（*Blackmail*，1929）、阿斯奎斯的《逃出达特穆尔》（*A Cottage on Dartmoor*，1930）、沃

尔特·福德（Walter Forde）的《罗马快车》（*Rome Express*，1932）等都属于上乘之作。

20世纪30年代，英国电影经历了短暂的繁荣，其中由亚历山大·柯达爵士（Sir Alexander Korda）导演的《英宫艳史》（*The Private Life of Henry VIII*，1933）最为有名。该片是第一部非好莱坞拍摄的获得学院奖（Academy Award）的影片。

二战期间，英国的主流电影为爱国电影，代表作有《48小时》（*Went the Day Well?*，1942）、《与祖国同在》（*In Which We Serve*，1942）等影片。一批优秀的纪录片也及时问世，鼓舞了英国民众。其他题材的影片表现得较为突出的有柯达的《巴格达窃贼》（*The Thief of Bagdad*，1940）、梭罗德·迪金森（Thorold Dickinson）的《煤气灯》（*Gaslight*，1940）和《首相》（*The Prime Minister*，1941）、巴兹尔·迪安（Basil Dean）的《二十一天》（*21 Days*，1940）、盖布里埃尔·帕斯卡（Gabriei Pascal）的豪华历史剧《恺撒和克莉奥佩特拉》（*Caesar and Cleopatra*，1945）、大卫·利恩（David Lean）的浪漫戏剧影片《相见恨晚》（*Brief Encounter*，1945）等。

20世纪50年代晚期，"英国新浪潮"（British "New Wave"）和"自由电影运动"（Free Cinema Movement）蓬勃发展，这个时期的电影特点是反映社会现状，重视劳动阶级，强调自由和人的重要性，注重日常生活的意义。代表作有由林赛·安德森（Lindsay Anderson）执导的影片《如此运动生涯》（*This Sporting Life*，1961）和托尼·理查德森（Tony Richardson）的《蜜的滋味》（*A Taste of Honey*，1961）等。

20世纪60年代，英国电影进入多元化时期，经典硬汉角色开始出现在荧屏上，代表作有"继续"（Carry On）系列电影和"詹姆斯·邦德"（James Bond）系列电影。

20世纪70年代为英国电影的困顿期；80年代，英国电影重新振作，代表作有由休斯·赫德森（Hugh Hudson）执导的《烈火战车》（*Chariots of Fire*，1981），理查德·艾登保禄（Richard Attenborough）的《甘地传》（*Gandhi*，1985）一举获得八项奥斯卡奖。其他如詹姆斯·伊沃里（James Ivory）的《看得见风景的房间》（*A Room with a View*，1986）、《尘与热》（*Heat and Dust*，1983）等也都获得了广泛的国际声誉。

20世纪90年代，英国电影继续辉煌，由迈克·李（Mike Leigh）导演的《秘密与谎言》（*Secrets and Lies*，1996）、伯纳德·罗斯（Bernard Rose）的《安娜·卡列尼娜》（*Anna Karenina*，1997）、戴米思·奥唐纳（Damien O'Donnell）的《东就是东》（*East Is East*，1999）、罗杰·米歇尔（Roger Michell）的《诺丁山》（*Notting Hill*，1999）、理查德·柯蒂斯（Richard Curtis）的《真爱至上》（*Love Actually*，2003）等电影都获得了成功。

（三）21世纪的英国电影

进入21世纪，奇幻类和传记类电影成为英国电影的亮点。前者的代表作有"哈利·波特"系列（*Harry Potter*，2001—2011）和根据英国作家 J. R. R 托尔金（J. R. R. Tolkien）作品改编的"指环王"系列（*Lord of the Rings*，2001—2003），影响当今一代人的成长。后者的代表作有《伊丽莎白：黄金时代》（*Elizabeth: The Golden Age*，2007）、《女王》（*The Queen*，2006）、《铁娘子》（*The Iron Lady*，2011）等。

（四）英国电影的学术研究

英国的大电影制片厂有松林制片厂（Pinewood Studios）、艾尔斯特里工作室（Elstree Studios）等；主要的电影教育机构有伦敦电影学校（The London Film School）、皇家艺术学院（Royal College of Art）等；主要的电影研究机构为英国电影学院（British Film Institute，1933 年成立）；主要的电影节有四年一度的伦敦国际电影节（London Film Festival），它是国际著名的电影节；主要的电影出版物有《画面与音响》（*Sight & Sound*，1932 年创刊）和《银幕》（*Screen*，1959 年创刊）。

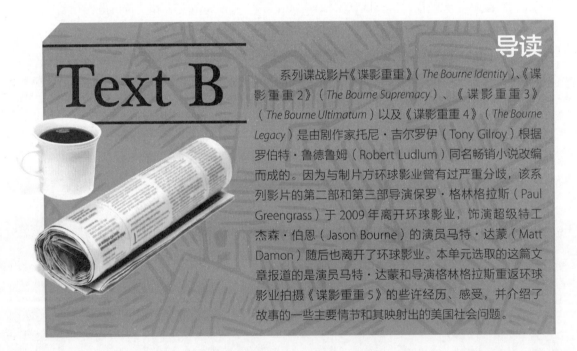

Text B

导读

系列谍战影片《谍影重重》（*The Bourne Identity*）、《谍影重重 2》（*The Bourne Supremacy*）、《谍影重重 3》（*The Bourne Ultimatum*）以及《谍影重重 4》（*The Bourne Legacy*）是由剧作家托尼·吉尔罗伊（Tony Gilroy）根据罗伯特·鲁德鲁姆（Robert Ludlum）同名畅销小说改编而成的。因为与制片方环球影业曾有过严重分歧，该系列影片的第二部和第三部导演保罗·格林格拉斯（Paul Greengrass）于 2009 年离开环球影业，饰演超级特工杰森·伯恩（Jason Bourne）的演员马特·达蒙（Matt Damon）随后也离开了环球影业。本单元选取的这篇文章报道的是演员马特·达蒙和导演格林格拉斯重返环球影业拍摄《谍影重重 5》的些许经历、感受，并介绍了故事的一些主要情节和其映射出的美国社会问题。

Damon is Bourne again

Spy thriller franchise back with more political intrigue, amped-up action

By Steven Zeitchik

Las Vegas[1]—On a trip to Los Angeles about 18 months ago, the London-based filmmaker Paul Greengrass sat down to lunch with Matt Damon and editor Christopher Rouse.

The latter two had come with stealth mission. Greengrass had long been unwilling to make his third Jason Bourne movie and for a time was even burned up about a spinoff done without him. But with the director wandering in a kind of decade-long exile making globalization cautionary tales, they thought it was time for him, in Bourne-ian terms, "to come in" and direct a new movie about Robert Ludlum's amnesiac assassin.

"I was skeptical [of the fact that] there was one to be done, I was skeptical [of the fact that] I wanted to do it and I was skeptical [of the fact that] it would hold up with the others," recalled Greengrass, 60. "But Matt said, 'We're really lucky to have an audience that loves this character.' Chris said, 'The world has really changed since *The Bourne Ultimatum* in 2007. I thought, 'Maybe I've been too negative to an old friend.'"

Greengrass told this story in Las Vegas, where his new movie Jason Bourne—starring and produced by Damon; edited by and co-written with Rouse—would later that day make its debut.

The figurative distance covered by the director is even greater. When the new Bourne arrives in theaters, Friday, it will land the one-time documentarian back in a tentpole fishbowl he'd long swum away from—while excitingly but potentially troublingly upping the political-realism ante above most Hollywood blockbusters. Jason Bourne expands the possibilities of—and tests the appetite for—serious issues in escapist cinema.

And it wasn't even supposed to exist—not after Universal[2] upset Greengrass by making 2012's *The Bourne Legacy* with rival director Tony Gilroy.

"I had," Damon said, "given up hope that we would get here."

With its trademark handheld cameras and edits faster than a croupier's fingers, Jason Bourne vibrates with the momentum fans know well. From its early set piece at an austerity riot in Athens to its fiery third-act car chase shot practically on the Vegas Strip, Bourne keeps the plot turns coming.

There's the ex-agent's new discoveries about his past, a fresh chapter with his comrade—roguery Nicky Parsons (Julia Stiles), slippery dealings with a murkily motivated cyber-analyst (Alicia Vicander) and a fraught relationship between new CIA[3] director Robert Dewey (Tommy Lee Jones) and Aaron Kalloor (Riz Ahmed), a Silicon Valley[4] mogul whose user database holds the key to Dewey's intelligence ambitions.

And yes, Bourne is again on the run from shadowy bosses as he tries to learn what brought him here. But you assumed all that. More novel are the social issues: The film's Athens-to-Vegas arc, for instance, which by going from a flailing economy to capitalist excess puts a spotlight on

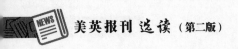

economic disenfranchisement. Or the privacy debate—when Kalloor and Dewey tensely hash out whether a tech company should give the government a backdoor, it so closely echoes the recent Apple-FBI controversy[5] over a terrorist's iPhone you'd think Greengrass shot it last month. [He didn't]

"We looked at the differences from *The Bourne Ultimatum* and it was shocking," Damon said. "We thought, if Jason was on the run, why not run him through today's landscape?"

Also, because Bourne now remembers what he's done, moral questions enter. Does he want to use his lethal skills to serve his country or does he refrain out of guilt—patriotism or conscience?

Crucially, every enemy and good guy is firmly within the U.S. government. This is a far cry from all other 21st-century thrillers and even from past Bourne movies (though *Ultimatum* gets close). No longer is the story about the U.S. versus its enemies. It's about the U.S. versus itself.

"In a sense all these films are anchored in identity, because Jason Bourne is trying to find out who he is. But with this one I think we're also asking how we want to define ourselves as a country." Rouse said.

Greengrass—who wears Harry Potter[6] glasses, shoulderlength white hair and a mien that in a certain light can make him look like Jay Leno—dedicated much of four years to *The Bourne Supremacy*, sequel to Doug Liman's *The Bourne Identity*, and then *Ultimatum*.

He imported his style of current-events research (he is known for being moved to direct films by seemingly unrelated writings; Paul Mason's global-uprising study *Why It's Kicking Off Everywhere* and a wired article about hacker recruitment in Vegas were the impetus for this one).

But his first two Bourne movies were, Greengrass admits, "painful in their processes." Because his spontaneity often led to key moments being omitted, he and a crew would be forced to return to various cities for reshoots, sometimes more than once.

Deciding in 2008—after Bourne scored three Oscars and global success—that he didn't want more stress, Greengrass walked away. He went off to make smaller-scale films. Damon, close with Greengrass, also stayed away.

But Universal, short on franchises and not wanting the rights to revert to the Ludlum estate, needed a movie. Soon Gilroy—who had written all three Bourne films but whose *Ultimatum* script Greengrass had almost entirely rewritten—was on board for a spinoff with Jeremy Renner, *The Bourne Legacy*.

Legacy performed modestly, but well enough to keep the franchise alive. Donna Langley, chairman of the Universal, said that she was proud of the movie and believed it had a beneficial effect on the public. She also hoped, soon after, that Greengrass might come back. And he did. The issues in Bourne are timely. Combine that with a documentary-style shoot and you're left with a movie of far more realism than most summer action film.

（From *Los Angeles Times*, Jul. 26, 2016）

NOTES

1. **Las Vegas**：拉斯维加斯，美国内华达州最大的城市，1905 年 5 月 15 日建市，位于沙漠边缘，全年高温。1931 年美国大萧条时期，为了度过经济难关，内华达州议会通过了赌博合法的议案，该市经济因此迅速崛起。拉斯维加斯现居世界四大赌城之首，是一座以赌博业为中心的世界知名度假城市。

2. **Universal**：此处指 Universal Pictures，环球影业公司，简称"环球影业"，成立于 1912 年 6 月 8 日。数十年来，环球影业与史蒂芬·斯皮尔伯格（Steven Spielberg）等著名导演合作，发行了诸如《大白鲨》（*Jaws*）、《外星人》（*E.T.*）、"侏罗纪公园"系列（The Jurassic Park series）、"谍影重重"系列（The Bourne series）、"速度与激情"系列（The Fast & Furious series）等影片。进入 21 世纪，环球影业成为好莱坞最擅长开发续集电影和喜剧片的大公司。

3. **CIA**：全称为 Central Intelligence Agency，（美国）中央情报局，1947 年成立，美国的情报机构之一，负责公开和秘密地收集和分析关于国外政府、公司、组织、个人、政治、文化、科技等方面的情报。中央情报局的总部在弗吉尼亚州的兰利市，其地位和功能相当于英国的军情六处（MI6）、苏联的克格勃（KGB）和以色列的摩萨德（Mossad），在美国情报体系中是一个独立的情报部门。

4. **Silicon Valley**：硅谷，美国电子工业重要基地，位于美国加利福尼亚州的旧金山经圣塔克拉拉至圣何塞近 50 公里的一条狭长地带。这是一个受益于微电子技术的高速发展、在 20 世纪 60 年代中期以后逐渐形成的基地。硅谷依托斯坦福大学、加州大学伯克利分校、加州理工学院等高校，既有思科（Cisco Systems, Inc.）、英特尔（Intel Corporation）、惠普（Hewlett-Packard Company）、朗讯（Lucent Technologies, Inc.）、苹果（Apple Inc.）等大公司，也汇聚着一大批拥有高新技术的中小公司，是一个融产、学、研为一体的基地。

5. **Apple-FBI controversy**：2016 年 2 月，据路透社报道，美国加利福尼亚州中央区地方法院法官谢里·皮姆（Sheri Pym）要求苹果公司帮助联邦调查局（Federal Bereau of Investigation，FBI）对枪击案凶手赛耶德·法鲁克（Syed Farook）拥有的苹果手机加以解锁，但苹果公司总执行官蒂姆·库克（Tim Cook）予以拒绝，即拒绝在用户手机上预先设计一个后门（back door）。这一纷争实际上涉及的是技术与政治的纷争，其焦点是智能手机该是一个值得公民信赖的通信手段还是应该成为政府探知公民隐私的某种工具。

（美国）联邦调查局成立于 1908 年，由美国司法部管辖。它的初期主要任务是调查违反联邦法律的犯罪行为，如偷盗、抢劫等，为地方、国家和国际机构提供帮助，同时在响应公众需要和忠实于美国宪法的前提下履行职责。联邦调查局曾对持不同政见者，如黑人运动领袖马丁·路德·金、卓别林、爱因斯坦等开展调查行动。2001 年 9 月 11 日的恐怖袭击后，联邦调查局将打击恐怖主义列为其首要任务。

6. **Harry Potter**：哈利·波特，英国作家 J. K. 罗琳（J. K. Rowling）所著的同名系列魔幻小说的主人公。该系列小说共七部，创作时间为 1997 年至 2007 年。前六部小说的情节围绕霍格沃茨魔法学校（Hogwarts School of Witchcraft and Wizardry）展开，讲述的是小说主人公——巫师学生哈利·波特六年的学习情况和冒险经历，第七部是关于哈利·波特在第二次巫师界大战中如何寻找魂器并消灭伏地魔（Lord Voldemort）的故事。该系列小说被翻译成 70 多种语言，为世界上最畅销小说系列之一，并于 2001 年由华纳电影公司搬上银幕，广受观众喜爱。

USEFUL WORDS

amnesiac	[æmˈniːziæk]	adj.	of a medical condition in which sb. partly or completely loses their memory 记忆缺失的
anchor	[ˈæŋkə(r)]	v.	to firmly base sth. on sth. else 使基于
austerity	[ɒˈsterəti]	n.	a situation when people do not have much money to spend because there are bad economic conditions 苦行；朴素；节衣缩食
blockbuster	[ˈblɒkbʌstə(r)]	n.	(informal) sth. very successful, especially a very successful book or film/movie （尤指）非常成功的书（或电影）
croupier	[ˈkruːpieɪ]	n.	a person whose job is to be in charge of a gambling table and collect and pay out money, give out cards, etc. （负责收付钱、发牌等的）赌台管理员
documentarian	[ˌdɒkjuˈmentriən]	n.	sb. who makes documentaries 纪录片导演（或制片人）
figurative	[ˈfɪɡərətɪv]	adj.	(of paintings, art, etc.) showing people, animal and objects as they really look 形象的
haunt	[hɔnt]	v.	to be always present as a nagging anxiety in the mind of 萦绕在……心头
lethal	[ˈliːθl]	adj.	causing or able to cause death 致死的，致命的
mogul	[ˈməʊɡl]	n.	a very rich, important and powerful person 有权势的人
momentum	[məˈmentəm]	n.	the ability to keep increasing or developing 动力，推动力
refrain	[rɪˈfreɪn]	v.	(formal) to stop sb. from doing sth., especially sth. that you want to do 抑制，克制
revert	[rɪˈvɜːt]	v.	(of property, rights, etc.) to return to the original owner again （财产、权利等）归还

roguery	['rəʊgərɪ]	*n.*	roguish behavior 无赖行为
score	[skɔː(r)]	*v.*	to win points, goal, etc. in a game or competition （在游戏或比赛中）得分
sequel	['siːkwəl]	*n.*	continuation (especially of a story) 续集，续篇
skeptical	['skeptɪkl]	*adj.*	having doubts that a claim or statement is true or that sth. will happen 怀疑性的
spinoff	['spɪnˌɒf]	*n.*	a book, a film/movie, a television program, or an object that is based on a book, film/movie or television series that has been very successful （根据成功的书籍、电影或电视系列剧制作的）派生作品
spontaneity	[ˌspɒntə'neɪəti]	*n.*	the quality of being spontaneous 自发性

✎ EXERCISES

I. Vocabulary

Choose among the four alternatives one word or phrase that is closest in meaning to the underlined part in each statement.

1. Greengrass had long been unwilling to make his third Jason Bourne movie and for a time was even <u>burned up</u> about a spinoff done without him.

    A. deeply hurt   B. completely stimulated

    C. greatly riled   D. excited by fire

2. "I was <u>skeptical</u> [of the fact that] there was one to be done, I was skeptical [of the fact that] I wanted to do it and I was skeptical [of the fact that] it would hold up with the others," recalled Greengrass, 60.

    A. hesitant   B. unbelievable   C. suspicious   D. thoughtful

3. There's the ex-agent's new discoveries about his past, a fresh chapter with his comrade—roguery Nicky Parsons (Julia Stiles), <u>slippery</u> dealings with a murkily motivated cyber-analyst (Alicia Vicander)...

    A. difficult to stand   B. difficult to handle   C. not trustworthy   D. very smooth

4. ...a <u>fraught</u> relationship between new CIA director Robert Dewey (Tommy Lee Jones) and Aaron Kalloor (Riz Ahmed)...

    A. worrying   B. troublesome   C. worried   D. false

5. Does he want to use his lethal skills to serve his country or does he <u>refrain</u> out of guilt—patriotism or conscience?

    A. restrain   B. sustain   C. obtain   D. ascertain

6. In a sense all these films are <u>anchored in</u> identity, because Jason Bourne is trying to find out who he is.

    A. firmly secured on   B. firmly based on   C. conducted in   D. fastened in

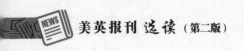

7. Greengrass—who wears Harry Potter glasses, shoulderlength white hair and a mien that in a certain light can make him look like Jay Leno—dedicated much of four years to *The Bourne Supremacy*, <u>sequel</u> to Doug Liman's *The Bourne Identity*, and then *Ultimatum*.

    A. an end

    B. the conclusion

    C. the outcome

    D. the follow-up

8. Because his <u>spontaneity</u> often led to key moments being omitted, he and a crew would be forced to return to various cities for reshoots, sometimes more than once.

    A. involuntary action

    B. forced action

    C. premeditated action

    D. impulsive action

9. Deciding in 2008—after Bourne <u>scored</u> three Oscars and global success—that he didn't want more stress, Greengrass walked away.

    A. marked   B. credited   C. got   D. cut

10. But Universal, short on franchises and not wanting the rights to <u>revert</u> to the Ludlum estate, needed a movie.

    A. reverse

    B. belong to

    C. return to a topic

    D. return to a former belief

II. Comprehension

Decide whether the following statements are true (T) or false (F) according to the information given in the press clipping. Mark T or F for each statement.

1. Matt Damon and Christopher Rouse's purpose of visiting Paul Greengrass is to persuade him to direct another film with Jason Bourne again as the hero.

2. Paul Greengrass is reluctant to direct another film about Robert Ludlum's assassin even though persuaded by Matt Damon and Christopher Rouse.

3. Tony Gilroy was a rival director of Paul Greengrass.

4. The hero Jason Bourne and his extremely exciting actions are well known to the audiences who love the series of the films.

5. Aaron Kalloor's user database is crucial to Robert Dewey's intelligence schemes.

6. There is a far cry between the issues touched by the past Bourne films and the issues which actually exist in American society.

7. Compared with the preceding ones, the plot of the new Bourne movie is closer to social issues.

8. "'But with this one I think we're also asking how we want to define ourselves as a country.' Rouse said." This sentence means that the film is an attempt to lead its audience to think about what a country America should be like.

9. The reason Universal had the intention to shoot another film of Jason Bourne is that Donna Langley, chairman of the Universal, was not satisfied with *The Bourne Legacy*, which was not directed by Paul Greengrass.

10. Donna Langley, chairman of the Universal, welcomed the return of Paul Greengrass.

III. Topics for Discussion

1. Spy thrillers are always exciting. What qualities make the genre so popular?

2. Have you ever seen any of the Bourne series? If so, what interests you most? And why?

3. Do you think it is a far cry between espionage illustrated by the Bourne series and the real life?

4. Edward Joseph Snowden (born on Jun. 21, 1983) is an American computer professional, former CIA employee and former contractor for the United States government who copied and leaked classified information from the National Security Agency in 2013 without prior authorization. How do you judge Snowden's behavior?

5. Have you ever seen any of the films starring Arnold Schwarzenegger? Can you make a comparison between the styles of Arnold Schwarzenegger and Matt Damon?

《读者文摘》简介

《读者文摘》（*Reader's Digest*）由德威特·华莱士（DeWitt Wallace）和丽拉·贝尔·艾奇逊·华莱士（Lila Bell Acheson Wallace）于 1922 年创刊，总部在纽约，是美国最普及的家庭阅读杂志。该杂志小巧紧凑，纸张大小为大多数美国杂志的一半左右，2005 年采用的口号就是"你口袋里的美国"（America in your pocket）。《读者文摘》每年出版 10 期，现在已发展至 50 个版本，以 21 种语言印刷，于世界 60 多个国家发行，为各个年龄、各种文化背景的读者提供资讯。

几十年来，该杂志每期都由 30 篇文章构成，此外还有词汇页、轶事页等页面。近些年，该杂志还配上了色彩华丽、吸人眼球的图形图画，并会在完整的文章间插入其他精短的信息。

《读者文摘》国际版占该杂志发行量的 50%，国际版的文章由各地的编辑委员会购买，并分享给美国和其他地方的版本。所有文章先由当地译员翻译，再由本族语编辑进行审稿，以便与美国版"受过良好教育的、非正式的"（well-educated, informal）风格保持一致。

Unit 7
Artists

报刊英语中的习语

习语指的是某一种语言在长期使用过程中形成的独特的、固定的表达法，其意义比较固定，但不是表达法中每个词义的简单叠加。习语是语言的精华，文化承载量最为丰富，其结构和含义都不能随意改变。从广义上讲，习语还包括格言、谚语、俚语、行话等。世界上历史悠久的语言都存在大量形式多样、比喻深刻的习语，英语也不例外。英语习语用词精简形象，能深刻地反映社会现象和习俗。一个民族的社会习俗、思维方式无不在习语中得到淋漓尽致的体现。

报刊作为一种传播文字资料的工具，早已成为人们认识社会的一个重要窗口，它在人们生活中起着举足轻重的作用，是人们生活中必不可少的一部分。报刊英语通常力求报道内容的准确性、语言的简洁度和结构条理的清晰感。这种准确、简洁的要求决定了新闻报道必然会使用习语。此外，有的报刊为了满足不同读者的需求，在文字表达方面更加多样化，更加贴近读者，也会使用习语。

对于习语的理解和学习，读者只能通过大量的阅读和平时的积累掌握，不能在阅读时进行随意猜测。报刊英语中经常出现的习语大致可以分为以下四类。

一、比喻性成语（figurative idiom）

学习任何一门语言，最困难的莫过于理解并运用成语。同汉语成语一样，英语成语也是颇具色彩的语言形式。英语中有 1.5 万多个成语，其中占多数的是比喻性成语。比喻性成语是指借助某一具体形象来表达意义的固定表达方式。严格意义上讲，只有包含比喻的固定词组才是真正意义上的成语，否则只能称之为"固定搭配"。因此，比喻性成语是英语成语的核心部分，其生动鲜明的形象通常会使人产生丰富的联想。例如：

● **Storms in a teacup**: The Jewish immigrants who changed British diets (*The Economist*, Aug. 31, 2019)

该习语的字面意思是"在茶杯中的风暴"，所谓"风暴"，多比喻来势猛烈、震动全社会的事件。而该习语中使用"茶杯"中的"风暴"，暗指新闻事件夸张有余，掀不起波澜。因此，该习语可用于比作有人不恰当地把小事当作大事来处理，含夸张的意思，对应汉语中的成语"小题大做"。又如：

● If these relaxations **are finally given the green light**, it will mark a pretty big turning point in Northern Ireland's recovery from lockdown. (*BBC*, May 20, 2021)

无论是在中国文化还是西方文化中，"绿灯"都是"可以通行"的意思，所以可以用give sb. the green light（给某人开绿灯）来比作"允许某工程或计划的启动"，此处指北爱尔兰的封城令。

二、谚语（proverb）

谚语类似于成语，大部分来源于劳动人民的生活实践经验，主要传达朴素而真实的哲理，流传途径通常以口耳相传为主。因此，谚语的口语性强，更通俗易懂，形式上大多为一两个短句或韵语。不同国家的谚语反映出不同国家民族的性格，而英语谚语是西方人民诸多智慧和普遍经验的规律性总结。正确地使用英语谚语，可以增加英语表达的鲜明性和生动性。在当代美英报刊中，作者大量引用谚语，使文章更贴近生活，并拉近其和读者之间的距离。例如：

● Smile and the whole world smiles with you, **cry and you cry alone**! (*The Economist*, Apr. 18, 2019)

cry and you cry alone 是一句英语谚语，全文为"Laugh and the world laughs with you; cry and you cry alone."，意思是"（如果你）笑，全世界（的人）都会跟你一起笑；（可是如果你）哭，你只好自己一个人哭"。这里仅选取英语谚语的一半，与汉语成语和歇后语常常省略后一半的情况相似，如"亡羊补牢""十五个吊桶打水"等。本例中该谚语有"福至人共享，祸来自承当"的意思。

以下列出美英报刊中频繁出现的部分常见谚语及其汉语释义：

● A baker's wife may bite of a bun, a brewer's wife may bite of a tun. （近水楼台先得月）
● A chain is no stronger than its weakest link. （一着不慎，满盘皆输）
● A crow is never the whiter for washing herself often. （江山易改，本性难移）
● A staff is quickly found to beat a dog with. （欲加之罪，何患无辞）
● A young idler, an old beggar. （少壮不努力，老大徒伤悲）
● All covet, all lose. （贪多嚼不烂）
● All feet tread not in one shoe. （众口难调）

- All is not gold that glitters.（闪光的未必都是金子）
- All rivers run into the sea.（殊途同归）
- Although the sun shine, leave not your cloak at home.（未雨绸缪）
- Behind the mountains there are people to be found.（天外有天，山外有山）
- Bread is the staff of life.（民以食为天）
- Cats hide their claws.（知人知面不知心）
- Diamond cut diamond.（棋逢对手）
- Do not teach fish to swim.（不要班门弄斧）
- Even woods have ears.（隔墙有耳）
- Every bean has its black.（金无足赤，人无完人）
- Every tub must stand on its own bottom.（人贵自立）
- Experience is the best teacher.（实践出真知）
- Experience teaches.（吃一堑，长一智）
- First impressions are half the battle.（先入为主）
- Full vessels sound least.（大智若愚）
- Go to the sea, if you would fish well.（不入虎穴，焉得虎子）
- Go while the going is good.（三十六计，走为上计）
- Good wine needs no bush.（酒香不怕巷子深）
- He that runs fastest gets the ring.（捷足先登）
- He travels the fastest who travels alone.（曲高和寡）
- Heaven helps those who help themselves.（求人不如求己）
- It is a silly fish that is caught twice with the same bait.（智者不上两次当）
- Keeping is harder than winning.（创业不易，守业更难）
- Kill two birds with one stone.（一箭双雕）
- Merry meet, merry part.（好聚好散）
- No fire without smoke.（无风不起浪）
- No work, no money.（不劳无获）
- The battle is to the strong.（两强相遇勇者胜）
- The best of friends must part.（天下没有不散的筵席）
- Unpleasant advice is a good medicine.（忠言逆耳利于行）
- You cannot have your cake and eat it.（事难两全其美）

三、典故（allusions）

典故的词典释义是指对文学作品间接、含蓄的引用。英语典故多来自古希腊、罗马神话传说和西方重要的宗教、文学作品，因此对于英语典故的理解往往要难于比喻性成语和谚语。

比如 Pandora's box（潘多拉魔盒）就出自古希腊神话。据说普罗米修斯（Prometheus）盗取天火来造福人类，主神宙斯（Zeus）十分恼怒。他命令儿子火神赫淮斯托斯（Hephaestus）用黏土制作了一个女人，取名为潘多拉（Pandora），并令诸神赋予她一切天赋。之后宙斯将潘多拉许给普罗米修斯的弟弟厄庇墨透斯（Epimetheus）为妻，嫁妆是一个密封的盒子，里面装满了各种灾难、祸患和瘟疫。潘多拉出于好奇私自打开了盒子，于是疾病、罪恶、嫉妒、偷窃、贪婪等一切祸害从盒子里飞出，散落到人间。据此，英语常借用 Pandora's box 一语喻指"灾祸之源"。

西方最重要的文学作品当属《圣经》，其地位至高无上，其中蕴含的典故在西方家喻户晓。比如 Moses' rod（摩西的杖）这一典故出自《出埃及记》（Exodus）第4章至第10章，指"克敌制胜的法宝"。

莎士比亚的作品也是英语典故的重要源头之一，比如 much ado about nothing（无事生非）就来自于莎士比亚的同名剧作。该剧是一出闹剧，讲述的是少年贵族克劳狄奥（Claudio）在结婚前夕听说未婚妻希罗（Hero）不贞的消息，气愤难当，于是在婚礼上当众羞辱她。不久他又得知那原来不过是小人作恶捏造的谣言而已，于是两人和好如初，重新举行了婚礼。

在当今的美英报刊中，合理地运用典故会使文章读起来回味无穷。例如：

- Thankfully, SARS was contained, and now seems to have disappeared in the wild. But the **bogeyman** status of coronaviruses has not diminished. (*The Economist*, Jan. 18, 2020)

bogeyman 在西方文化中原指大人想象出来的用来吓唬小孩的鬼怪，外国父母常对小孩讲"Be good, or the bogeyman will come and get you!"。此句新闻报道用 bogeyman 来代指人们对冠状病毒的恐惧。

四、俚语（slang）

俚语是一种高度口语化的语言，包含一些新词或者流行词语。可以说，俚语是英语中最活跃的语言部分。新闻报刊作为大众传媒，必须适合广大读者的阅读水平，语言应简洁精练且通俗易懂。同时，报刊面临着电视、广播、网络等其他传媒手段带来的挑战，因此其语言还要兼顾生动有趣。在美英报刊中，合理地使用俚语会使文章更加活泼、幽默、自然。

俚语最早被认为是军队、黑社会、牛仔、水手等亚文化群所讲的一种"粗俗的语言"，但随着社会的发展，人们的生活节奏日益加快，英语本身日趋通俗化和口语化。尤其近年来互联网的迅猛普及，使网络用语成为英语俚语的一大来源，比如 CU（再见）、cyberpunk（网友）、lady-killer（帅哥）等。同时，随着创造和使用俚语的人的文化层次在不断提高，俚语这种非标准英语逐渐从"难登大雅之堂"的尴尬地位变成公众认可的主流地带。有时，正确使用俚语还属时髦之举。因此，作为求新求快的媒介和社会风尚的导向标，美英新闻报刊自然会使用俚语。例如：

- As he began collecting albums, he became entranced by the **far-out** album sleeves of Pink Floyd and Led Zeppelin. (*The Guardian*, Feb. 27, 2021)

far-out 由俚语 far out 转变而来，意为"(informal terms) unconventional or avant-garde"（标新立异的），在非正式口语表达中可以翻译为"绝佳的"或"很酷"。本例中的 far-out 作为定语修饰名词 album sleeves，整句意为"他刚开始收集专辑时，就被平克·弗洛伊德和齐柏林飞艇**超酷**的专辑封面迷住了"。

俚语虽然能使报刊文章更加新潮时髦，拉进作者与读者之间的距离，但是不宜在报刊文章中大量使用，否则会破坏报刊英语的文体。只有正确地使用俚语，才能真正发挥其锦上添花的作用。

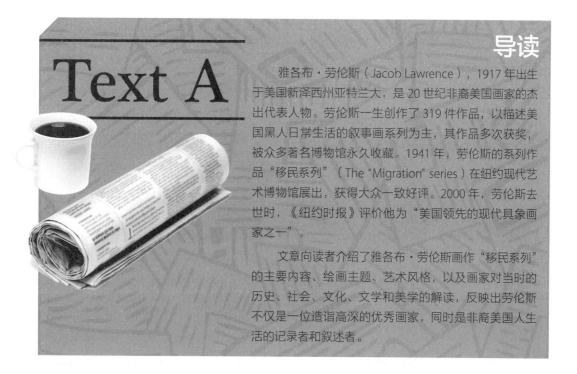

Text A

导读

雅各布·劳伦斯（Jacob Lawrence），1917 年出生于美国新泽西州亚特兰大，是 20 世纪非裔美国画家的杰出代表人物。劳伦斯一生创作了 319 件作品，以描述美国黑人日常生活的叙事画系列为主，其作品多次获奖，被众多著名博物馆永久收藏。1941 年，劳伦斯的系列作品"移民系列"（The "Migration" series）在纽约现代艺术博物馆展出，获得大众一致好评。2000 年，劳伦斯去世时，《纽约时报》评价他为"美国领先的现代具象画家之一"。

文章向读者介绍了雅各布·劳伦斯画作"移民系列"的主要内容、绘画主题、艺术风格，以及画家对当时的历史、社会、文化、文学和美学的解读，反映出劳伦斯不仅是一位造诣高深的优秀画家，同时是非裔美国人生活的记录者和叙述者。

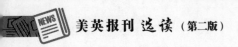

Jacob Lawrence's portraits of America

His landmark "Struggle" series, which reimagined the early days of the republic, has been brought together for the first time in over 60 years.

By Y. F.

By the mid-20th century Jacob Lawrence was one of the most celebrated artists in America. In a style described as "dynamic cubism[1]", he captured the joys and difficulties of the African-American experience and painted portraits of Toussaint L'Ouverture[2], a key figure in the Haitian Revolution[3], as well as of the abolitionists Frederick Douglass and Harriet Tubman. In 1940, aged only 23, he created his acclaimed "Migration" series: the story of the "Great Migration" of African-Americans from the rural south to the cities of the north, told across 60 panels. It earned him his first major solo exhibition, at the Museum of Modern Art[4] in New York.

In 1949 Lawrence sought a new project. He began visiting the New York Public Library[5], mining the archives for letters, diaries, public speeches, legal petitions and military reports that might spark an idea. After five years of research, he decided that he would reimagine the history of America itself. "I gradually began to appreciate not only the struggles of the Negro people, but also to appreciate the rich and exciting story of America and of all the peoples who emigrated to the 'New World' and contributed to the creation of the United States," he said. The new work would "depict the struggles of a people to create a nation and their attempt to build a democracy". The result was the 30-strong "Struggle" series, completed in 1956.

A new exhibition, "Struggle: From the History of the American People", at the Peabody Essex Museum[6] in Salem, Massachusetts, brings together most of the panels for the first time in over 60 years. (It took six years to track down the works in private collections; two paintings remain unaccounted for, and five others are too fragile to transport. They are represented by reproductions.) In the next two years the show will travel around the country—a recognition of Lawrence's status as one of the country's most celebrated artists, and of the enduring dispute over the nature of American democracy. It makes its next stop in June at the Metropolitan Museum of Art[7] in New York, moving to the Birmingham Museum of Art[8] and Seattle Art Museum[9], before concluding in the nation's capital at the Phillips Collection[10] in June 2021.

The "Struggle" paintings cover a period of almost 50 years, from 1770 to 1817. Lawrence revisited the events that Americans consider part of their country's origin story, such as the duel between Alexander Hamilton and Aaron Burr, and George Washington's crossing of the Delaware River (already the subject of a painting of 1851 by Emanuel Leutze[11]).

Yet his canvases emphasised a more inclusive history. In his version of the Boston Massacre[12], which historians often consider the trigger for the revolutionary war, the focal point of the scene is the fallen figure of Crispus Attucks, a man of African and Native American descent. In another panel, entitled "And a Woman Mans a Cannon", Lawrence painted Margaret Cochran Corbin, who took up her husband's post when he was killed in battle. Astride a blue cannon and carrying a pistol, Corbin's yellow dress spreads over the canvas.

Famous quotations often lent the pictures their titles. The final sentence of the Declaration of Independence, "We mutually pledge to each other our Lives, our Fortunes and our sacred Honour", was used for a panel depicting a farmer bearing a heavy load of hay, suggesting the need for collective effort. Lawrence borrowed a line from Patrick Henry[13], a founding father, for his first panel: "Is life so dear or peace so sweet as to be purchased at the price of chains and slavery?" Responding to this rallying cry, the men in the image raise their fists—a gesture used during the civil rights movement, which was gaining momentum at the time of the painting's creation.

The formal choices Lawrence made in the service of these ideas are surprising. At a time when the large canvases of the abstract expressionists seemed the very picture of innovation and modernity, he insisted on figurative painting. He combined this style with a cubist sensibility, which both instilled a sense of movement and encouraged the viewer to linger over the image. Lawrence painted the skin of his figures in a palette of dark reds, browns and ochres. "It is intentionally ambiguous, because what he is putting forth is the idea of a much more inclusive and complex understanding of who was actually at these events, who was fighting, and on what side people were," Lydia Gordon, one of the curators, has said.

The series grew out of the political unrest of the mid-20th century, as a country struggled to live up to the Constitution's promises of "a more perfect union" and "secure the blessings of liberty". Lawrence's paintings argued that every American has a part to play in that struggle. He saw his work as "a symbol showing man's constant search for the perfect society in which to live".

"Jacob Lawrence: The American Struggle" continues at the Peabody Essex Museum until April 26th. It will then travel to New York, Birmingham, Seattle and Washington.

(From *The Economist*, Feb. 12, 2020)

NOTES

1. **cubism**：立体派，亦译为"立方主义"，1908 年始于法国，是前卫艺术运动的一个流派，对 20 世纪初期的欧洲绘画与雕塑产生了极为重要的影响。立体派艺术家通过碎裂、解析、重新组合的形式来绘制分离的画面，并从不同角度来描写某一对象，同时将多种角度的描写汇总在同一个画面之中，以此来展现该对象最完整的形象。立体派通过背景与画面主题交互穿插的表现手法，创造出一个二维空间的绘画特色，其代表人物为乔治·布拉克（Georges Braque）与帕布罗·毕加索（Pablo Picasso）。

2. **Toussaint L'Ouverture**：杜桑·卢维杜尔（1741—1803），海地革命领导者之一，海地历史上最伟大的人物之一。杜桑·卢维杜尔是一名奴隶之子，生于法属圣多明戈（Saint-Domingue）种植园的一个黑奴家庭。1791 年，海地北部省突然发生奴隶暴动，卢维杜尔带领 1,000 余名奴隶加入起义队伍，展开游击活动。1794 年，他与法军联合将西班牙殖民军逐出海地北部，宣布废除奴隶制度。1798 年，卢维杜尔将法国殖民军逐出海地西部，迫使法军投降。1801 年，他率军统一整个海地岛，建立革命政权，颁布海地第一部宪法。

3. **Haitian Revolution**：海地革命（1791—1804），指海地推翻了西班牙和法国的殖民统治，成为一个独立的国家，这是西半球第一场奴隶起义成功的革命。在杜桑·卢维杜尔的领导下，海地历经十余年的挣扎，先后击败入侵海地的西班牙和法国军队，最后于 1804 年 1 月发表了《海地独立宣言》。

4. **Museum of Modern Art**：纽约现代艺术博物馆，位于美国纽约州曼哈顿西第 53 街，藏有众多重要的现代艺术作品，与大都会艺术博物馆。

5. **New York Public Library**：纽约公共图书馆，主建筑物位于美国纽约州曼哈顿第五大道，是美国主要的图书馆之一。由于藏有《古腾堡圣经》（Gutenberg Bible，即《四十二行圣经》）和牛顿的《自然哲学的数学原理》（Philosophiæ Naturalis Principia Mathematica），纽约公共图书馆被认为是世界著名的图书馆之一。

6. **Peabody Essex Museum**：皮博迪·埃塞克斯博物馆，是一座位于美国马萨诸塞州塞勒姆的艺术和文化博物馆。其历史可以追溯至 1799 年，它是美国最古老且一直开放的博物馆，也是美国最大的收藏和展出亚洲艺术的博物馆之一。馆内收藏了从 18 世纪至今的非洲、美洲、中国、印度、日本、韩国、北美印第安、大洋洲等地的艺术藏品，约达 180 万件，包括油画、雕塑、照片、纺织品、建筑、海事装备、装饰品、罕见书籍、手稿等。

7. **Metropolitan Museum of Art**：大都会艺术博物馆，位于美国纽约州曼哈顿中央公园旁，是世界上最大的、参观人数最多的艺术博物馆之一。其主建筑物面积约有 8 公顷，展出面积有 20 多公顷。馆藏超过 200 万件艺术品，在众多艺术收藏品中，包括许多出众的古典艺术品、古埃及艺术品、欧洲油画以及大量美国视觉艺术和现代艺术作品。该博物馆还收藏了大量的非洲、亚洲、大洋洲、拜占庭风格和伊斯兰教艺术品。

8. **Birmingham Museum of Art**：伯明翰艺术博物馆，位于美国亚拉巴马州伯明翰，成立于 1951 年，美国东南部最好的博物馆之一。馆内主要收藏了亚洲、欧洲、美洲、非洲、前哥伦布时期以及美洲原住民的杰出艺术作品。

9. **Seattle Art Museum**：西雅图艺术博物馆，位于美国华盛顿州西雅图城区。

10. **Phillips Collection**：菲利普收藏馆，美国第一家现代艺术博物馆，也是华盛顿特区最受欢迎的艺术博物馆。馆内藏品包括印象派画家雷诺阿（Pierre-Auguste Renoir）的伟大杰作《游船上的午餐》（*Luncheon of the Boating Party*），以及其他印象派代表人物梵高（Vincent Willem van Gogh）、莫奈（Claude Monet）、德加（Edgar Degas）和塞尚（Paul Cézanne）的绘画作品。

11. **Emanuel Leutze**：埃玛纽埃尔·洛伊茨（1818—1868），德裔美国画家，以作品《华盛顿横渡特拉华河》（*Washington Crossing the Delaware*）著名。该画作描绘了美国独立战争期间，美国国父乔治·华盛顿在 1776 年 12 月 25 日横渡特拉华河的场景。

12. **Boston Massacre**：波士顿大屠杀，英国称之为"国王街事件"（Incident on King Street），美国则习惯称之为"波士顿大屠杀"。1770 年，在北美殖民地波士顿的国王街，英军士兵和平民之间发生冲突，有五名平民被枪杀身亡，另有六人受伤。

13. **Patrick Henry**：帕特里克·亨利（1736—1799），美国政治家，美国独立战争时期卓越的领导人。他与塞缪尔·亚当斯（Samuel Adams）和托马斯·佩因（Thomas Paine）同为最具影响力的美国革命和共和主义倡导者。

USEFUL WORDS

abolitionist	[ˌæbəˈlɪʃənɪst]	*n.*	a person who favors the abolition of a practice or institution, especially capital punishment or (formerly) slavery 废奴主义者
blessing	[ˈblesɪŋ]	*n.*	God's favor and protection 幸事
canvase	[ˈkænvəs]	*n.*	a strong, coarse unbleached cloth made from hemp, flax, cotton, or a similar yarn, used to make items such as sails and tents and as a surface for oil painting 油画布
collective	[kəˈlektɪv]	*adj.*	done by people acting as a group 共同的
curator	[kjʊəˈreɪtə(r)]	*n.*	a keeper or custodian of a museum or art gallery, etc. （博物馆等收藏机构的）馆长
democracy	[dɪˈmɒkrəsi]	*n.*	a system of government by the whole population or all the eligible members of a state, typically through elected representatives 民主制度
dispute	[dɪˈspjuːt]	*n.*	a disagreement, argument, or debate 争议
duel	[ˈdjuːəl]	*n.*	a contest with deadly weapons arranged between two people in order to settle a point of honor 决斗
emigrate	[ˈemɪɡreɪt]	*v.*	to leave one's own country in order to settle permanently in another 移居国外
expressionist	[ɪkˈspreʃənɪst]	*n.*	a painter, writer, or composer who is an exponent of

expressionism, seeking to express through their work the inner world of emotion rather than external reality 表现主义艺术家

modernity	[mə'dɜːnəti]	*n.*	the quality or condition of being modern 现代性
palette	['pælət]	*n.*	a thin board or slab on which an artist lays and mixes colors 调色板
petition	[pə'tɪʃn]	*n.*	a formal written request, typically one signed by many people, appealing to authority with respect to a particular cause 请愿书
pistol	['pɪstl]	*n.*	a small firearm designed to be held in one hand 手枪
portrait	['pɔːtreɪt]	*n.*	a painting, drawing, photograph, or engraving of a person, especially one depicting only the face or head and shoulders （尤其指刻画面部、头部和肩部的）肖像
rally	['ræli]	*v.*	(of troops) to come together again in order to continue fighting after a defeat or dispersion 集合
reproduction	[ˌriːprə'dʌkʃn]	*n.*	a copy of a work of art, especially a print or photograph of a painting 复制品
slavery	['sleɪvəri]	*n.*	the practice or system of owning slaves 奴隶制

EXERCISES

I. Vocabulary

Choose among the four alternatives one word or phrase that is closest in meaning to the underlined part in each statement.

1. By the mid-20th century Jacob Lawrence was one of the most celebrated artists in America.

    A. notorious   B. renowned   C. overt   D. infamous

2. In 1949 Lawrence sought a new project. He began visiting the New York Public Library, mining the archives for letters, diaries, public speeches, legal petitions and military reports that might spark an idea.

    A. set off   B. inspire   C. cease   D. break off

3. The new work would "depict the struggles of a people to create a nation and their attempt to build a democracy".

    A. delineate   B. outline   C. narrate   D. relate

4. It took six years to track down the works in private collections; two paintings remain unaccounted for, and five others are too fragile to transport.

    A. unnamed   B. unidentified   C. misplaced   D. missing

5. In the next two years the show will travel around the country—a recognition of Lawrence's status as one of the country's most celebrated artists, and of the <u>enduring</u> dispute over the nature of American democracy.

    A. continuing   B. tolerating   C. remaining   D. lingering

6. Yet his canvases emphasised a more <u>inclusive</u> history.

    A. general   B. dominant   C. comprehensive   D. counting

7. The final sentence of the Declaration of Independence, "We mutually <u>pledge</u> to each other our Lives, our Fortunes and our sacred Honour", was used for a panel depicting a farmer bearing a heavy load of hay, suggesting the need for collective effort.

    A. promise   B. commit   C. engage   D. bind

8. He combined this style with a cubist sensibility, which both instilled a sense of movement and encouraged the viewer to <u>linger over</u> the image.

    A. expatiate on   B. elaborate on   C. dwell upon   D. harp on

9. "It is intentionally <u>ambiguous</u>, because what he is putting forth is the idea of a much more inclusive and complex understanding of who was actually at these events, who was fighting, and on what side people were," Lydia Gordon, one of the curators, has said.

    A. dubious   B. equivocal   C. multivocal   D. unfixed

10. The series grew out of the political <u>unrest</u> of the mid-20th century, as a country struggled to live up to the Constitution's promises of "a more perfect union" and "secure the blessings of liberty".

    A. dismay   B. restlessness   C. disturbance   D. uneasiness

II. Comprehension

Decide whether the following statements are true (T) or false (F) according to the information given in the press clipping. Mark T or F for each statement.

1. In the style of "dynamic cubism", Jacob Lawrence mainly described the real life of the African-Americans.

2. Jacob Lawrence became famous all over the U.S. at the age of 23 thanks to his work named "Migration" series.

3. The topic of the 30-strong "Struggle" series was finally decided after Jacob Laurence's five years of research in various archives from the New York Public Library.

4. The exhibition of "Struggle: From the History of the American People" marked Jacob Lawrence's status as one of the most famous artists in the United States.

5. Both Emanuel Leutze and Jacob Lawrence painted such events as the duel between Alexander Hamilton and Aaron Burr and George Washington's crossing of the Delaware River.

6. For the theme of the "Struggle" paintings, Jacob Lawrence not only revisited the events that Americans consider part of their country's origin story but also emphasized a more inclusive history.

7. The Boston Massacre is historically considered the trigger for the American Revolutionary War.

8. In Patrick Henry's opinion, black people should raise their fists to earn a peaceful and sweet life.

9. In the "Struggle" series, Jacob Lawrence combined the figurative painting with a cubist sensibility, making the skin of his figures in a palette of dark red, browns and ochres.

10. Jacob Lawrence saw his work as "a symbol showing man's constant search for the perfect society in which to live" because he reimaged the history of America itself in his "Struggle" series.

III. Topics for Discussion

1. Have you ever visited any art museums before? If so, what is your most impressive painting? Please make a brief description of it.

2. What is your opinion on Jacob Lawrence's work in the style of "dynamic cubism"?

3. In terms of American history, what is your understanding of the following quotation from the Declaration of Independence, "We mutually pledge to each other our Lives, our Fortunes and our sacred Honour"?

4. Considering the struggles of a people to create a nation and build democracy in the United States, what do you think of the sentence in the text "Life is so dear or peace so sweet as to be purchased at the price of chains and slavery"?

5. Black Lives Matter (BLM) is a decentralized movement advocating for non-violent civil disobedience in protest incidents of police brutality and all racially motivated violence against black people. The broader movement and its related organizations typically advocate against police violence towards black people, as well as for various other policy changes considered to be related to black liberation. Please make your comments on this social movement considering Jacob Lawrence's work.

美英两国的艺术博物馆

　　博物馆的英文为 museum，由希腊词汇 *mouseion* 和 *mousa* 演变而来，原指祭祀文艺科学女神缪斯（Muses）的神庙。公元前 3 世纪，埃及的亚历山大城建了一座专门收藏文化珍品的缪斯神庙，被公认为人类历史上最早的"博物馆"。这一缪斯神庙设有研究室，陈列天文、医学和文化艺术藏品，但并不对外开放，仅作为一个学者进行研究活动的专门机构。

　　文艺复兴时期，欧洲的王室贵族开始在王宫中设陈列室，用于收藏珍品，但仅允许贵族参观。早期的博物馆主要陈列富有的个人、家庭或艺术机构收藏的私人物品，而且，这时的私人艺术收藏主要依据藏品主人及陈列室负责人的意愿而定。

　　与古代博物馆不同，现代博物馆是收集、典藏、陈列和研究代表自然和人类文化遗产实物的场所，是为公众提供知识、教育和欣赏自然或文化艺术品机会的文化教育机构或者社会公共机构。博物馆一般为艺术博物馆、历史博物馆、科学博物馆等多种类型。其中，艺术博物馆以保存和展示艺术作品为主，通常以视觉艺术为中心，涉及绘画、雕刻、装饰艺术、实用工艺和工业艺术等展示内容，有的还会展示古物、民俗和原始艺术。艺术博物馆的主要的目的是提供展示空间，兼具推广与文化相关的教育、研究等功能，譬如举办音乐会或诗歌朗诵会等艺术活动。

一、美国

艺术博物馆在美国具有重大的政治意义，它不仅是美国国家财富的象征，更是美国民主信念的表达。美国的艺术博物馆的建设受到法国卢浮宫（Louvre Museum）和英国南肯辛顿博物馆（The South Kensington Museum）的影响，一开始就坚持向大众开放，它收藏珍宝是为了满足全体国民的利益。

在美国，艺术博物馆的兴起主要依靠 19 世纪富有的工业家，他们是艺术赞助和博物馆建设的主力军。1857 年经济危机的出现，使富商们意识到货币的资产价值可能会严重萎缩，而艺术品的精神价值不可估量，所以艺术收藏不失为一种理想的投资途径，并且这不仅是自身社会地位的有力彰显，同时是成功、财富和权力的象征。1917 年，美国通过的联邦收入法案规定，捐赠宗教、慈善、科学研究、文学艺术和教育机构的款项可以抵消其他方面的收入税，后来也包括捐赠物品。因此，在这种税收制度下，对收藏者来说，把收藏的艺术品捐赠出来显然比卖出去更有利可图，更利于实现利益最大化。与此同时，捐赠行为还为其赢得了社会声誉，可谓经济利益与声望名誉的双丰收。在此时期，美国艺术博物馆的藏品迅速丰富。美国政府通过建立艺术博物馆，不仅将其打造成经济之都，更使之成为文化和艺术之都。

现今美国拥有很多规模较大的艺术博物馆，较受欢迎的有以下这些，如表 7.1 所示：

表 7.1　美国著名艺术博物馆一览

英语原名	汉语译名	建立时间	所在地
Metropolitan Museum of Art	大都会艺术博物馆	1870	纽约
Boston Museum of Fine Arts	波士顿美术博物馆	1876	波士顿
Philadelphia Museum of Art	费城艺术博物馆	1876	费城
Detroit Institute of Arts	底特律艺术博物馆	1885	底特律
The Art Institute of Chicago	芝加哥艺术博物馆	1879	芝加哥
Dallas Museum of Art	达拉斯艺术博物馆	1903	达拉斯
Museum of Modern Art	纽约现代艺术博物馆	1929	纽约
Whitney Museum of American Art	惠特尼美国艺术博物馆	1931	纽约
Nelson-Atkins Museum of Art	纳尔逊 – 阿特金斯艺术博物馆	1933	堪萨斯
San Francisco Museum of Modern Art	旧金山现代艺术博物馆	1935	旧金山

续表

英语原名	汉语译名	建立时间	所在地
National Gallery of Art	美国国家艺术馆	1937	华盛顿特区
Getty Center	盖蒂中心	1997	洛杉矶

二、英国

英国建立艺术博物馆的初衷是发展商业。早期的艺术藏品主要来自私人捐赠，且主要用于研究，参观者也大多是特权阶层。17 世纪至 18 世纪，英国萌发的启蒙运动，掀起了批判专制主义和宗教愚昧，宣传自由、平等和民主的社会思潮。新的公共博物馆由此产生，并将对公众开放作为对这些思潮的积极响应。随着开放程度的日益扩大，博物馆逐渐成为普通大众集会的社会场所。1753 年，英国政府决定建立大英博物馆（The British Museum），这是世界上第一个对普通公众开放的大型博物馆。1824 年，英国国家美术馆（The National Gallery）设立，所有公众都能欣赏到伟大的绘画作品，他们的欣赏水平和艺术素养得到了普遍提升。

英国的艺术博物馆大多位于交通极为便利的市中心，均设有停车场、咖啡店和纪念品商店。英国的艺术博物馆通过展览发挥着巨大的潜移默化的导向作用，不仅提高了公众的审美水平，还净化和愉悦了公众的心灵，真正起到了文化传播的桥梁作用。

现今英国较受欢迎的艺术博物馆如表 7.2 所示：

表 7.2　英国著名艺术博物馆一览

英语原名	汉语译名	建立时间	所在地
Ashmolean Museum	阿什莫尔博物馆	1683	牛津
The British Museum	英国国家博物馆（大英博物馆）	1753	伦敦
The National Gallery	英国国家美术馆（国家画廊）	1824	伦敦
Montrose Museum and Arts Gallery	蒙特罗斯博物馆与画廊	1842	安格斯
Victoria and Albert Museum	维多利亚和阿尔伯特博物馆	1852	伦敦
Elgin Museum	埃尔金博物馆	1856	埃尔金
National Portrait Gallery	国家肖像馆	1856	伦敦
Kelvingrove Art Gallery and Museum	凯文葛罗夫艺术博物馆	1901	格拉斯哥
National Museum of Scotland	苏格兰国家博物馆	1931	爱丁堡
The Hunt Museum	汉特博物馆	1974	利默里克
Tate Modern	泰特现代美术馆	2000	伦敦

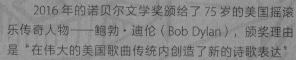

导读

2016 年的诺贝尔文学奖颁给了 75 岁的美国摇滚乐传奇人物——鲍勃·迪伦（Bob Dylan），颁奖理由是"在伟大的美国歌曲传统内创造了新的诗歌表达"（having created new poetic expressions within the great American song tradition）。鲍勃·迪伦因此成为继黑人小说家托妮·莫里森 1993 年获奖后的首位美籍诺贝尔文学奖得主。时任美国总统奥巴马立刻送上祝福，并称鲍勃·迪伦是他最喜欢的诗人之一，获此殊荣是实至名归。

鲍勃·迪伦的获奖引发了人们对于摇滚歌词是否属于文学这一话题的持久争议。支持者将其比作美国的"莎士比亚"、游吟诗人的杰出继承者，他的歌词被视作经典广为引用。本文以此为主题，报道了不同人群对鲍勃·迪伦获得诺贝尔文学奖这一事件的具体看法，反映出不同观点背后人们对文学概念的不同解读。

Bob Dylan wins Nobel Prize in Literature

By Tribune News Services, Contact Reporter

Bob Dylan, Nobel laureate. In the book world's equivalent of a Supreme Court ruling, the Nobel judges declared Thursday that Dylan is not just a rock star but a poet of the very highest order.

Dylan, 75, becomes the first musician in the 115-year history of the Nobel to win the prize in literature. He was honored for "having created new poetic expressions within the great American song tradition".

It is the ultimate ascension for the man who set off a lasting debate over whether lyrics, especially rock lyrics, can be regarded as art. Dylan, who gave the world "Like a Rolling Stone", "Blowin' in the Wind" and dozens of other standards, now finds himself on a list that includes Samuel Beckett[1], Toni Morrison[2] and T. S. Eliot[3], whom Dylan referred to in his epic song "Desolation Row".

"Congratulations to one of my favorite poets, Bob Dylan, on a well-deserved Nobel," tweeted President Barack Obama, who in 2012 presented the singer-songwriter with a Presidential Medal of Freedom.

Dylan rarely gives interviews, and a representative said the star had no immediate comment.

He is on tour and was scheduled to play in Las Vegas on Thursday night.

The startling announcement out of Stockholm[4] was met with both euphoria and dismay.

Many fans already quote Dylan as if he were Shakespeare, there are entire college courses and scholarly volumes devoted to his songs, and judges work Dylan quotations into their legal opinions all the time, such as "The times they are changing" and "You don't need a weatherman to know which way the wind blows".

With this year's Nobel announcement, many people, especially Americans, weren't scratching their heads and asking "Who?!" the way they did after hearing the names of such winners as Patrick Modiano[5] and J. M. G. Le Clézio[6].

Others, though, lamented a lost moment for books.

"An ill-conceived nostalgia award wrenched from the rancid prostates of senile, gibbering hippies," wrote *Trainspotting*[7] novelist Irvine Welsh. "I totally get the Nobel committee," tweeted author Gary Shteyngart. "Reading books is hard." The Vatican newspaper *L'Osservatore Romano*[8] said some "real writers" probably aren't pleased.

But several leading authors praised the news.

Nobel laureate Toni Morrison said in a statement that she was pleased and that Dylan was "an impressive choice". Salman Rushdie, who has written songs with U2's[9] Bono[10], tweeted that Dylan is "the brilliant inheritor of the bardic tradition. Great choice". Perennial Nobel candidate Joyce Carol Oates tweeted that "his haunting music and lyrics have always seemed, in the deepest sense, literary".

Dylan's award also was welcomed by a venerable literary organization, the Academy of American Poets[11].

"Bob Dylan receiving the Nobel Prize in Literature acknowledges the importance of literature's oral tradition, and the fact that literature and poetry exist in culture in multiple modes," executive director Jennifer Benka said in a statement.

Critics can argue whether "Visions of Johanna" is as literary as "Waiting for Godot", but Dylan's stature among musicians is unchallenged. He is the most influential songwriter of his time, who brought a new depth, range and complexity to rock lyrics and freed Bruce Springsteen, Joni Mitchell and countless other artists to break out from the once-narrow boundaries of love and dance songs.

Dylan already was the only rock star to receive a Pulitzer Prize (an honorary one), and is, in fact, an author, too: He was nominated for a National Book Critics Circle[12] prize for his memoir,

Chronicles: Volume One.

He is the first American to win the Nobel literature prize since Morrison in 1993, and his award probably hurts the chances of such older American writers as Philip Roth and Don DeLillo, since the Nobel judges try to spread the honors around.

"Rather doubt Philip Roth and Don DeLillo wish they'd written 'Mr. Tambourine Man' vs. *American Pastoral* and *Underworld*," tweeted Roth biographer Blake Bailey, referring to acclaimed novels by Roth and DeLillo. "But sure, OK."

Dylan's life has been a hybrid of popular and literary influences. A native of Duluth, Minnesota, he worshipped Elvis Presley and James Dean as a boy, but also read voraciously and seemed to absorb virtually every style of American music.

His lyrics have referred to (and sometimes lifted from) the Bible, Civil War poetry and Herman Melville[13]. He has contended that his classic "Blood on the Tracks" album was inspired by the stories of Anton Chekhov.

His songs can be snarling and accusatory ("Idiot Wind," "Positively 4th Street"); apocalyptic ("A Hard Rain's A-Gonna Fall"); dense and hallucinatory ("Desolation Row"); tender and wistful ("Visions of Johanna"); bracingly topical ("Hurricane" and "Only a Pawn in Their Game"); and enigmatic and absurdist ("Stuck Inside of Mobile with the Memphis Blues Again").

"Blowin' in the Wind" was an instant protest anthem for the 1960s, yet sounded as if it had been handed down through the oral tradition from another century, with such lines as "How many times must the cannon balls fly before they're forever banned?"

"Like a Rolling Stone", his takedown of a rich and pampered young woman forced to fend for herself, was pronounced the greatest song of all time by *Rolling Stone* magazine. The six-minute recording from 1965 is regarded as a landmark that shattered the notion a hit song had to be three minutes.

His career has been such a complicated pastiche of elusive, ever-changing styles that it took six actors—including Cate Blanchett—to portray him in the 2007 movie based on his life, *I'm Not There*. He won an Oscar in 2001 for the song "Things Have Changed" and received a lifetime achievement award from the Academy of Recording Arts and Sciences[14] in 1991.

Dylan is the most unorthodox Nobel literature prize winner since 1997, when the award went to Italian playwright Dario Fo, whose works some say also need to be performed to be fully appreciated. By a sad coincidence, Fo died Thursday at 90.

The literature award was the last of this year's Nobel Prizes to be announced. The six awards will be handed out on Dec. 10, the anniversary of prize founder Alfred Nobel's death in 1896.

（From *Chicago Tribune*, Oct. 13, 2016）

NOTES

1. **Samuel Beckett**：塞缪尔·贝克特（1906—1989），爱尔兰前卫小说家、剧作家、诗人，荒诞派戏剧的重要代表人物，20 世纪最有影响力的作家之一。1969 年，塞缪尔·贝克特荣获诺贝尔文学奖，其代表作品有《等待戈多》（*Waiting for Godot*，1952）。

2. **Toni Morrison**: 托妮·莫里森（1931—2019），美国黑人女作家、编辑，普林斯顿大学荣誉退休教授。她的小说以史诗般的主题、生动的对话和对人物细致的刻画见长，代表作品有《最蓝的眼睛》（*The Bluest Eye*，1970）、《苏拉》（*Sula*，1973）、《所罗门之歌》（*Song of Solomon*，1977）和《宠儿》（*Beloved*，1987）。由她主编的《黑人之书》（*The Black Book*，1974），被誉为"美国黑人史的百科全书"。1993 年，由于其作品被认为"具有极其丰富的想象力和诗意的表达方式"，她赢得了诺贝尔文学奖，也是文学史上第一位获得诺奖的黑人女作家。

3. **T. S. Eliot**：T. S. 艾略特（1888—1965），英国诗人、散文家、剧作家和文学社会批评家。生于美国密苏里州圣路易斯，25 岁时移居英国，39 岁时放弃美国国籍，正式加入英国国籍。艾略特在 1915 年发表的诗歌《阿尔弗雷德·普鲁弗洛克的情歌》（*The Love Song of J. Alfred Prufrock*），被视为现代派运动的经典之作。1948 年，他因"对现代诗歌杰出、开拓性的贡献"获得诺贝尔文学奖。其代表作品有《荒原》（*The Waste Land*，1922）、《四个四重奏》（*Four Quartets*，1943）等。

4. **Stockholm**：斯德哥尔摩，瑞典首都，享有"北方威尼斯"的美誉。斯德哥尔摩是阿尔弗雷德·诺贝尔（Alfred Nobel）的故乡，也是诺贝尔奖颁奖仪式的举行地。

5. **Patrick Modiano**：帕特里克·莫迪亚诺（1945—），法国小说家。莫迪亚诺与 2008 年诺贝尔文学奖得主让 – 马里·古斯塔夫·勒·克莱齐奥、乔治·佩雷克（Georges Perec）并称为"法国当代作家三杰"。2014 年，莫迪亚诺获得诺贝尔文学奖，因为他的作品"唤起了对最不可捉摸的人类命运的记忆"。其代表作有《暗店街》（*Rue des Boutiques Obscures*，1978）、《八月的星期天》（*Dimanches d'août*，1986）等。

6. **J. M. G. Le Clézio**：让 – 马里·古斯塔夫·勒·克莱齐奥（1940—），法国著名文学家，20 世纪后半期法国新寓言派代表作家之一，现今法国文坛的领军人物之一。在 1994 年的法国读者调查中，勒·克莱齐奥成为最受读者欢迎的作家。2008 年，勒·克莱齐奥获得了诺贝尔文学奖，被认为是"一位标志文学新开端的作家，一位书写诗歌历险、感官迷醉的作者，是在主导文明之外和之下探索一种人性的探索者"。

7. *Trainspotting*:《猜火车》，是苏格兰著名作家欧文·威尔士（Irvine Welsh，1958— ）所写的一部小说，真实地描绘了苏格兰地区下层人民的生活。

8. *L'Osservatore Romano*：《罗马观察报》，于 1861 年在梵蒂冈创刊，主要刊登有关宗教的讲话，报道圣座的活动和天主教及世界各地的新闻，也刊登文化类评论。

9. **U2**：U2 乐队，一支爱尔兰四人制摇滚乐乐队，于 1976 年在爱尔兰都柏林成立。自 1980 年代走红之后，直到今日，该乐队仍活跃于全球流行乐坛。因其广泛的知名度和良好的形象，U2 乐队成为爱尔兰重要的国家象征之一。

10. **Bono**：博诺，U2 乐队的主唱，本名保罗·大卫·休森（Paul David Hewson，1960—）。

11. **Academy of American Poets**：美国诗人学会，1934 年在纽约成立，是会员制的非营利组织，宗旨是推动诗歌艺术的发展。学会每年还会主办各种评奖活动，包括华莱士·斯蒂文斯终生成就奖（Wallace Stevens Award）、沃尔特·惠特曼奖（Walt Whitman Award）以及哈罗德·莫顿·兰登翻译奖（Harold Morton Landon Translation Award）等。

12. **National Book Critics Circle**：美国全国书评家协会，1974 年在纽约成立。该协会是非营利性组织，是美国书评编辑和评论家的专业联盟。该协会每年三月会颁发美国国家书评人协会奖。

13. **Herman Melville**：赫尔曼·梅尔维尔（1819—1891），美国小说家、诗人。他被视为象征主义文学大师，与纳撒尼尔·霍桑（Nathaniel Hawthorne）齐名，其代表作品有《泰比》（*Typee*，1846）、《大白鲸》（*Moby-Dick*，1851）等。

14. **Academy of Recording Arts and Sciences**：美国国家录音艺术与科学学院，由美国音乐家、制片人、录音师和录音专业人士成立的组织，也是格莱美奖的举办方。该学院成立于 1957 年，总部位于美国加利福尼亚州圣莫尼卡。

USEFUL WORDS

accusatory	[əˈkjuːzətəri]	*adj.*	containing or expressing accusation 责问的
acknowledge	[əkˈnɒlɪdʒ]	*v.*	to accept or recognize (as); to recognize the fact or existence 承认
ascension	[əˈsenʃn]	*n.*	a movement upward 上升
contend	[kənˈtend]	*v.*	to claim; to say with strength 主张
enigmatic	[ˌenɪɡˈmætɪk]	*adj.*	mysterious and difficult to understand 神秘难解的
euphoria	[juːˈfɔːriə]	*n.*	a feeling of intense happiness and excitement 狂喜
fend	[fend]	*v.*	~*for* to look after oneself without relying on help from anyone else 照料（自己）
lament	[ləˈment]	*v.*	to express sadness, regret, or disappointment about sth. 感到遗憾
laureate	[ˈlɒriət]	*n.*	a person who is honored with an award for outstanding, creative, or intellectual achievement 获奖者
lyric	[ˈlɪrɪk]	*n.*	(*pl. lyrics*) words of a song 歌词
nominate	[ˈnɒmɪneɪt]	*v.*	to suggest or name (sb.) officially for election to a position, office, honor, etc. 提名
perennial	[pəˈreniəl]	*adj.*	recurring again and again 反复发生的

present	['preznt]	v.	to give (sth.) away, especially at a ceremonial occasion 授予；颁发
prostate	['prɒsteɪt]	n.	an organ in the body of male mammals situated at the neck of the bladder that produces a liquid which forms part of semen 前列腺
ruling	['ruːlɪŋ]	n.	an official decision made by a judge or court 裁决
shatter	['ʃætə(r)]	v.	to break into a lot of small pieces 粉碎
stature	['stætʃə(r)]	n.	the importance and reputation that a person has 名望
tweet	[twiːt]	v.	(a small bird) to make a short, high-pitched sound （小鸟）啾鸣，吱吱地叫
voraciously	[və'reɪʃəsli]	adv.	in an eagerly voracious manner 非常渴望地
wrench	[rentʃ]	v.	to pull hard with a twisting or turning movement 猛扭

EXERCISES

I. Vocabulary

Choose among the four alternatives one word or phrase that is closest in meaning to the underlined part in each statement.

1. "Congratulations to one of my favorite poets, Bob Dylan, on a well-deserved Nobel," tweeted President Barack Obama, who in 2012 <u>presented</u> the singer-songwriter with a Presidential Medal of Freedom.

   A. demonstrated B. represented C. submitted D. awarded

2. He is on tour and was <u>scheduled</u> to play in Las Vegas on Thursday night.

   A. forced   B. required   C. arranged   D. docketed

3. "An ill-conceived nostalgia award <u>wrenched from</u> the rancid prostates of senile, gibbering hippies," wrote *Trainspotting* novelist Irvine Welsh.

   A. hurled away B. twisted off C. did away with D. got away from

4. Salman Rushdie, who has written songs with U2's Bono, tweeted that Dylan is "the brilliant <u>inheritor</u> of the bardic tradition. Great choice".

   A. heir   B. hare   C. inhabitor   D. inherence

5. "Bob Dylan receiving the Nobel Prize in Literature <u>acknowledges</u> the importance of literature's oral tradition, and the fact that literature and poetry exist in culture in multiple modes," executive director Jennifer Benka said in a statement.

   A. reflects   B. recognizes C. notices   D. realizes

6. He was <u>nominated</u> for a National Book Critics Circle prize for his memoir, *Chronicles: Volume One*.

   A. constituted B. proposed   C. assigned   D. appointed

7. "Rather doubt Philip Roth and Don DeLillo wish they'd written 'Mr. Tambourine Man' vs. *American Pastoral* and *Underworld*," tweeted Roth biographer Blake Bailey, referring to <u>acclaimed</u> novels by Roth and DeLillo. "But sure, OK."

    A. derogatory   B. praised   C. laudatory   D. accelerant

8. He has <u>contended</u> that his classic "Blood on the Tracks" album was inspired by the stories of Anton Chekhov.

    A. competed   B. struggled   C. asserted   D. argued

9. The six-minute recording from 1965 is regarded as a landmark that shattered the notion a <u>hit</u> song had to be three minutes.

    A. successive   B. popular   C. well-written   D. elaborate

10. The six awards will be <u>handed out</u> on Dec. 10, the anniversary of prize founder Alfred Nobel's death in 1896.

    A. bestowed   B. distributed   C. allocated   D. portioned

II. Comprehension

Decide whether the following statements are true (T) or false (F) according to the information given in the press clipping. Mark T or F for each statement.

1. The Nobel Prize in Literature has become the world's most prestigious literature prize.

2. Bob Dylan is the first American poet in the 115-year history of the Nobel to win the prize in literature.

3. There is a consensus that rock lyrics can be regarded as art. Therefore, the announcement of Nobel laureate is met with euphoria.

4. Bob Dylan is one of the favorite poets of the former President Barack Obama.

5. Bob Dylan was ecstatic when he got the news that he won the Nobel Prize in Literature, so he gave an interview immediately.

6. Many people, especially Americans, weren't shocked with this year's Nobel announcement because they already quote Bob Dylan as if he were Shakespeare.

7. Bob Dylan is the most influential songwriter of his time, because he brought a new depth, range and complexity to rock lyrics.

8. Being the first American to win the Nobel Prize in Literature, Bob Dylan is an epoch-making people in the history of the United States of America.

9. Dylan's life has been a hybrid of popular and literary influences. He reads avidly and absorbs every style of American music.

10. "Like a Rolling Stone" is the only poem written by Bob Dylan, depicting a rich and pampered woman forced to look after herself.

III. Topics for Discussion

1. Nobel Prize was established by Alfred Nobel for the greatest benefit to mankind. How much do you know about Alfred Nobel and the Nobel Prize? Can you name some Nobel laureates?

2. The link between music and great poetry goes back at least as far as ancient Greece. Yet song lyrics are not generally considered serious literature today. Do you agree that music is an important oral form of literature?

3. Almost a week after Bob Dylan was named the winner of the Nobel Prize in Literature, no one knew how he felt about the prestigious award—not even the Nobel judges. They couldn't establish direct contact with Bob Dylan. Please comment on Dylan's muted reaction.

4. Some people say, "Nobody would expect a singer to win a Nobel." Japanese writer Haruki Murakami is rumored to better deserve a Nobel Prize in Literature. Do you think so? Why or why not?

5. Chen Xiaoming, a professor specializing in literary criticism from Peking University, comments on the win that Bob Dylan just elicits a sense of nostalgia. What do you think about it?

《新闻周刊》简介

　　《新闻周刊》（Newsweek）与《时代周刊》（Time）、《美国新闻和世界报道》（U.S. News & World Report）并称为美国三大周刊。《新闻周刊》主要报道最新时政，辟有多个专栏对国际时事、前沿科技、商业、文化和政治进行深度分析，并配有大量照片和图表。

　　《新闻周刊》最初的英语名是News-Week，创刊于1933年，创始人为托马斯·马丁（Thomas Martyn）。1937年，马尔柯姆·米尔（Malcolm Muir）出任主编及总裁，将News-Week改为Newsweek，并引入新的署名专栏和国际版面。1961年，华盛顿邮报公司将其收归旗下。在归属华盛顿邮报公司逾半个世纪之后，《新闻周刊》于2010年8月2日以1美元的价格出售给91岁的美国大亨、慈善家西德尼·哈曼（Sidney Harman），力图实现以平面媒体向全媒体的华丽转型。受网络发展的冲击，该周刊的广告量严重下滑，发行量大幅下跌，读者大量流失。2012年12月24日，《新闻周刊》发布了创刊80年的最后一本纸质杂志，并宣布退出纸质媒体市场。2014年3月7日，《新闻周刊》再次付梓，回归传统纸媒市场，开始在美国和欧洲发行，首期发行7万册。

　　《新闻周刊》的报道犀利、大胆、自由。自由派游说组织"美国民主行动"曾对美国媒体的倾向进行打分——100分表示立场最倾向自由派，《新闻周刊》的得分高达72分，完全超过《时代周刊》《纽约时报》等报刊。《新闻周刊》曾在克林顿性丑闻事件等负面报道中一马当先。

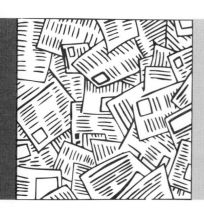

Unit 8
Education

📰 报刊英语中的文体风格

所谓文体是指文本构成的模式，反映了文本从内容到形式的整体特点，是内容和形式的高度统一。文本内容决定了使用什么样的文体，而文体一旦形成，又反作用于表达内容。新闻报刊由于受到大众性、简洁性、趣味性、时效性和客观性的制约，要求其内容既要客观报道最新发生的新闻事实，又要文字精练、通俗易懂、生动有趣。这种文本内容决定了报刊英语独特的文体风格，而这一文体风格又对文本内容起到了一定的制约作用。了解美英报刊的各种文体风格及文字特色，有助于读者更好地理解新闻英语报道所传递的信息，提高其美英报刊阅读能力。

根据美英报刊的行文结构，报刊英语的文体风格主要体现在标题精练浓缩和内容丰富多样两个方面。

📖 一、标题精练浓缩

报刊标题是新闻内容的精华提炼和高度概括，是新闻报道的点睛之笔。读者通常通过扫视标题来选择自己感兴趣的新闻报道，因此标题是新闻报道给读者的第一印象。新闻界有"1/3 时间写标题、1/3 时间写导语、1/3 时间写主题"的说法，由此可见标题的重要性。

报刊标题有其独特的排版、文字、语法、修辞等方面的文体特色。常见的英语报刊标题排版有三种：垂直式标题、单行式标题和缩进式标题。垂直式标题不以标题长度来显示重要性，主要通过标题的厚度（多层）来呈现，讲究层次分明，《时代周刊》常采用这种排版方式。这不仅方便读者阅读大部分标题，还能够突出新闻。单行式标题能简洁地反映新闻消息的主要事实。缩进式标题一般为两到三行，每行向右逐步缩进。这种标题形式新颖，易于激发读者兴趣。英语报刊标题在文字上多使用首字母缩略词、截短词、小词、短词等；在语法上常使用省略手法，多使用一般现在时态、动词不定式、现在分词和过去分词；常用的修辞手法有押韵、比喻、典故、习语、对照、夸张等。报刊文章标题在第三单元已做详细介绍，在此不再赘述。

二、内容丰富多样

美英报刊的文章内容丰富、涵盖范围广，涉及政治、经济、科技、文化、体育、军事、社会、娱乐、天气等领域。按照不同的报道形式，报刊英语的文体风格主要可以分为四类：消息报道、专栏、社论和广告。

（一）消息报道类文体风格

美英报刊消息报道类文章文体的最大特点是简洁。简洁的标准是精确、清晰和简练。为了达到这个标准，消息报道通常采用以下两种基本写法。

1. 倒金字塔体（the inverted pyramid style）

倒金字塔体，也称为"倒卷帘体"或"倒叙法"，是新闻英语写作的标准文体或规范形式。当今报纸约有90%的消息都是用倒金字塔体写成的。倒金字塔体先写消息中最重要的事实，随之是次要事实，最后以最次要的事实结尾。倒金字塔体起源于美国南北战争时期。当时，记者稿件通过电报传送时常中断，为了及时传送消息，记者就把战况写在最前面，之后按照事实的重要性依次写完。后来这种写法被《纽约时报》的编辑采用，一直使用至今。

倒金字塔体中最重要的是导语，它是整条消息的核心部分，要求用最有限的版面来表达尽可能多的内容，而消息的主体是对导语的扩展。导语中一般涵盖了由 5W1H 构成的新闻六要素：什么人（who）、什么事（what）、什么时间（when）、什么地点（where）、为什么（why）和怎么样（how）。例如：

Biden's first formal press conference slated for next week

Joe Biden will hold his first formal press conference as president next week in office, the White House said Tuesday, capping off a long dry spell that attracted criticism from his political opponents.

...

(*The New York Daily News*, Mar. 16, 2021)

美国总统拜登自 2021 年 1 月 20 日上任至发稿，任职已过 50 天，但仍未举行过一场正式的新闻发布会，创下了美国 100 年以来未有之纪录。通过本篇消息报道的导语，读者了解到美国新任总统拜登（who）将于下周（when）在办公室（where）举办任职后首次正式的新闻发布会（what & how），平息政治对手对他的批评和指责（why）。

2. 编年史体（the chronological style）

编年史体又称为"顺序法"或者"香肠式"，是指按照新闻事实发生的时间顺序来写报道，这种写法层层推进消息内容，事件高潮多出现在最后，能起到引人入胜的效果。编年史体多用于体育比赛、商业发展或新闻人物讣告类的报道。

（二）专栏类文体风格

专栏是指由一些具有某种共同点的文章构成的自成格局的局部版面。这些文章具有某些共同的特征，或是同一主题，或是同一内容，抑或是同一体裁等。专栏虽然只是报纸上的一块方寸之地，但对于活跃报纸版面、丰富报纸内容起着举足轻重的作用。可以说，专栏是报纸的"指南针"（葛密艳，2015）。专栏通常是叙事兼说理的表达方式，即作者的个人思想在说理中得到充分表达。在行文风格上，专栏可以采取第一人称，将"我"置身于评论当中，以个人的身份发表见解，这有利于作者与读者之间进行平等的交谈与沟通，避免产生生硬感。例如：

How John Coltrane has sustained me during the pandemic

...

In my own life those tragedies arrived in every shape and form. There was the day our library closed—no new books for the kids during lockdown. There was the day we told my parents they could no longer see their grandchildren. Later in the year, there was the first day we knew someone who died of COVID-19, a neighbor. Then the hardest day, in November, when my father-in-law, a man we loved, admired and enjoyed in equal measure, slipped from a ladder, fractured his spine and died. That was the day we wondered if my husband should go see him in the hospital to say goodbye. Was it worth the risk?

He went. A week later we stood at the small funeral. I sang "Amazing Grace" through my mask. We could not hug anyone—perhaps that has been the most distressing part of all. In a year of unbearable loss, we cannot do the one physical act we need in such moments. We cannot hold each other up. Maybe that's why now I am sad and tired and losing hope, oddly, when there are finally reasons to hope.

This is where John Coltrane comes in. Specifically, "A Love Supreme". An album with an uncanny, multiyear history that begins with Coltrane being fired by Miles Davis(!), it includes a quest for sobriety, self-inflicted isolation, intense prayer and

Coltrane's demand for artistic control. I've probably listened to it 50 times during the pandemic. I return to "A Love Supreme" the same way I returned to Rothko's paintings years ago, for one simple reason: It holds me up.

...

(*Los Angeles Times*, Mar. 15, 2021)

本篇报道的作者将"我"在新冠疫情时期的经历娓娓道来，即"敬爱的公公临终时，丈夫能否去医院见最后一面都是未知；去世后只能为公公举办小型葬礼，而且囿于社交距离不能相互拥抱给予安慰"。读者作为特殊时期的共同经历者，可以感同身受，代入感极强。

（三）社论类文体风格

社论作为代表媒体观点的评论性文章，堪称报刊的灵魂。一般来说，美英报刊的社论在政治性和社会舆论导向工具性方面有着较大自由度。新闻界的最高奖项普利策奖自 1917 年设立以来，就有社论写作奖（the Pulitzer Editorial Prize）。迄今为止，社论版仍是美国报刊中生命力最强的部分。当代美国大中型报纸一般设有每天刊登的社论版，如《纽约时报》几乎每天都会发三四篇社论，《华盛顿邮报》每天也会维持两到三篇的发表数量。

社论是报刊英语中最严肃的一种文体。黑、白、灰三色的运用使社论版显得更加理性和庄严。社论版的版头通常与要闻版的头版处于同一水平线，内容上用词正式、严谨，句式上多用长句和复杂句，篇章上通常采用"提出论点—正 / 反论证—得出结论"的结构。美英报刊社论版的选题不局限于社会要闻，还包括读者在日常生活中会遇到的一些问题，这不仅不会破坏这一文体的权威性，反而会提高读者对社论版的关注度。比如"Make the District a place to die with dignity"（*The Washington Post*, Oct. 1, 2016）这则社论，探讨的就是晚期的重症病人选择安乐死的自主权问题。即使是严肃的话题，社论作者也可以运用幽默等修辞手法使写作风格更加个性化。

（四）广告类文体风格

美英报刊上的广告多使用大幅照片或图画，并配以简洁生动的文字。这种图文搭配的方式很好地起到了吸引读者注意力、帮助读者了解宣传事物并接受该事物的作用。

报刊英语的广告中会频繁使用 make、get、give、have、see、buy、come、go、know、keep 等特定动词，new、crisp、good、fine、free、big、fresh、great、delicious、real 等形容词，使用如 you、we 等代词的频率也要高于一般文体，这样能更好地拉近商家和客户之间的距

离。在句法上，报刊广告多使用简单句、分裂句、非主谓句、省略句和主动结构，并频繁使用疑问句和祈使句来加强广告的说服力。比如"Give the gift they'll open every day."（*The New York Times*, Mar. 6, 2020）这则订购广告，语言简洁明了，祈使句的使用会让读者觉得《纽约时报》就是最好的礼物。此外，广告的说服性要求广告英语需要具有较强的艺术感染力，所以广告英语可以说是最具修辞色彩的应用文体，常常使用拟人、夸张、比喻、双关等修辞手法。例如：

- Service that sparkles. Discover Tiffany's personalized shopping experience in store, over the phone or online. We are here to make sure you find exactly what you're looking for. (*The New York Times*, Mar. 6, 2020)

这是蒂芙尼钻石（Tiffany & Co.）在《纽约时报》上刊登的一则广告。广告语中巧妙地使用了 sparkle 一词，具有一语双关的作用：它既指钻石的闪耀光芒，又暗示着蒂芙尼可以为顾客提供全方位且满意的服务。

值得说明的是，网络的发展催生了各类新媒体，比如微博、今日头条等。媒介融合下报刊英语的文体风格也随之发生变化，新闻的原创性和独家性要求大大提高，"手机文体""网络文体"等新型新闻报道文体相继产生，视觉新闻也逐渐成为新闻报道的重要组成部分。可以说，科技的每一次突破都会影响到新闻写作，进而影响到报刊英语的文体风格。

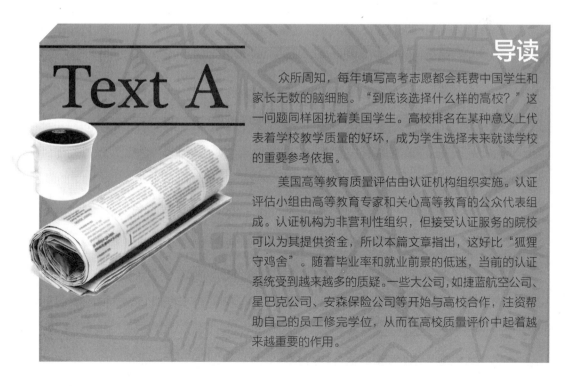

Text A

导读

众所周知，每年填写高考志愿都会耗费中国学生和家长无数的脑细胞。"到底该选择什么样的高校？"这一问题同样困扰着美国学生。高校排名在某种意义上代表着学校教学质量的好坏，成为学生选择未来就读学校的重要参考依据。

美国高等教育质量评估由认证机构组织实施。认证评估小组由高等教育专家和关心高等教育的公众代表组成。认证机构为非营利性组织，但接受认证服务的院校可以为其提供资金，所以本篇文章指出，这好比"狐狸守鸡舍"。随着毕业率和就业前景的低迷，当前的认证系统受到越来越多的质疑。一些大公司，如捷蓝航空公司、星巴克公司、安森保险公司等开始与高校合作，注资帮助自己的员工修完学位，从而在高校质量评价中起着越来越重要的作用。

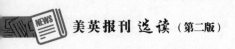

Will employers gain influence in rating the quality of a college degree?

By Jeffrey J. Selingo

It's an anxiety-ridden decision for millions of students each year: how to compare the quality of the colleges they're considering so they can ensure a pay off from what will likely turn out to be the largest investment of their lifetime.

While a plethora of college rankings serve as a crude proxy for quality among thousands of colleges in the U.S., most students don't attend the brand-name institutions that tend to top the rankings. In reality, students are often limited by finances, academics, or family and job obligations and have just a few choices about where to go. According to a recent study by the American Council on Education[1], the average freshman at a public university attends a campus that is within 100 miles of home.

Quality control of higher education is governed by a national network of regional accreditors approved by the U.S. Department of Education[2]. Without accreditation, a college can't access federal financial aid for its students. But accreditors are run and financed by the colleges themselves. It's kind of like the fox guarding the hen house[3]. Colleges determine quality measures they need to ultimately meet.

In recent years, such self-regulation has come under increased scrutiny as questions have been raised about colleges that continue to operate with low graduation rates or that produce graduates deep in debt and without any job prospects. Last month, an advisory board within the Education Department voted to strip one of the largest accreditors in the country of federal recognition because of its lax oversight.

While there is widespread agreement among college officials and policymakers that the current accreditation system is broken, this is less consensus on what should replace it. While that debate rages on, a group that is the largest consumer of college graduates is increasingly taking on a greater role in quality control: employers.

Employers are beginning to define quality in higher education through their tuition-assistance programs. Some 71 percent of employers offer tuition benefits to their workers, according to Deloitte, and spend nearly $22 billion on the benefit annually. Most employers offer a flat-rate benefit each year and have long controlled how that money is used—for classes related to a person's job or other positions in the organization. Now, employers want more oversight in where their dollars are used.

"Busy workers don't have time to distinguish between colleges and universities," Bonny

Simi, president at JetBlue[4] Technology Ventures, said during a panel discussion I moderated at a U.S. Education Department summit last week. "They probably haven't heard about the problems at some institutions and don't pay attention to graduation rates or accreditation. We're doing that work for them and eliminating some of the complexity."

Simi leads JetBlue Scholars, a new program started by the airline that takes the place of the traditional tuition benefit (JetBlue never offered tuition assistance before starting the program earlier this year). About 6,000 of JetBlue's 18,000 employees have a bachelor's degree, Simi said. Many more have some college credit but no degree.

JetBlue Scholars is designed to get employees with at least 15 credits to complete their degree. The airline works with just seven pre-approved providers, including Straighterline and Saylor.org. They evaluate credits that can be awarded for workers' previous work experience or military service and offer one course at a time to employees.

All the costs are covered by JetBlue. The course work is completed virtually at Thomas Edison State University[5] in New Jersey, which awards the degrees. Some 400 employees are enrolled in the program. Their average age is 42.

JetBlue is far from alone. Other large employers are taking similar approaches in picking one or just a small group of colleges where employees can use their educational benefit.

Starbucks[6], for example, has partnered with Arizona State University[7] to allow employees in the U.S. who have earned at least two years' worth of credits to complete their degree for free (like JetBlue, just a quarter of Starbucks employees had a bachelor's degree). And Anthem Inc., one of the nation's largest health benefits companies, has joined up with Southern New Hampshire University[8] to offer free self-paced associate and bachelor's degree programs for their employees.

In making these exclusive deals, the companies are often not only negotiating lower tuition prices than they would pay if the employees enrolled on their own, but they are also making judgments about quality. Like students worried about wasting their money at a sub-par college, employers are also trying to reduce their risks.

Given how much money employers spend on tuition benefits, where companies decide to spend their dollars has ripple effects. Already, for-profit colleges have seen their enrollments plummet, in part because fewer adults are using tuition benefits at their institutions.

Employers have long played a part in determining quality in higher education by simply deciding where to recruit traditional undergraduates into full-time jobs. Now as colleges and policymakers debate how to measure outcomes and regulate institutions that receive $150 billion in federal aid each year, employers are making their own assessments that just might put some colleges with poor outcomes out of business.

（From *The Washington Post*, Jul. 8, 2016）

NOTES

1. **American Council on Education**：美国教育委员会，美国较有影响力的高等教育组织，创立于 1918 年，位于华盛顿哥伦比亚特区。目前该委员会拥有 1,800 个成员机构，包括被认可的学位授予高校和与高等教育相关的协会、组织或企业。该委员会就与高等教育相关的重大问题进行公共政策倡议、调研等，对美国高等教育的发展起到了重要的领导作用。

2. **U.S. Department of Education**：美国教育部，1980 年和其他联邦机构合并成立。截至 2023 年，有大约 4,400 名雇员，其宗旨是发展优质教育，并确保人人都享有平等受教育的机会。不同于其他国家的教育部，美国教育部不参与课程标准的设置，而是主要负责编写联邦补助方案以及执行联邦关于民权及隐私的教育法案。

3. **the fox guarding the hen house**：狐狸守鸡舍，此处比喻美国的高等教育质量监管体制存在的问题，即大学制订自己最终要达到的教学质量标准。

4. **JetBlue**：捷蓝航空公司，成立于 1999 年，总部坐落于美国纽约市皇后区，最大枢纽设于约翰·肯尼迪国际机场。该航空公司是一家廉价航空公司，也是美国第五大航空公司。"9·11 事件"后，美国航空业比较低迷，但捷蓝航空公司仍是几家能盈利的航空公司之一。

5. **Thomas Edison State University**：托马斯·爱迪生州立大学，原名为 Thomas Edison State College，创办于 1972 年，位于美国新泽西州特伦顿。作为新泽西州 11 所公立大学之一，该大学提供 100 多个研究领域的学位课程和证书课程。

6. **Starbucks**：星巴克，全球最大的咖啡连锁公司，成立于 1971 年，总部坐落于美国华盛顿州西雅图市。星巴克于 1998 年进入中国台湾，于 1999 年 1 月在北京中国国际贸易中心开设中国大陆第一家门店。星巴克的商标是一幅 16 世纪斯堪的纳维亚的双尾美人鱼木雕图案。

7. **Arizona State University**：亚利桑那州立大学，创办于 1885 年，位于美国亚利桑那州的州府和最大城市菲尼克斯，是一所研究型公立大学。该校的学术研究在世界上享有盛名，比如航天、光学、计算机、商业管理等专业均处于美国乃至世界领先地位。

8. **Southern New Hampshire University**：南新罕布什尔大学，原名为 New Hampshire College。该校创建于 1932 年，位于美国曼彻斯特市的市郊，离商业重镇波士顿仅一个小时车程。该校被列为北新英格兰地区最好的商业教育机构，其中 MBA 专业和在线教育项目曾赢得"最佳商业教育"的荣誉。

USEFUL WORDS

access	['ækses]	*v.*	to reach, enter or use sth. 使用；到达；进入
accreditation	[əˌkredɪ'teɪʃn]	*n.*	the act of granting credit or recognition (especially with respect to an educational institution that maintains suitable standards) 委托；委派
consensus	[kən'sensəs]	*n.*	a general agreement among a group of people 共识
distinguish	[dɪ'stɪŋgwɪʃ]	*v.*	~ *between/from* to mark as different 辨别；区分
eliminate	[ɪ'lɪmɪneɪt]	*v.*	to remove completely 根除
evaluate	[ɪ'væljueɪt]	*v.*	to calculate the value or degree of 评定……的价值；评价
exclusive	[ɪk'skluːsɪv]	*adj.*	not divided or shared with other 独有的
flat	[flæt]	*adj.*	(of taxes) not increasing as the amount taxed increases （费率等）固定的
lax	[læks]	*adj.*	not careful or strict about maintaining high standards 松懈的；不严格的
moderate	['mɒdərət]	*v.*	to preside over 主持（会议）
obligation	[ˌɒblɪ'geɪʃn]	*n.*	a duty; necessity 义务；责任；必要
panel	['pænl]	*n.*	a group of speakers who answer questions to inform or amuse the public, usually on a radio or television show （广播或电视中的）答问小组，座谈小组 ~ *discussion*（在听众面前进行的有组织的、预先选定的）专题讨论会；座谈会
plethora	['pleθərə]	*n.*	an amount that is greater than you need, want, or can cope with 过剩
plummet	['plʌmɪt]	*v.*	to fall steeply or suddenly 垂直落下；骤然跌落
proxy	['prɒksi]	*n.*	a person or thing that is acting or being used in the place of sb. or sth. else 代理人；代替者；替代物
rage	[reɪdʒ]	*v.*	~ *on* to continue in a violent way 猛烈地继续；激烈地进行
recruit	[rɪ'kruːt]	*v.*	to register formally as a participant or member 招收；招募
scrutiny	['skruːtənɪ]	*n.*	the act of examining sth. closely (as for mistakes) 仔细研究；仔细观察
strip	[strɪp]	*v.*	~ *of* to take away possessions from sb. 剥夺
sub-par	[ˌsʌb'pɑː(r)]	*adj.*	under the average standard 平均标准以下的；低于一般水准的

EXERCISES

I. Vocabulary

Choose among the four alternatives one word or phrase that is closest in meaning to the underlined part in each statement.

1. In reality, students are often limited by finances, academics, or family and job <u>obligations</u> and have just a few choices about where to go.

    A. requirements   B. responsibilities   C. categories   D. regulations

2. Without accreditation, a college can't <u>access</u> federal financial aid for its students.

    A. spend   B. apply   C. approach   D. obtain

3. Colleges determine quality measures they need to <u>ultimately</u> meet.

    A. finally   B. intimately   C. basically   D. ulteriorly

4. Last month, an advisory board within the Education Department voted to strip one of the largest accreditors in the country of federal recognition because of its lax <u>oversight</u>.

    A. rule   B. organization   C. supervision   D. procedure

5. "Busy workers don't have time to <u>distinguish</u> between colleges and universities," Bonny Simi, president at JetBlue Technology Ventures, said during a panel discussion I moderated at a U.S. Education Department summit last week.

    A. differentiate   B. discuss   C. distinct   D. disguise

6. They <u>evaluate</u> credits that can be awarded for workers' previous work experience or military service and offer one course at a time to employees.

    A. withdraw   B. assess   C. admit   D. evolve

7. Some 400 employees are <u>enrolled</u> in the program.

    A. passed   B. awarded   C. registered   D. empowered

8. Other large employers are taking similar <u>approaches</u> in picking one or just a small group of colleges where employees can use their educational benefit.

    A. approvals   B. measures   C. adornments   D. methods

9. Already, for-profit colleges have seen their enrollments <u>plummet</u>, in part because fewer adults are using tuition benefits at their institutions.

    A. summit   B. comet   C. drop   D. increase

10. Employers have long played a part in determining quality in higher education by simply deciding where to <u>recruit</u> traditional undergraduates into full-time jobs.

    A. employ   B. find   C. persuade   D. introduce

II. Comprehension

Decide whether the following statements are true (T) or false (F) according to the information given in the press clipping. Mark T or F for each statement.

1. It is difficult for millions of students each year to decide which university they should go to.

2. Students in the United States can choose brand-name universities as they like with the financial support from the government.

3. Colleges should determine quality measures they need to ultimately meet, because they know students and the requirements of the employers very well.

4. With the current accreditation system, even a high-quality college may operate with low graduation rates or produce graduates deep in debt and without any job prospects.

5. Both college officials and policymakers agree that the broken accreditation system should be replaced by a new system.

6. Employers begin to offer money to help their employees to complete their degree.

7. JetBlue is the only one to offer free degree programs for the employees so far.

8. Starbucks has partnered with Southern New Hampshire University to allow employees in the U.S. who have earned at least two years' worth of credits to complete their degree for free.

9. Employers are also making judgments about quality because they do not want to waste their money.

10. Where companies decide to spend their dollars has a great effect on some colleges or universities.

III. Topics for Discussion

1. Choosing colleges is an anxiety-hidden decision to make. Do you still remember the moment you made such a decision?

2. Most students would like to attend the brand-name universities that top the rankings. How about you?

3. It is necessary to rank the universities or colleges because it will help students as a reference. Do you agree with this statement? What do you think about the ranking of universities or colleges?

4. Some experts suggest the quality of a college or university should be judged by its graduate employment rate. Please comment on this viewpoint.

5. Some big companies, such as JetBlue, Starbucks, and Anthem Inc., cooperate with some universities to offer free courses for their employees to complete their degrees. How do you understand this statement?

美英两国的教育体制

一、美国

美国现行的教育体制有两个理想的前提：一是保证所有人接受小学和初中阶段的基础教育；二是保证所有人都有进一步接受更高教育的机会和权力（理查德·卡特等，2004）。按照法律规定，任何年龄阶段的美国公民，无论信仰什么宗教、来自什么民族或属于什么阶级，都可以平等地接受教育。这是美国教育制度一个显著的特点，也被称为"单轨制"。这种单轨制从 19 世纪中期就开始实行，保障了美国公民平等接受教育的权利。经过一个多世纪的发展，美国的教育体制受到社会变迁和政治、经济等因素的影响，逐步趋于完善。

美国的教育体制由各州为主体负责。虽然联邦政府设有教育部，但其主要是教育政策的研究和咨询机构，负责制订教育政策，并不参与政策的执行，也不监管地方学校。美国的学校分为公立和私立两类：公立学校由联邦政府和州政府拨款，须遵守各州议会制订的有关教育法律，接受各州州政府的监督；私立学校根据国家有关规定自行筹集资金，基本不受任何政府监管。家长和教师联合会以及专业性的私营教育机构对学校的政策制订与执行具有一定影响力。

美国的教育体制大体可以分为四个阶段：学前教育（pre-school education）、初等教育（elementary education）、中等教育（secondary education）和高等教育（higher education）。学前教育包括托儿所（nursery school）和幼儿园（kindergarten）。托儿所和幼儿园阶段旨在辅助家庭帮助儿童养成良好习惯，为儿童进入小学做好身心准备。初等教育通常指六年制的小学教育，部分州也实行五年制。小学教育旨在发展儿童的社会认知，促进儿童的心智健康发展，培养他们的创造力。中等教育包括三年的初中（middle school）和四年的高中（high school）。只要学生顺利完成高中学业，就可以拿到高中文凭；未获得高中文凭的学生可以参加普通教育发展测试（General Educational Development Texts），取得同等学历证书。在美国，初等和中等教育都属于国家义务教育。美国的高等教育比较发达，高校数量多、类型多，并且有公立和私立之分，比如哈佛大学、耶鲁大学、麻省理工学院、斯坦福大学都是比较知名的私立大学。美国的高中生毕业后可进入两年制学院（two-year college）的初级学院（junior college），学习相当于四年制大学一、二年级的课程，完成高等教育的初级阶段，毕业后可以拿到准学士学位（Associate's degree）。社区学院（community college）也属于两年制学院，为学生提供职业教育，所开课程为学生毕业后的就业做准备。两年制学院的目标是推广普及高等教育，招生要求不高，学费低廉，这是美国高中生能有半数以上进入高等院校的原因之一。美国的高等教育还包括四年制学院（four-year college）和综合性大学

（comprehensive university）。四年制学院又称为文理学院，规模较综合性大学偏小，注重本科教育，没有研究院，但教授对学生的关注度高，旨在培养文理兼长、平衡博学的人才。学生毕业时可获得学士学位（Bachelor's degree）。综合性大学集本科教育、研究生教育和学术研究为一体，除提供学士学位以外，还提供硕士学位（Master's Degree）和博士学位（Doctor of Philosophy，Ph.D）。

美国的教育投资位居世界之首，这一高投入带来的高产出是高水平的文化教育，从而极大促成了美国在世界科技方面的领先地位。自 1901 年诺贝尔奖设立至今，约四成诺贝尔奖获得者来自美国，这与其健全、完善、优质的教育体制密不可分。

二、英国

大约 6 世纪时，基督教传入英国，学校教育在英国拉开帷幕，并深深烙上宗教的印记。此后，随着资本主义的发展和工业革命的出现，英国的教育从宗教化走向世俗化，国家通过出台各种政策为各阶层民众创造接受学校教育的机会。漫长的历史沉淀和一系列的变革使英国的教育体制呈现出传统和创新的双重特点。

按照课程设置和学制划分，英国存在英格兰、威尔士、北爱尔兰教育体制和苏格兰教育体制两种，本部分主要介绍前者。英国的教育体制大体可以分为三个阶段：义务教育（compulsory education）、延续教育（further education）和高等教育（higher education）。英国是世界上最早实施义务教育的国家之一，1870 年便颁布了《初等教育法》，以保障儿童和青少年受教育的机会。1973 年，《教育法》规定英国的义务教育年限为 12 年，要求 5 岁到 16 岁青少年必须接受义务教育，即适龄儿童强制入学，享受全免费的国家福利。16 岁以后，英国的学生可以根据自己的情况选择继续学习或工作。继续学习便进入延续教育阶段，这是英国教育体制中比较有特色的部分，它分两个方向：学术方向和职业方向。学术方向重点培养学术研究人才，要求学生继续学习两年，并参加高级普通教育证书（General Certificate of Education Advanced Levels，A-levels）考试。职业方向重点培养在各行各业中具有专门知识和技能的人才，开设职业课程和部分本科课程，学生修完课程之后就可以获得英国国家高等教育文凭（Higher National Diploma），之后可以选择就业或继续接受高等教育。英国的高等教育在世界上负有盛名，除白金汉大学是唯一一所私立非营利性大学以外，其余均为公立大学。英国的大学由古典大学、近代大学、新大学和开放大学构成。古典大学主要指牛津大学和剑桥大学。19 世纪末以来，牛津大学和剑桥大学一直是培养英国统治阶层和科学家的场所。截至 2023 年，从牛津大学共走出 30 名英国首相，从剑桥大学共走出 96 名诺贝尔奖获得者。近代大学成立于 19 世纪上半叶，包括伦敦大学和杜伦大学。新大学是指 20 世纪 60 年代由国家创办的大学，包括约克大学等。开放大学是 20 世纪 70 年代出现的以广播、电视、函授与暑期学校相结合的高等教育机构。英国的大学既是教学中心，也是科研中心，提供学士、硕士和博士学位。

正如中国驻英国大使馆前教育参赞王百哲所说："英国是一个有悠久教育传统的国家。它的教育体系经过几百年的沿革，相当的完善和复杂，且具有非常大的灵活性。英国的教育是鼓励式教育，不断地鼓励学生独立解决问题，以各种方法激励学生越来越好地学习。"（晓晓，2012）

导读

传统教育重视课堂教学和系统知识的传授，紧紧围绕教学目标要求展开，教师在当中发挥了充分的主导作用。但是随着社会的发展，就业市场的要求发生了变化，智能手机和互联网改变了年轻人获取知识的方式，教育必然要随之进行改革和发展。

德国柏林有一所福音学校，彻底颠覆了传统的教育方式。学生在 15 岁之前不分年级，没有固定的上课时间表，可以自行决定想要学习的课程以及考试时间。固定的科目只设有数学、德语、英语和社会研究，更多的是一些像"责任"和"挑战"之类的课程。正如校长玛格丽特所说："学校能传授给学生最重要的技能是自主能动性，学校的使命是使学生能勇于面对改变，甚至期待改变。"

No grades, no timetable: Berlin school turns teaching upside down

By Philip Oltermann

Anton Oberländer is a persuasive speaker. Last year, when he and a group of friends were short of cash for a camping trip to Cornwall[1], he managed to talk Germany's national rail operator into handing them some free tickets. So impressed was the management with his chutzpah that they invited him back to give a motivational speech to 200 of their employees.

Anton, it should be pointed out, is 14 years old.

The Berlin teenager's self-confidence is largely the product of a unique educational institution that has turned the conventions of traditional teaching radically upside down. At Oberländer's school, there are no grades until students turn 15, no timetables and no lecture-style instructions. The pupils decide which subjects they want to study for each lesson and when they want to take an exam.

The school's syllabus reads like any helicopter parent's[2] nightmare. Set subjects are limited to maths, German, English and social studies, supplemented by more abstract courses such as "responsibility" and "challenge". For challenge, students aged 12 to 14 are given €150 (£115) and sent on an adventure that they have to plan entirely by themselves. Some go kayaking; others work on a farm. Anton went trekking along England's south coast.

The philosophy behind these innovations is simple: As the requirements of the labour market are changing, and smartphones and the Internet are transforming the ways in which young people process information, the school's headteacher, Margret Rasfeld, argues, the most important skill a school can pass down to its students is the ability to motivate themselves.

"Look at three or four year olds—they are all full of self-confidence," Rasfeld says. "Often, children can't wait to start school. But frustratingly, most schools then somehow manage to untrain that confidence."

The Evangelical School Berlin Centre (ESBC) is trying to do nothing less than "reinvent what a school is", she says. "The mission of a progressive school should be to prepare young people to cope with change, or better still, to make them look forward to change. In the 21st century, schools should see it as their job to develop strong personalities."

Making students listen to a teacher for 45 minutes and punishing them for collaborating on an exercise, Rasfeld says, were not only out of sync with the requirements of the modern world of work, but counterproductive. "Nothing motivates students more than when they discover the meaning behind a subject of their own accord."

Students at her school are encouraged to think up other ways to prove their acquired skills, such as coding a computer game instead of sitting a maths exam. Oberländer, who had never been away from home for three weeks until he embarked on his challenge in Cornwall, said he learned more English on his trip than he had in several years of learning the language at school.

Germany's federalised education structure, in which each of the 16 states plans its own education system, has traditionally allowed "free learning" models to flourish. Yet unlike Sudbury[3], Montessori[4] or Steiner[5] schools, Rasfeld's institution tries to embed student self-determination within a relatively strict system of rules. Students who dawdle during lessons have to come into school on Saturday morning to catch up, a punishment known as "silentium". "The more freedom you have, the more structure you need," says Rasfeld.

The main reason why the ESBC is gaining a reputation as Germany's most exciting school is that its experimental philosophy has managed to deliver impressive results. Year after year,

Rasfeld's institution ends up with the best grades among Berlin's *gesamtschulen,* or comprehensive schools, which combine all three school forms of Germany's tertiary system[6]. Last year's school leavers achieved an average grade of 2.0, the equivalent of a straight B—even though 40% of the year had been advised not to continue to *Abitur*[7], the German equivalent of A-levels[8], before they joined the school. Having opened in 2007 with just 16 students, the school now operates at full capacity, with 500 pupils and long waiting lists for new applicants.

Given its word-of-mouth success, it is little wonder that there have been calls for Rasfeld's approach to go nationwide. Yet some educational experts question whether the school's methods can easily be exported: In Berlin, they say, the school can draw the most promising applicants from well-off and progressive families. Rasfeld rejects such criticisms, insisting that the school aims for a heterogenous mix of students from different backgrounds. While a cross adorns the assembly hall and each school day starts with worship, only one-third of current pupils are baptised. Thirty percent of students have a migrant background and 7% are from households where no German is spoken.

Even though the ESBC is one of Germany's 5,000 private schools, fees are means tested and relatively low compared with those common in Britain, at between €720 and €6,636 a year. About 5% of students are exempt from fees.

However, even Rasfeld admits that finding teachers able to adjust to the school's learning methods can be harder than getting students to do the same.

Aged 65 and due to retire in July, Rasfeld still has ambitious plans. A four-person "education innovation lab" based at the school has been developing teaching materials for schools that want to follow the ESBC's lead. About 40 schools in Germany are in the process of adopting some or all of Rasfeld's methods. One in Berlin's Weissensee district recently let a student trek across the Alps[9] for a challenge project. "Things are only getting started," says Rasfeld.

"In education, you can only create change from the bottom—if the orders come from the top, schools will resist. Ministries are like giant oil tankers: It takes a long time to turn them around. What we need are lots of little speedboats to show you can do things differently."

（From *The Guardian*, Jul. 1, 2016）

NOTES

1. **Cornwall**：康沃尔郡，位于英格兰西南部，西北毗邻凯尔特海，南部靠近英吉利海峡，东部是塔玛河流经的德文郡。康沃尔郡拥有约 53 万人口，占地 3,563 平方公里。特鲁罗（Truro）是康沃尔郡郡治。

2. **helicopter parent**：直升机父母，指像直升机一样整天盘旋在孩子的身边、时刻等待孩子召唤的父母。凡事代劳、过分操控的父母只会使子女的自理能力低下。

3. **Sudbury**：指 University of Sudbury，萨德伯里大学，创立于 1913 年，位于加拿大安大略省萨德伯里，是一所罗马天主教大学。该校为英语和法语双语授课，开设课程有宗教研究、哲学、土著研究和民俗学（法语），是劳伦森大学联合会的创始成员。

4. **Montessori**：蒙台梭利学校。这类学校的教育特点是鼓励通过发现和玩耍来发展儿童的自然能力。其创始人为玛利亚·蒙台梭利（Maria Montessori）。她出生于 1870 年 8 月 31 日，是意大利第一位女医学博士，也是一位杰出的幼儿教育家。她创立了蒙氏教育法，代表作品有《发现孩子》《童年的秘密》《教育人类学》等。蒙台梭利认为要为儿童准备可以最大限度进行自由活动的环境，不能盲目限制儿童的自由行动，而是要鼓励孩子自由地探索与发展，培养他们的好奇心。

5. **Steiner**：斯坦纳学校，又名华德福学校。1919 年，德国创立了第一所华德福学校，课程设置以学生的意志、感觉和思考的发展需求为目标，促进学生身心和精神的平衡、和谐发展，培养他们成为一个具有创造性、道德感、责任感和独立思维的人。

6. **Germany's tertiary system**：第三级高等教育。德国的教育体系共分为五个部分：第一级基础教育、第二级初阶教育、第二级进阶教育、第三级高等教育，以及衍生教育。在第三级高等教育中，大约有 400 所高等院校，包括综合大学、神学院和教育学院，69% 的学生在这些学校里接受教育。此外，还有 215 所应用技术大学，约有 29% 的学生在此学习。其余为艺术院校，约有 2% 的学生在该类院校就读。

7. *Abitur*：德国中学生的毕业考试，其重要性不亚于中国的高考。该考试的成绩评定不是基于一次考试的成绩，而是综合高中阶段最后两年内不同学科的成绩，并和毕业考试的成绩加权计算，得出一个综合成绩。1.0 分是最高分，4.0 分以上为不及格。

8. **A-levels**：全称为 General Certificate of Education Advanced Levels，是英国高中学生的大学入学考试课程以及大学入学标准。A-levels 被全球 110 多个国家和地区认可，因此被誉为"世界高考"和"全球大学入学的金牌标准"。

9. **Alps**：阿尔卑斯山，欧洲最高、最长的山脉，呈弧形，长约 1,200 千米，最高峰为勃朗峰（Mount Blanc），海拔约 4,810 米。阿尔卑斯山共跨越八个国家：奥地利、法国、德国、意大利、列支敦士登、摩纳哥、斯洛文尼亚和瑞士，被世人称为"大自然的宫殿"和"真正的地貌陈列馆"。

USEFUL WORDS

adorn	[əˈdɔːn]	*v.*	to make sth. look more beautiful 装饰
chutzpah	[ˈhutspə]/[ˈxutspə]	*n.*	the quality of being not afraid or embarrassed to do or say things that shock, surprise, or annoy other people 胆识
collaborate	[kəˈlæbəreɪt]	*v.*	to work together with sb. in order to produce or achieve sth. 合作；协作
convention	[kənˈvenʃn]	*n.*	(an example of) generally accepted social behavior 惯例；

习俗

counterproductive	[ˌkaʊntəprə'dʌktɪv]	*adj.*	tending to hinder the achievement of a goal 产生相反结果的
dawdle	['dɔːdl]	*v.*	to waste time; to be slow 混日子；磨蹭
embark	[ɪm'bɑːk]	*v.*	~ *on* to set out on (an enterprise or subject of study) 开始从事
embed	[ɪm'bed]	*v.*	to fix firmly and deeply 嵌入
exempt	[ɪg'zempt]	*adj.*	~ *from* to state officially that sb. is not affected by a particular rule, duty, or obligation 免除
heterogenous	[ˌhetə'radʒənəs]	*adj.*	not originating within the body; of foreign origin 异种的；异源的
kayak	['kaɪæk]	*n.*	a light canoe in which the part where you sit is covered over 独木舟；单人划子
motivate	['məʊtɪveɪt]	*v.*	to give an incentive for action 激发……的积极性
persuasive	[pə'sweɪsɪv]	*adj.*	likely to persuade a person to believe or do a particular thing 有说服力的
radically	['rædɪkəlɪ]	*adv.*	thoroughly, completely 彻底，完全
speedboat	['spiːdbəʊt]	*n.*	a small power-driven boat built for high speed 快速汽艇
supplement	['sʌplɪmənt]	*v.*	to make additions to 补足；增补
syllabus	['sɪləbəs]	*n.*	(*pl. ~buses or ~bi*) an arrangement of subjects for study, especially a course of studies leading to an examination 教学大纲；课程提纲
tertiary	['tɜːʃəri]	*adj.*	third in order, third in importance, or at a third stage of development 第三的
transform	[træns'fɔːm]	*v.*	to change completely in form, appearance, or nature 改变；转变
trek	[trek]	*v.*	to journey on foot, especially in the mountains 徒步旅行

EXERCISES

I. Vocabulary

Choose among the four alternatives one word or phrase that is closest in meaning to the underlined part in each statement.

1. The Berlin teenager's self-confidence is largely the product of a unique educational institution that has turned the <u>conventions</u> of traditional teaching radically upside down.

    A. assemblies   B. patterns   C. agreements   D. custom

2. The school's <u>syllabus</u> reads like any helicopter parent's nightmare.

    A. curriculum   B. name   C. summary   D. sketch

3. Set subjects are limited to maths, German, English and social studies, <u>supplemented</u> by more abstract courses such as "responsibility" and "challenge".

    A. subscribed   B. supplied   C. complemented   D. accelerated

4. But <u>frustratingly</u>, most schools then somehow manage to untrain that confidence.

    A. dishearteningly   B. heartbrokenly   C. unexpectedly   D. excitingly

5. Making students listen to a teacher for 45 minutes and punishing them for <u>collaborating</u> on an exercise, Rasfeld says, were not only out of sync with the requirements of the modern world of work, but counterproductive.

    A. laboring   B. cooperating   C. confirming   D. surpassing

6. Germany's federalised education structure, in which each of the 16 states plans its own education system, has traditionally allowed "free learning" models to <u>flourish</u>.

    A. glamour   B. foster   C. flush   D. thrive

7. Students who <u>dawdle</u> during lessons have to come into school on Saturday morning to catch up, a punishment known as "silentium".

    A. dismiss   B. absent   C. linger   D. dwell

8. The main reason why the ESBC is gaining a reputation as Germany's most exciting school is that its experimental philosophy has managed to <u>deliver</u> impressive results.

    A. present   B. impress   C. restrict   D. disclose

9. Even though the ESBC is one of Germany's 5,000 private schools, fees are <u>means</u> tested and relatively low compared with those common in Britain, at between €720 and €6,636 a year.

    A. methods   B. averages   C. classifications   D. varieties

10. About 40 schools in Germany are in the process of <u>adopting</u> some or all of Rasfeld's methods.

    A. adapting   B. adjusting   C. accepting   D. absorbing

II. Comprehension

Decide whether the following statements are true (T) or false (F) according to the information given in the press clipping. Mark T or F for each statement.

1. Anton Obeländer succeeded in getting some free tickets from Germany's national rail operator to continue his camping trip to Cornwall.

2. ESBC's curriculum is appreciated by helicopter parents.

3. The mission of a traditional school should be to prepare young people to cope with change, or better still, to make them look forward to change.

4. According to Margret Rasfeld, the most important responsibility of school is to motivate students.

5. The best way of motivating students is to let them discover the meaning behind a subject voluntarily.

6. Students in the ESBC enjoy absolute freedom because the school advocates students' self-determination.

7. The ESBC is so innovative that few students would like to go there.

8. Educational experts assert that the ESBC's methods can easily be exported.

9. According to the news, it is very expensive to study in the ESBC.

10. It is difficult to find teachers who are able to adjust to the ESBC's learning methods.

III. Topics for Discussion

1. Before entering universities, we had received elementary and secondary education. Say something about your educational experience.

2. Can you briefly introduce to the Western people the education system in China?

3. In China, attitudes towards National College Entrance Examination ("gaokao") vary from person to person. Some people believe that "gaokao" should be abolished because it is too stressful, while others say it is the only fair way for students and hence, it should be maintained. What's your opinion?

4. If you are short of cash for a camping trip, a situation that Anton Oberländer and his friends encountered, what would you do?

5. Do you think it is necessary to advocate an innovation in Chinese education? Why or why not?

《时代周刊》简介

　　《时代周刊》（*Time*），简称《时代》，是在美国纽约市出版的一份新闻类周刊，创刊于 1923 年 3 月 3 日，是美国三大时事性周刊之一，在美国乃至全世界都颇有影响力。其报道内容广泛，不仅立足美国，更是放眼全球，对国际问题发表主张，并跟踪国际重大事件，有世界"史库"之称。

　　《时代周刊》最初的名字是《事实》（*Facts*），创始人为布里顿·哈登（Briton Haddon）和亨利·卢斯（Henry Luce）。他们强调简洁性，主张即使是忙人也可以在一个小时内读完，所以改名《时代周刊》，并使用口号"简约《时代》，方以遣暇"（Take Time—It's Brief）。写给"忙人"看的宗旨使读者能迅速地找到自己最需要了解和关注的报道，能在最短的时间获得最多的信息量，从而切实满足他们的要求，因此《时代周刊》自 20 世纪 30 年代起开始迅速流行起来。

　　《时代周刊》最初的写作文体极为独特，常用倒装句。标志性的红色边框从 1927 年使用至今，期间只变过四次：第一次是在"9·11"恐怖袭击事件发生之后，使用黑色边框以示哀悼；第二次是在 2008 年 4 月 28 日的地球日使用绿色边框；第三次是在 2011 年 9 月 19 日使用金属银色边框，以纪念"9·11 事件"十周年；第四次是在 2012 年 12 月 31 日同样使用了银色边框，庆祝奥巴马当选《时代周刊》年度人物。《时代周刊》对新闻的关注极其敏锐，记者的身影和笔端触及世界的每一个角落。除美国主版、国际版以外，《时代周刊》还有出版于伦敦的欧洲版（*Time Europe*，旧称 *Time Atlantic*），出版于中国香港的亚洲版（*Time Asia*）和出版于悉尼的南太平洋版（*Time South Pacific*）。涉及外国国家时，《时代周刊》会拿美国版和其他国际版进行比较，通过援引它们的政治情况，追溯报道事件的来龙去脉，并借助图表等信息帮助读者理解复杂的国际问题。

《时代周刊》的特色专刊有 20 世纪最有影响力的 100 人（*Time 100*）、年度风云人物（*Person of the Year*）和红叉封面（*Red X Covers*）。《时代周刊》还曾为迈克尔·杰克逊（Michael Jackson）和史蒂夫·乔布斯（Steve Jobs）创办过纪念特刊。

Unit 9
Travel

报刊英语中的修辞手法

　　修辞手法是指在语言使用过程中，根据不同的交际内容、语言环境，运用多种语言手段和表达方式以达到特定语言效果的一种语言活动。报刊英语中经常会灵活运用一些修辞手法，以增加文章的生动性和有趣性，达到用精练语言表达丰富内容的文体效果。本章将就报刊英语中几种常用的修辞手法进行分析，探讨其修辞效果。

一、比喻

　　比喻是报刊英语中常见的一种修辞手法，能使语言更加精练和生动。下面将分别以明喻（simile）、隐喻（metaphor）、借喻（metonymy）和提喻（synecdoche）四种常见的修辞手法逐一举例说明。

（一）明喻

　　如果两种不同的事物之间具有某种相似的特征，则可构成可比性基础，通过明喻词将具有可比性基础的本体和喻体串连起来，即构成了明喻。报刊英语中常用的明喻词有 as、like 等。明喻的使用可以让表达更加生动形象。例如：

● "Drugs have always been depicted **as this extraordinary enemy** requiring extraordinary tactics," says Matthew Pembleton, a historian at American University in Washington. "It's always been a way to do things differently, ...to use tools or force that otherwise could never be justified. It's true that drugs are a problem with real social consequences. But [dealing with them] has always served as justification for state power." (*The Christian Science Monitor*, Jul. 29, 2021)

　　美国的毒品问题由来已久。这篇报道发表于 2021 年，美国历史学家马修·彭布尔顿

（Matthew Pembleton）在谈及美国毒品问题时指出，对待美国的毒品就要像对待"需要非凡战术的非凡敌人"一样。他同时指出毒品问题具有严重的社会后果，这也为行使国家权力提供了正当理由。

- According to Tom Lutz, the author of *Crying: The Natural and Cultural History of Tears*, it was common in the 18th century for upper-class men to cry—in fact, "They were viewed **as brutes** if they didn't," he said. (*The New York Times*, May 3, 2020)

本例选自一篇标题为 "Leaders Are Crying on the Job. Maybe That's a Good Thing" 的新闻，讨论的是政客在公众面前哭泣是好还是坏的问题。文章提到，在 18 世纪的上层社会，如果男子不会在公众面前哭泣，就会被视为像野兽一样，是一种野蛮的行为，进而受到歧视。

（二）隐喻

隐喻是报刊英语中比较常见、涵盖范围很广的一种比喻手段，常被称为"简缩的明喻"。它是指两种不同的事物之间也具有某种相似之处，但是因为该相似性是隐含的，所以不便用像 as、like 这样的比喻词，而是直接把本体说成喻体，直接把复杂、抽象的本体喻化为人们熟悉的喻体，直接变抽象为具体，使呆板的本体变得生动形象，进而增强语言的表现力。例如：

- The British Monarchy Is **a Game**. Harry and Meghan Didn't Want to Play. (*The New York Times*, Aug. 16, 2020)

这是《纽约时报》针对英国王子哈里和王妃梅根宣布退出皇室后进行的一篇新闻报道的标题。本标题中，把"英国的君主制"比喻成"一场游戏"，暗指英国的君主制政体中充满了复杂的规则和不确定性，哈里和梅根不想参与这种游戏，宁愿选择放弃皇室身份。

- What to make of this whirling dervish? Mr. Johnson is notoriously a **"Marmite"** politician: Fans forgive him anything; enemies regard him as a dangerous buffoon. The latter group now includes his former chief adviser, Dominic Cummings, who this week told the BBC that the very idea of Mr. Johnson being prime minister "obviously is ludicrous". (*The Economist*, Jul. 24, 2021)

Marmite 指马麦酱，又称为黑酱或酵母酱，在英国较为常见，最先是 19 世纪一个德国科学家用啤酒的发酵提取物制作而成的。它的营养丰富，味道非常独特。有一句经典广告词是 "You either love it or hate it."，说的就是它特别有争议的味道，喜欢这种味道的人视之为蜜糖，讨厌这种味道的人则避之不及。此新闻把鲍里斯·约翰逊比作英国人熟悉的 Marmite：支持者认为他做的一切都对，无条件地喜欢、包容他；反对者则极度讨厌他，认为他是臭名昭著的小丑。这种隐喻非常形象地指出了鲍里斯·约翰逊在英国极有争议的公众形象。

（三）借喻

借喻是指通过相近的联想，不直接说出人和事物的名称，而是用一个事物的名称指代另一事物。借喻是新闻写作中常用的一种修辞手法，它可以节省篇幅，避免重复，增加语言的形象性和表达效果（端木义万等，2013）。比如可以用地名指代机构名，常用的有 Pentagon 指代"美国国防部"、Big Apple 指代"纽约城"等。例如：

- "COVID-19 Updates: **White House** Will Keep Travel Bans in Place" (*The New York Times*, Jul. 27, 2021)

这个新闻标题指出在新冠疫情下，美国政府将继续执行关于旅行的禁止令。用 White House（白宫）指代美国政府，这是比较常用的表达。

- More people are being pinged because COVID infections are out of control. But **No. 10** has its head in the sand. (*The Guardian*，Jul. 26, 2021)

这个片段选自《卫报》，新闻标题为 "England's 'pingdemic' is a convenient distraction from the real problem"。面对英国疫情局势失控，媒体指责英国政府抗击疫情不力。No.10 指的是"唐宁街 10 号"，即英国行政机构所在地，英国首相在此办公。

（四）提喻

提喻又称为举隅法，即基于两事物的部分相似性，用一个事物指代另一事物，但不直接说出后者的名称。提喻通常以局部代全部、具体代抽象、单个代类别；或者反之。例如：

- Biden's **thin skin** also was on display in January when an Associated Press reporter pointed out that his goal of 1 million COVID-19 vaccinations per day had already been accomplished by the Trump administration. "Come on, gimme a break, man! It's a good start," Biden said in a serious tone. (*New York Post*, Jul. 26, 2021)

本部分选自新闻 "Biden slams 'pain in the neck' reporter for off-topic question on breaking news"，描述的是当拜登被媒体问及自己不喜欢的话题时的反应。当形势或者问题对自己不利时，人们的惯常反应是对媒体反问或顾左右而言他。此处的 thin skin 暗指拜登的这一薄弱点。当记者质疑他承诺的每天一百万新冠疫情疫苗接种的目标，其实早在特朗普政府时期就已经实现时，拜登的反应再次佐证了他的这一弱点。

二、委婉语

委婉语（euphemism）是指使用较含蓄的词汇来表达不便直言或不文雅的事情，从而避免粗俗和不雅，包括生理疾病、死亡、卖淫等令人尴尬、不快或充满禁忌的话题。有的委婉语较文雅、礼貌，有的含糊其辞，以使听者顺耳、读者舒服（周学艺，2010），这是报刊英语中委婉语正面的、积极的意义。委婉语通常在社会领域使用较多，如"残疾人"一般不会直接称为 the disabled、the retarded 等，而以 the physically challenged、the physically inconvenient 等委婉表述。准确理解这些委婉语的意义有助于对新闻内容的精准把握。例如：

- Children are often charged hundreds of dollars to join soccer clubs in the United Kingdom. In some of **the more disadvantaged neighborhoods**, it can be nearly impossible to find parks or public spaces that are suited to play in, members of the soccer club said. (*The Washington Post*, Oct.1, 2016)

本例中，the more disadvantaged neighborhoods 实际上指的是"贫民区"。原文使用"更不利的社区"委婉地表达了"该社区比较贫穷"之义，因此引出下文中"经济上不可能提供公园或广场让孩子进行足球练习"。又如：

- The first major doping allegation from the Tokyo Summer Olympics happened shortly after the men's 200-meter backstroke on Thursday night, which was late Friday morning in Japan. And it was an American accusing a Russian swimmer of being "**not clean**". (*Newsweek*, Jul. 30, 2021)

在东京奥运会男子 200 米仰泳比赛中，美国选手墨菲输给了俄罗斯选手雷洛夫，获得亚军。赛后，墨菲对比赛结果不满意，暗示雷洛夫"不干净"，not clean 的说法看上去比较委婉，但实际上是在质疑雷洛夫可能在比赛中使用违禁毒品。

在政治领域，委婉语通常是为政客和政治服务的一种手段。不可避免的是，有人会故意歪曲事实，将丑陋隐匿于看似美好的大话、空话之中，这是委婉语在新闻报道中消极的一面。

三、排比

排比（parallelism）是指一组三个或三个以上的短语或句子并列使用，通常结构相同或相似、内容相关、语气一致、字数大体相等。排比结构通常工整对仗、节奏鲜明、气势较强，能起到很好的强调效果。该修辞手法多用于报刊文章、政治演讲、广告等文体中。例如：

- The Obama administration is **to blame** and Democratic governors are **to blame** and the people getting sick are **to blame** and the so-called infectious disease experts who keep saying the nation needs a coordinated federal response are **to blame** and the media are **to blame** and hospitals are **to blame**. (*Chicago Tribune*, May 20, 2020)

特朗普政府应对新冠疫情措施不力，导致美国新冠疫情蔓延泛滥，但该政府却把这一责任推给了包括奥巴马在任时的政府、民主党州长、病人、专家、媒体，甚至医院，对他们大肆挞伐。本例用一系列 to blame，凸显了"滥加指责"这一语势，也间接表达了记者对这一做法不认同的态度。

四、夸张

夸张（hyperbole）是指有意夸大或缩小所叙述之事，以达到突出事物的本质特征、强化表达效果的目的。在报刊英语中，夸张的修辞手法使用得较为频繁，一定程度上成为报刊英语追求新奇的手段之一。夸张通常运用充满想象力、夸大其词的语言来突出强调效果。例如：

● Nearly two-thirds of Trump's lies (65 percent) were self-serving. Examples included: "They're big tax cuts—**the biggest cuts** in the history of our country, actually" and, about the people who came to see him on a presidential visit to Vietnam last month: "They were really lined up in the streets by **the tens of thousands.**" (*Chicago Tribune*, Dec. 8, 2017)

本例中，特朗普政府在执行税收政策时，自我吹嘘该政策是"美国历史上最大的税收减免"。特朗普还提到自己在越南访问时的受欢迎程度——两边街道上"成千上万的人"夹道欢迎他。以上体现了他惯用夸张的手法进行自我吹嘘和标榜的做法。

除上面列举的几种修辞手法以外，报刊英语中还包括音韵修辞、拟人、典故、矛盾等多种修辞手法。在新闻报道中，作者需要根据具体的语境选择合适的修辞手法。合理运用修辞手法不仅能帮助作者用更生动形象的语言来表达主题，而且能有效增加读者的阅读兴趣并使其充分领会文章的内涵。

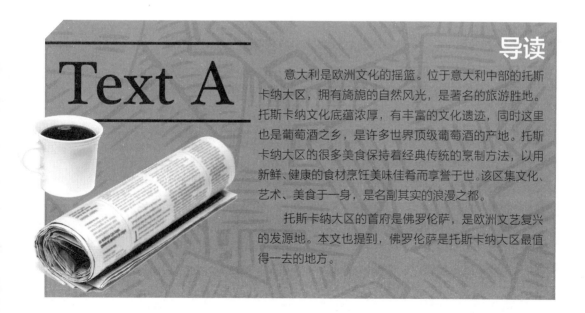

导读

意大利是欧洲文化的摇篮。位于意大利中部的托斯卡纳大区，拥有旖旎的自然风光，是著名的旅游胜地。托斯卡纳文化底蕴浓厚，有丰富的文化遗迹，同时这里也是葡萄酒之乡，是许多世界顶级葡萄酒的产地。托斯卡纳大区的很多美食保持着经典传统的烹制方法，以用新鲜、健康的食材烹饪美味佳肴而享誉于世。该区集文化、艺术、美食于一身，是名副其实的浪漫之都。

托斯卡纳大区的首府是佛罗伦萨，是欧洲文艺复兴的发源地。本文也提到，佛罗伦萨是托斯卡纳大区最值得一去的地方。

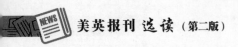
Plan the ultimate Tuscany[1] trip, from private cooking lessons to hot spring dips

By Alex Palmer

There's no shortage of highlights that make Tuscany an ideal place to visit—the cypress-accented landscape, friendly locals, and a wealth of history, to name a few. But a top draw for anyone visiting this region of central Italy is the food.

Tuscan food isn't fussy. Most dishes are just a few ingredients, prepared quick without elaborate presentation. But those ingredients are fresh and local—often sourced from farms a few miles away—and that preparation follows customs that have developed over centuries. It's about as far as you can get from the revolving door of trends and hot new restaurants that define New York's foodie scene.

Italy's efficient train system makes it easy to get from one major city to another, to experience the Tuscan countryside, rent a car. This allows you to visit hole-in-the-wall restaurants and wineries, trace the rolling hills and expansive valleys, and spot local wildlife. (Yes, the roads are narrow and windy, but it's worth it.)

Book a few nights at the Renaissance Tuscany[2] for a taste of the Tuscan countryside. Set atop a hillside on the Il Ciocco estate, the hotel showcases the local landscape, with stunning views of the Apuan Alps[3] and the Tuscan-Emilian Apennines mountain range. And the property's menu includes dishes created from local ingredients, like gnocchi made from chestnut flour or a plate of cured meats including hare and wild boar, caught on the Il Ciocco property.

For a deeper dive into Tuscan cuisine, the Renaissance Tuscany offers a menu of indigenous culinary experiences. Those who sign up accompany chef Alessandro Manfredini on a trip to the farmers market in the nearby medieval city of Barga, selecting ingredients based on your own preferences. Then join him in the kitchen to whip up a multi-course Italian feast (we made fresh tagliatelle and veal scallopini with local porcini mushrooms) that can be enjoyed for lunch or dinner.

This private cooking experience with the chef for dinner only (includes everything except the visit to the market with the chefs) costs about $166 per person at current exchange rates. The full experience, with a market visit, ranges from $200 to $266 per person, depending on the day of the week.

Of course, no Italian meal is complete without wine, so pay a visit to Podere Cóncori, a family-owned biodynamic winery[4] just a few minutes from the Renaissance Tuscany. While the Garfagnana region, where Podere Cóncori is located, is not known for its wines as much as other parts of Tuscany, this winery has created a thriving operation, with its aromatic Melograno ("pomegranate" in Italian) well worth trying.

About 30 miles south of Barga lies the provincial capital of Lucca[5], a rampart-enclosed city of cobblestone streets and clock towers that offers local crafts and high-end shopping that could compete with Fifth Ave. For lunch, stop by Buca di Sant'Antonio , which has been serving terrific Tuscan food since 1782. Copper pots and brass musical instruments decorate the walls and ceiling, and local specialties such as prosciutto toscano and mushroom risotto grace the menu.

As charming as Lucca is, the must-see city in Tuscany remains Florence[6], birthplace of the Renaissance and home to Michelangelo's[7] *David* statue, the famed Ponte Vecchio bridge, and the astonishing Duomo. It also houses no shortage of excellent restaurants, from the friendly and delicious Taverna del Bronzino (built in the former studio of a Renaissance artist), to the high-end Il Santo Graal in the city's trendy Oltrano neighborhood, on the south side of the Arno River.

There is so much to explore in Florence that visitors would be wise to stay here for at least two or three days—or better yet, stay just outside the city, at the Il Salviatino. This luxury hotel built in a refurbished 15th century palazzo sits less than three miles from Florence, providing terrific views of the city from the serenity of an expansive Italian garden—and a free shuttle to and from Florence every hour.

Visitors can enjoy terrific Tuscan food without leaving the property. Il Salviatino's La Cucina restaurant, set in the stunning library of the hotel, serves a rotating menu of classic dishes, such as *gnudi* with ricotta and spinach, as well as *pici* (a thick noodle pasta you're likely only to find in the area) with porcini mushrooms and wild fennel. But any meat-eater will want to order the *bistecca alla Florentina*—a Tuscan T-bone steak, prepared rare, sliced tableside and drizzled with olive oil. It's a substantial meal, even for two people, but for fans of steak, it will be a culinary highlight.

One of Tuscany's most popular natural resources is its hot springs. Going back centuries, locals have enjoyed the comfort and healing properties of the mineral-rich water. The Lunigiana territory in the north and the Val d'Orcia region in the south boast dozens of public springs where visitors can drop in for the day.

But for those interested in experiencing Tuscan hot springs on a more involved level, consider checking in at Fonteverde Tuscan Resort & Spa. It offers eight pools infused with mineral water from hot springs, including an expansive infinity pool, a spiral-shaped "bioacquam" pool, and even a small wading pool just for dogs.

Wellness is on the menu as well, with health-oriented spreads for breakfast and lunch, including fresh juice, salads, and fish. And don't miss aperitivo hour. It's a much classier version of American happy hour, where instead of discounted drinks, you sip on cocktails like Negronis and snack on small appetizers—olives, potato chips, or finger sandwiches. It's hard to beat the aperitivo hour at Fonteverde's Il Falconiere Bar.

The property is about a 45-minute drive from a few of Italy's best wine regions, such as Montalcino and Montepulciano. The latter is a medieval city dotted with restaurants, shops, and wine stores, most of which offer free tastings of the area's famed Vino Nobile wine, as well as pairings with cheese or local cured meats.

Consider going out of the city to visit one of the many wineries in the area, such as Bindella (bindella.it). Opened about three decades ago, it has established a reputation for itself as a local favorite. In a region with so much history and tradition, there's still room for new arrivals.

（From *New York Daily News*, Jul. 14, 2016）

NOTES

1. **Tuscany**：托斯卡纳，意大利中部一个大区，其首府是佛罗伦萨，意大利文艺复兴的发源地。托斯卡纳以风光秀丽、物产丰富以及历史悠久而闻名，比如盛产红酒。

2. **Renaissance Tuscany**：全称为 Renaissance Tuscany Il Ciocco Resort & Spa，托斯卡纳西科度假酒店。该酒店位于托斯卡纳大区的中世纪小镇——巴尔加（Barga）的山坡上，是一家豪华型酒店，拥有现代化的配置，酒店周围环绕着占地约 600 公顷的庄园。

3. **Apuan Alps**：阿普安阿尔卑斯山（意大利语为 Alpi Apuane），意大利托斯卡纳大区北部的一个山脉，是亚平宁山脉（Apennine Mountains）的一部分。

4. **biodynamic winery**：生物动力酿酒厂，属于生物动力农业。针对农业发展方向问题，奥地利社会哲学家鲁道夫·施泰纳博士（Dr. Rudolf Steiner）在 1924 年首次提出用传统的肥料代替化学肥料和杀虫剂，从而建立可持续发展的生态农业，也就是"生物动力农业"。此外，他还强调农业是一个完整有机的系统，包括土壤、月亮、行星等都是有机联系的整体，动植物的生长要与这些因素相配合，建立良好的、相互促进的平衡关系。近年来，生物动力农业很流行，但关于此种方法是否值得推崇，一直存有争议。

5. **Lucca**：卢卡，意大利中部城市，位于托斯卡纳大区，卢卡省的省会城市。它是比萨和佛罗伦萨之间的一座平原小城，建于公元前 180 年，城中的古迹保存比较完善，比如著名的景点卢卡城墙。

6. **Florence**：佛罗伦萨（意大利语为 Firenze），旧译为"翡冷翠"。佛罗伦萨是托斯卡纳大区的首府，也是意大利文艺复兴的中心，是意大利最美丽的城市之一。佛罗伦萨保存着大量的艺术作品、精美建筑以及历史遗迹，号称"中世纪的雅典"。

7. **Michelangelo**：米开朗基罗（1475—1564），意大利文艺复兴时期著名的雕塑家、画家、建筑师和诗人，对西方艺术的发展起着无可比拟的影响。其代表性的雕塑作品有两个：一个是《圣母怜子像》（*Pieta*），另一个是本文中提到的《大卫》。

✎ USEFUL WORDS

accent	[æk'sent]	*v.*	to emphasize a part of sth. 强调；突出
aromatic	[ˌærə'mætɪk]	*adj.*	having a pleasant smell that is easy to notice 芳香的，有香味的
cobble	['kɒbl]	*n.*	(also *cobblestone*) a stone worn round and smooth by water and used for paving （用以铺路的）圆形鹅卵石
dip	[dɪp]	*n.*	act of bathing, putting in or into a liquid for a moment 浸，蘸
elaborate	[ɪ'læbəreɪt]	*adj.*	very detailed and complicated; carefully prepared and finished 复杂的；精心制作的
expansive	[ɪk'spænsɪv]	*adj.*	able or tending to expand or characterized by expansion; spacious 广阔的
fennel	['fenl]	*n.*	yellow-flowered herb, used as a flavoring 茴香（用来调味）
foodie	['fuːdi]	*n.*	a person devoted to refined sensuous enjoyment (especially good food and drink) 美食家
fussy	['fʌsi]	*adj.*	(of dress, style, etc.) over-ornamented; having too many unimportant details, etc. （指衣服、风格等）装饰过分的；有太多不重要细节的
gnocchi	['njɒki]	*n.*	(Italian) a small dumpling made of potato or flour or semolina that is boiled or baked and is usually served with a sauce or with grated cheese （面粉或马铃薯做的）汤团；团子
healing	['hiːlɪŋ]	*adj.*	tending to cure or restore to health 有治疗功能的；能治愈的
highlight	['haɪlaɪt]	*n.*	the best, most conspicuous or prominent part of sth. 最显著的部分；最精彩的部分
hole-in-the-wall	[ˌhəulɪnðə'wɔːl]	*adj.*	small and dark 狭小的；简陋的
indigenous	[ɪn'dɪdʒənəs]	*adj.*	~ *to* native, belonging naturally 土生的；天生的
infuse	[ɪn'fjuːz]	*v.*	to fill, as with a certain quality 注入；倾注
refurbish	[ˌriː'fɜːbɪʃ]	*v.*	to make clean or bright again; to make or polish (as if new) 使清洁；翻新，革新
revolve	[rɪ'vɒlv]	*v.*	to (cause to) go round in a circle （使）旋转
serenity	[sə'renəti]	*n.*	the state of being calm, peaceful and untroubled 宁静；沉着

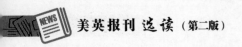

| substantial | [səbˈstænʃl] | *adj.* large in amount, value or importance 相当可观的；大量的；重大的 |
| whip | [wɪp] | *v.* ~ *up* to prepare or cook quickly or hastily 匆匆做（饭等） |

EXERCISES

I. Vocabulary

Choose among the four alternatives one word or phrase that is closest in meaning to the underlined part in each statement.

1. Plan the ultimate Tuscany trip, from private cooking lessons to hot spring <u>dips</u>.

    A. erosion   B. bathing   C. scouring   D. rinsing

2. There's no shortage of highlights that make Tuscany an ideal place to visit—the cypress-<u>accented</u> landscape, friendly locals, and a wealth of history, to name a few.

    A. intensified   B. italicized   C. emphasized   D. peculiar

3. Most dishes are just a few ingredients, prepared quick without <u>elaborate</u> presentation.

    A. tedious   B. devious   C. complicated   D. forthright

4. This allows you to visit hole-in-the-wall restaurants and wineries, trace the rolling hills and <u>expansive</u> valleys, and spot local wildlife.

    A. horizontal   B. profound   C. confined   D. spacious

5. Set atop a hillside on the Il Ciocco estate, the hotel <u>showcases</u> the local landscape, with stunning views of the Apuan Alps and the Tuscan-Emilian Apennines mountain range.

    A. embodies   B. displays   C. reflects   D. obstructs

6. Then join him in the kitchen to <u>whip up</u> a multi-course Italian feast (we made fresh tagliatelle and veal scallopini with local porcini mushrooms) that can be enjoyed for lunch or dinner.

    A. prepare for   B. tidy up   C. lash   D. gulp

7. While the Garfagnana region, where Podere Cóncori is located, is not known for its wines as much as other parts of Tuscany, this winery has created a <u>thriving</u> operation, with its aromatic Melograno ("pomegranate" in Italian) well worth trying.

    A. boisterous   B. distressing   C. prosperous   D. blooming

8. This luxury hotel built in a <u>refurbished</u> 15th century palazzo sits less than three miles from Florence, providing terrific views of the city from the serenity of an expansive Italian garden—and a free shuttle to and from Florence every hour.

    A. spruced   B. redesigned   C. excavated   D. repolished

9. Going back centuries, locals have enjoyed the comfort and <u>healing</u> properties of the mineral-rich water.

    A. remedying   B. specializing   C. trimming   D. preventing

10. It offers eight pools <u>infused</u> with mineral water from hot springs, including an expansive infinity pool, a spiral-shaped "bioacquam" pool, and even a small wading pool just for dogs.

    A. imparted   B. filled   C. implanted   D. covered

II. Comprehension

Decide whether the following statements are true (T) or false (F) according to the information given in the press clipping. Mark T or F for each statement.

1. Tuscany boasts distinctive landscape, friendly locals, and a wealth of history. But the food there is the biggest attraction for visitors.

2. Most dishes in Tuscany are easy to cook, and the ingredients are fresh and local. The preparation of foods in this area still follows the customs.

3. In Tuscany, if you want to have a private cooking experience with the chef for dinner, it will only cost about $166 per person at current exchange rates.

4. The provincial capital of Lucca is located in the south of Barga, and is a place which could compete with Fifth Ave for the similarity they share in food.

5. Florence, as the birthplace of the Renaissance, offers both some famous arts and excellent restaurants. Compared with Lucca, Florence is more charming.

6. II Salviatino, a luxury hotel, is located outside Florence. And from this hotel, there is a free shuttle to and from Florence every hour.

7. Tuscany's most popular natural resource is its hot springs. Both the locals and the visitors could dip in for the day.

8. If you are interested in experiencing hot springs on a more involved level, you may refer to the Lunigiana territory in the north where you can enjoy eight pools infused with mineral water from hot springs.

9. Tuscany has the best wine regions in Italy, such as Montalcino and Montepulciano. They offer both free tastings of the area's famed Vino Nobile wine and pairings with cheese or local cured meats.

10. According to the text, we may infer the author might be from America. What the author enjoys most in Tuscany is its hot springs.

III. Topics for Discussion

1. To travel on the spur of the moment has been popular recently. Do you agree to this fashion? While we are visiting scenic spots, apart from merely taking pictures, what are the other ways to appreciate the beauty and the local culture?

2. "It's about as far as you can get from the revolving door of trends and hot new restaurants that define New York's foodie scene." Why does the author mention New York while being in Tuscany? Please explain the sentence based on the context.

3. Visitors come to Tuscany for many reasons. Some come for beautiful landscapes, some explore its rich culture, and others like to enjoy its cuisine. If you were a visitor, what would you come for? And why?

4. What does the last sentence "In a region with so much history and tradition, there's still room for new arrivals" possibly imply? Please discuss with your partner.

5. Supposing you have just finished your trip to Tuscany and come back, what are the most impressive experiences you would like to share with your friends?

美英两国的著名景点掠影

一、美国

（一）科罗拉多大峡谷（Grand Canyon）

科罗拉多大峡谷又称"美国大峡谷"，是世界上最为壮观的自然奇迹之一。大峡谷位于亚利桑那州西北部，以小科罗拉多河（Little Colorado River）为起点，是全长 2,190 千米的科罗拉多河（Colorado River）在科罗拉多高原上侵蚀切割形成的 19 个主要峡谷中最长、最宽、最深、最著名的一个，其山石多为红色。大峡谷的主要特色有两个：一是被称为"活着的地质教科书"，从大峡谷底部到顶部分布着从寒武纪到新生代各个不同地质年代的代表性生物化石，并且从下到上有不同的气候、鲜明的植物群和动物生物化石群；二是拥有马蹄形的玻璃走廊（Skywalk），从大峡谷的崖边向外伸延出 21 米，使在峡谷崖边空中漫步成为可能，该走廊也被称为"21 世纪的世界奇观"。1919 年，托马斯·威尔逊总统将大峡谷地区辟为"大峡谷国家公园"（Grand Canyon National Park）。

（二）黄石国家公园（Yellowstone National Park）

黄石国家公园主要位于怀俄明州。1872 年，美国总统尤利西斯·格兰特许可建立该公园，总面积达 8,985 平方公里，是美国最古老的国家公园。该公园以喷泉和温泉而闻名，有超 3,000 个温泉，其中最著名的是"不老泉"（Old Faithful），每隔几小时就会喷出巨大的水柱直冲天空，每次时间持续长达 4 分钟。黄石国家公园拥有美丽的瀑布、起伏的丘陵和丰茂的山谷，是很多珍稀野生动物的家园，因此以拥有良好的生态环境而著名。

（三）自由女神像（Statue of Liberty）

自由女神像是法国在 1886 年为纪念美国独立战争期间美法联盟而送给美国的礼物，位于纽约市纽约港口的自由岛上，游客乘坐游轮即可前往岛上参观。雕像由金属铸造，是非常巨大的新古典主义艺术品，由法国雕塑家弗雷德里克·奥古斯特·巴托尔迪（Frédéric Auguste Bartholdi）设计，历时 10 年完成。雕塑是身着希腊风格服饰的女神形象，头戴象征着世界七大洲的冠冕，手持火炬并高高举起，象征着自由精神。整座雕像高 46 米，加上基座共 93 米，重达 225 吨，整体非常雄伟，是美国最著名的旅游景点之一。

（四）尼亚加拉瀑布（Niagara Falls）

尼亚加拉瀑布位于加拿大的安大略省和美国纽约州边界的尼亚加拉河上，是三个瀑布的总称。这三个瀑布分别是马蹄形瀑布（Horseshoe Falls）（位于加拿大境内）、美利坚瀑布（American Falls）和新娘面纱瀑布（Bridal Veil Falls）（后两个都位于美国境内）。由于河流落差大，瀑布喷射出的水从几公里外就可以看到，形成的水势澎湃非凡，并发出雷鸣般的响声，景象非常壮观、震撼。

二、英国

（一）伦敦

伦敦是英国乃至欧洲最大的城市，拥有悠久浓厚的历史底蕴和众多的风景名胜，是世界著名的旅游胜地。

1. 泰晤士河（Thames River）：全长 346 公里，贯穿整个伦敦城。它被英国前首相温斯顿·丘吉尔称为"穿过英国历史的河流"，见证了英格兰的历史变迁。伦敦城的主要建筑物大多分布在泰晤士河的两岸。

2. 伦敦塔（Tower of London）：位于泰晤士河的北岸，是一座拥有悠久历史的城堡。伦敦塔是一组塔群，包括珍宝馆、白塔和格林塔等。1066 年，威廉征服者（William the Conqueror）征服英格兰后开始营建。从 1100 年至 1952 年，伦敦塔被作为监狱使用。

3. 大本钟（Big Ben）：建于 1859 年，位于泰晤士河畔。2012 年，为庆祝英国女王（Queen Elizabeth II）登基 60 周年，它被改名为 Elizabeth Tower（伊丽莎白塔）。大本钟同时朝向四个方向，钟楼高 95 米，直径 7 米，重 13.5 吨。大本钟每 15 分钟响一次，是英国的地标性建筑。

4. 白金汉宫（Buckingham Palace）：位于威斯敏斯特城内，是一座四层楼的正方形围院建筑。它是英国君主居住和办公的地方，也是一些重要的国家庆典活动场所。

5. 唐宁街 10 号（No. 10 Downing Street）：位于威斯敏斯特城的白厅（Whitehall）街旁，是英国首相的官邸，因其黑色木门上的白色数字"10"十分醒目，故名为"唐宁街 10 号"。与之相近的白厅街，连接着议会大厦和唐宁街，是一条重要的知名大街。因为在这条街上分布着国防部、财政部、外交部、内政部、海军部等多个英国中央政府机构，所以"白厅"常作为英国行政部门的代名词使用。

6. 大英博物馆（British Museum）：世界上历史最悠久的博物馆，始建于 1753 年，1759 年正式开放。该馆也是世界上规模最大的综合性博物馆，是历史、艺术和文化的收藏中心，馆内藏品来自世界各地，数量超过 800 万件。就藏品的数量和丰富程度而言，大英博物馆在全球首屈一指。

（二）英国巨石阵（Stonehenge）

巨石阵位于英格兰的威尔特郡，又叫"圆柱石林"，是著名的史前建筑遗迹，也是世界上最壮观的巨石文物之一。巨石阵由许多整块的兰砂岩组成，其主体是几十根巍峨的石柱，排成几个完整的同心圆。考古学家推测巨石阵建于公元前 3000 年至公元前 2000 年之间。关于巨石阵到底是如何建成的，至今仍然是人类未解之谜。

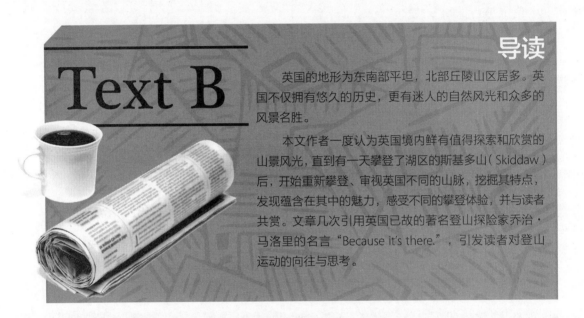

Text B

导读

英国的地形为东南部平坦，北部丘陵山区居多。英国不仅拥有悠久的历史，更有迷人的自然风光和众多的风景名胜。

本文作者一度认为英国境内鲜有值得探索和欣赏的山景风光，直到有一天攀登了湖区的斯基多山（Skiddaw）后，开始重新攀登、审视英国不同的山脉，挖掘其特点，发现蕴含在其中的魅力，感受不同的攀登体验，并与读者共赏。文章几次引用英国已故的著名登山探险家乔治·马洛里的名言"Because it's there."，引发读者对登山运动的向往与思考。

'The spaciousness is breathtaking…' In praise of Britain's mountains

By Simon Ingram

The beauty of the UK's uplands, from the Highlands to the Lakes, is that you don't have to travel far to find adventure, spectacle or solitude, says Simon Ingram.

Why climb a mountain? Don't say "Because it's there.[1]" It's said that when the great, doomed mountaineer George Mallory[2] used the phrase in 1923, it was uttered dismissively, without the gravitas it later gained. Just because climbing a mountain may serve no obvious practical purpose, there are plenty of better reasons to get to its summit than its mere existence. Far better.

I didn't walk to the top of anything high until I was 20, when I was dragged. Until then—as with many people who look overseas rather than exploring their own backyard—I was considering emigrating, to Canada. I believed the nonsense about Britain being a claustrophobic place where you could never find the crystalline magnificence you visualise when you think of escape, wilderness and all that stuff.

Then that day I climbed Skiddaw, in the Lake District[3], I saw layers of blue mountains spilling from my feet, only one and a half hours from where I'd lived all of my life, and realised I'd been missing something. In 2004, I took a job on *Trail* magazine (which I now edit), and learned two things quickly: The more you see of Britain, the bigger Britain gets; and you haven't seen it at all until you've seen it from a mountain.

So first, get it out of your head that a mountain is a thing. A bollard is a thing. Mountains are places. Things are just there. But in places, things happen. They appear on maps, cover ground, create weather and bear life.

Our ancient peoples saw them as the homes of gods and monsters. Our greatest poets found muses in them. They've harboured scientists, smugglers, occultists and ghost hunters. They were, and are, uninhabited, inhospitable islands of wild. Agriculturally barren and obstinate to passage, mountains are the last landscapes to become useful, and so are left to the fringes.

And being the wonderful geological hotchpotch Britain is, you don't have to travel far to feel a complete shift in the way the mountains cut their dash. There is true variety here: the volcanic summits of the Cuillin ridge on the Isle of Skye[4]; the strange, free-standing peaks of Assynt, northwest Scotland, eulogised by poet Norman MacCaig; the exquisite tapestry of mountains, lakes and slate villages of the Lake District that were such an inspiration for Turner[5], Wordsworth[6], Ruskin[7] and Coleridge; Snowdonia, with its Tolkeinian mines, climbs and folk tales—all underpinned by its splintered mountains…

The most wonderful attribute of all of these is their scale. They can all be explored on foot, mostly in a weekend. Leave London—or other cities en route—by sleeper train on a Friday night and you'll wake up in the Highlands on Saturday morning. A flight covers the distance between London and Inverness quicker than you can cross London by tube.

Once in the uplands, you can have a real adventure with few of the collateral hazards of other mountain areas. You can camp safe in the knowledge that no animals will pull you shrieking from your tent into the night. You won't get altitude sickness. You're never more than 10 miles from a road. There are no crevasses to fall into, no deserts to get lost in or hostile tribes to be wary of. And there's so much freedom here: In many countries, you keep out unless told otherwise. Thanks to the right to roam, in most parts of Britain it's the other way around.

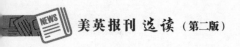

That said, our mountains do have teeth. That old joke about Qomolangma[8] being good training for the Highlands of Scotland is only funny if you've never experienced the Cairngorms in winter, or looked up at Snowdon's sharp summit when it's white. It's alarming how extreme Britain can be: The first taste of this engenders a mixture of sudden, shocked respect. Chuck it in the deep freeze and suddenly, electrifyingly, Britain stops playing nice.

But you'll come to crave the feelings. The chill, the silence and the space. The darkest night you've ever seen from the window of a stove-lit bothy. The tired-happy exhilaration of being a mile high having walked there. The thrill of holding on for your life, and living. Of swinging a bag on to your back that contains all you need to sustain yourself, then doing it. The act of boiling life down to the basics—get up, move, eat, sleep, get down—is the ultimate in perspective realignment. And the few who make the effort to get into Britain's wild rafters share the biggest secret of all: Up above the millions in this crowded…this apparently suffocatingly crowded nation, the spaciousness and enormity is breathtaking.

"Because it's there" is the last reason to climb a mountain. Perhaps another of George Mallory's comments carries more truth: "What we get from this adventure is sheer joy. And joy is, after all, the end of life." Qomolangma, Helvellyn[9], Snowdon[10], Ben Nevis[11]. To those who know, that joy inhabits the same lofty step—where the mountains of Britain stand as tall as any in the world. One of Mallory's gifts to Qomolangma was to name its great valley the Western Cwm, a Welsh word, because it reminded the mountaineer of Snowdon.

Mallory's mentor was another mountaineer-philosopher, Geoffrey Winthrop Young. A line from his poem, "A Hill", about the implacability of the British mountains' lure, gave me a title for my book about the same:

Only a hill, but all of life to me,

Up there between the sunset and the sea

So, why climb a mountain? Stop asking. Just climb one.

Note: Simon Ingram is the author of *Between the Sunset and the Sea*.

（From *The Guardian*, Jun. 14, 2016）

NOTES

1. **Because it's there.**： "因为它就在那里。" 1923 年，英国著名登山探险家乔治·马洛里打算挑战世界最高峰——珠穆朗玛峰，这是记者采访他时他说的一句话。这句话后来成为登山界的名言。

2. **George Mallory**：乔治·马洛里（1886—1924），英国著名的登山探险家。在 20 世纪 20 年代早期，他曾三次参加英国组织的征服珠穆朗玛峰的探险。1924 年，他和队友安德鲁·欧文（Andrew Irvine）第三次攀登珠峰，在接近珠峰顶端的东北部时，他们与地面失去联系。直到 1999 年，康拉德·安克（Conrad Anker）带领探险队找到了马洛里的尸体。关于马洛里和他的队友在遇难前是否已经到达了珠峰的峰顶，仍然是个谜。

3. **Lake District**：全称为 Lake District National Park，湖区国家公园，位于英国的西北部，方圆大约 2,300 平方公里，因拥有湖泊（主要的有 14 个）、山峰和树林而闻名。文中的斯基多山，就是位于湖区的一座山。湖区的最高山是斯可斐峰（Scafell Pike）。另外，湖区因 19 世纪英国文学史上著名的"湖畔派"诗人居住于此而闻名，尤其是威廉·华兹华斯（William Wordsworth）常年生活在湖区内，并在此写下了很多著名的诗篇，如《水仙》（The Daffodils）等。著名儿童文学家毕翠克丝·波特（Beatrix Potter）也是这个湖区的常客，备受全世界儿童喜欢的《彼得兔的故事》（*The World of Peter Rabbit and His Friends*，1902）就是受湖边的美景启发而来的。

4. **Cuillin ridge on the Isle of Skye**：Isle of Skye 指斯凯岛，又名天空岛，是位于苏格兰西北部的一个岛屿，因风景秀丽而闻名。库林山（Cuillin）是位于这个岛屿上的山，又名 Black Cuillin，最高海拔为 992 米。

5. **Turner**：全名为 Joseph Mallord William Turner（1775—1851），约瑟夫·马洛德·威廉·透纳，英国绘画史上最著名的艺术家之一，擅长风景画，被称为"光之画家"。

6. **Wordsworth**：全名为 William Wordsworth（1770—1850），威廉·华兹华斯，英国浪漫主义诗人，1843 年获得英国"桂冠诗人"的称号，和塞缪尔·泰勒·柯勒律治（Samuel Taylor Coleridge，1772—1834）、罗伯特·骚塞（Robert Southey，1774—1843）同被称为"湖畔派"诗人（Lake Poets），他们都是英国文学史上浪漫主义时期的早期代表。

7. **Ruskin**：全名为 John Ruskin（1819—1900），约翰·罗斯金，英国维多利亚时代的艺术评论家，同时也是作家、艺术家、哲学家，代表作品为著作《现代画家》（Modern Painters）。

8. **Qomolangma**：珠穆朗玛峰，喜马拉雅山（the Himalayas）的最高峰，岩面高程为 8,848.86 米，终年被积雪覆盖。珠穆朗玛峰因其高度和险峻而闻名世界，许多登山爱好者以征服此山作为人生梦想，本文提到的乔治·马洛里就是其中之一。

9. **Helvellyn**：赫尔维林山，位于湖区国家公园的一座山，英格兰的第三高峰，海拔为 950 米。

10. **Snowdon**：雪墩山，威尔士最高山峰，海拔为 1,085 米，位于雪墩国家公园（Snowdonia National Park，仅次于湖区国家公园的第二大国家公园）。

11. **Ben Nevis**：本尼维斯山，位于苏格兰，英国最高峰，海拔为 1,343 米。此山南坡缓、东北坡陡，山顶终年积雪。

📖 USEFUL WORDS

barren ['bærən] *adj.* unproductive; completely wanting or lacking 贫瘠的；无效的

claustrophobic	[ˌklɒstrəˈfəʊbɪk]	*adj.*	suffering from claustrophobia (a morbid fear of being closed in a confined space); abnormally afraid of closed-in places （患）幽闭恐惧症的；引起幽闭恐惧的
collateral	[kəˈlætərəl]	*adj.*	connected with sth. else, but in addition to it and less important 并行的；附属的
crevasse	[krəˈvæs]	*n.*	deep, open crack, especially in ice on a glacier（冰河等的）裂缝，破口
crystalline	[ˈkrɪstəlaɪn]	*adj.*	transmitting light; able to be seen through with clarity 水晶（般）的，水晶做的；透明的
dismissively	[dɪsˈmɪsɪvli]	*adv.*	in a way that shows that you do not believe a person or thing to be important or worth considering 轻蔑地；不屑一顾地
doomed	[duːmd]	*adj.*	marked by or promising bad fortune 命中注定的
eulogise	[ˈjuːləˌdʒaɪz]	*v.*	to praise formally and eloquently 表扬，赞扬
exhilaration	[ɪɡˌzɪləˈreɪʃn]	*n.*	the feeling of lively and cheerful joy 高兴，兴奋
gravitas	[ˈɡrævɪtɑːs]	*n.*	formality in bearing and appearance 庄严的举止；庄严
hotchpotch	[ˈhɒtʃpɒtʃ]	*n.*	a motley assortment of things 杂烩；混杂
implacability	[ɪmplækəˈbɪlɪti]	*n.*	the quality of having strong opinions or feelings that are impossible to change 难以安抚的性质或状态
lofty	[ˈlɔːfti]	*adj.*	of high moral or intellectual value; elevated in nature or style 崇高的，高尚的
muse	[mjuːz]	*n.*	a person or spirit that gives a writer, painter, etc. ideas and the desire to create things （作家、画家等的）灵感；创作冲动的源泉
obstinate	[ˈɒbstɪnət]	*adj.*	tenaciously unwilling or marked by tenacious unwillingness to yield 固执的，倔强的；不易屈服的
solitude	[ˈsɒlɪtjuːd]	*n.*	the state or situation of being alone 孤独；独居；荒僻的地方
splinter	[ˈsplɪntə]	*v.*	to break up into splinters or slivers 破裂；组成小派别
suffocate	[ˈsʌfəkeɪt]	*v.*	to cause or have difficulty in breathing （使）窒息，（使）呼吸困难
tapestry	[ˈtæpəstri]	*n.*	a heavy textile with a woven design, used for curtains and upholstery 挂毯
underpin	[ˌʌndərˈpɪn]	*v.*	to support from beneath 从下端支持，支撑

EXERCISES

I. Vocabulary

Choose among the four alternatives one word or phrase that is closest in meaning to the underlined part in each statement.

1. The beauty of the UK's uplands, from the Highlands to the Lakes, is that you don't have to travel far to find adventure, spectacle or solitude, says Simon Ingram.

   A. strange scene   B. remarkable scene   C. desolate scene   D. horrible scene

2. It's said that when the great, doomed mountaineer George Mallory used the phrase in 1923, it was uttered dismissively, without the gravitas it later gained.

   A. solemnly   B. gravely   C. indifferently   D. joyously

3. Agriculturally barren and obstinate to passage, mountains are the last landscapes to become useful, and so are left to the fringes.

   A. shallow   B. fertile   C. arid   D. unproductive

4. There is true variety here: the volcanic summits of the Cuillin ridge on the Isle of Skye; the strange, free-standing peaks of Assynt, north-west Scotland, eulogised by poet Norman MacCaig...

   A. praised   B. mentioned   C. repudiated   D. confounded

5. Once in the uplands, you can have a real adventure with few of the collateral hazards of other mountain areas.

   A. horizontal   B. vertical   C. diagonal   D. accompanying

6. You can camp safe in the knowledge that no animals will pull you shrieking from your tent into the night.

   A. screaming   B. weeping   C. roaring   D. grieving

7. It's alarming how extreme Britain can be: The first taste of this engenders a mixture of sudden, shocked respect.

   A. presumes   B. causes   C. endangers   D. accumulates

8. The tired-happy exhilaration of being a mile high having walked there.

   A. exclamation   B. excitement   C. howl   D. reminiscence

9. To those who know, that joy inhabits the same lofty step—where the mountains of Britain stand as tall as any in the world.

   A. humble   B. course   C. high   D. intrigue

10. A line from his poem, "A Hill", about the implacability of the British mountains' lure, gave me a title for my book about the same...

    A. repression   B. exclusion   C. resistance   D. attraction

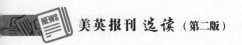

II. Comprehension

Decide whether the following statements are true (T) or false (F) according to the information given in the press clipping. Mark T or F for each statement.

1. Before starting for Mount Qomolangma in 1923, when interviewed by the reporter, George Mallory was very passionate and confident to conquer the highest point on the Earth.

2. The author used to think Britain did not have any mountains which could arouse his interest to explore. It was not until the day he climbed Skiddaw that he realized he had missed something about British mountains.

3. According to the news, mountains tend to be areas unsuitable for cultivation, for it is agriculturally barren and obstinate to passage.

4. The Lake District occupies exquisite tapestry of mountains, lakes and slate villages, which is an inspiration for literature figures, such as Wordsworth and MacCaig.

5. "The most wonderful attribute of all of these is their scale" means that in Britain the mountains are low enough for most of people to conquer within a short time.

6. Climbing British mountains seems to be very safe, and no animals will attack you while camping because wild animals are preserved in certain areas.

7. To climb a mountain in Britain might be an amazing experience, which involves sudden, shocked respect.

8. Britain is a crowded nation for the large population, but the mountains in this country are very spacious, for the comparatively larger area they occupy.

9. In Mount Qomolangma there is a valley Western Cwm named by George Mallory, for it reminded him of Snowdon in Britain.

10. The attitude towards mountains in Britain held by the author has changed from being negative to positive, and the author gradually began to extoll British mountains.

III. Topics for Discussion

1. "Because it's there" is the famous quote from George Mallory in 1923 before he took the third attempt to conquer Mount Qomolangma. Based on the text, please describe what kind of person George Mallory was, and share with your partner your understanding of his remarks.

2. Have you ever been to Britain? How much do you know about mountains in this country? Please refer to the Internet and find more information.

3. "Mountains are places. Things are just there. But in places, things happen." These sentences seem a little confusing, while rich in meanings. Could you distinguish what "mountains" and "things" respectively refer to?

4. Climbing a mountain, especially a steep, intimidating one, is very challenging, but some mountaineers deliberately challenge those treacherous mountains which are seemingly impossible to be conquered. What are the motives driving them to face these challenges?

5. At the end of the text, the author quotes a line from Geoffrey Winthrop Young, who was George Mallory's mentor. What does the author intend to convey by quoting this?

《卫报》简介

　　《卫报》（*The Guardian*）是英国的一份全国性日报，是著名的综合性报刊。《卫报》与同在卫报传媒集团（Guardian Media Group，GMG）下的《观察者报》（*The Observer*）是"姐妹报"，与《泰晤士报》《每日电讯报》（*The Daily Telegraph*）合称为"英国三大报"。《卫报》是定位于高端市场的主流大报，在一定程度上是严肃、可信、独立新闻的代名词，其读者主要为政界人士、白领和知识分子。

　　《卫报》原名为《曼彻斯特卫报》（*The Manchester Guardian*），1821 年由约翰·爱德华·泰勒（John Edward Taylor）创刊于曼彻斯特，当时是一份地方周报，每周六出版。1872年，查尔斯·普里斯维奇·史考特（Charles Prestwich Scott）成为该报的总编，并在 1907 年从泰勒的儿子手中买下这份报纸。在他当总编的 57 年间，该报纸逐渐被整个英国所认可，奠定了其成为英国高品质报纸的基础。1936 年，其儿子约翰·罗素·斯科特（John Russell Scott）放弃继承权，并把报纸的所有权全部转给斯格特信托基金（Scott Trust），这一举措保证了报纸的独立性和高品质，使其不依赖于任何政党，坚守自由民主立场的办报传统，同时赢得了世界的瞩目。1955 年，该报纸改为日报进行发行；1959 年，去掉 Manchester 这一地方色彩的字眼，由《曼彻斯特卫报》改为现名进行发行；1964 年，总部迁往伦敦，但曼彻斯特和伦敦都有其印刷厂。《卫报》现在仍偶尔被称为 Grauniad，源于英国杂志《私家侦探》（*Private Eye*，专门以讽刺、揭发各种丑闻出名）曾给《卫报》起的绰号讽称为 Grauniad（缩写为 Graun），因为《卫报》早期曾把 Guardian 误拼为 Gaurdian。

　　2005 年 9 月起，《卫报》宣布从使用对开面改为使用柏林报纸版式，成为英国第一家使用这种版式的报纸。这种版式通常的尺寸为 470 mm × 315 mm，其优点在于比小报的版式略宽，比大报的版式又略小，非常便于折叠、携带和阅读。改版后，《卫报》的发行量一度迅速上涨。

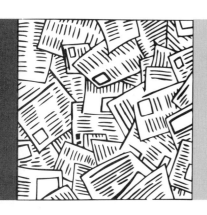

Unit 10
Global Spotlight

报刊英语中的话语权力

　　报刊是大众传媒的重要方式之一。新闻报道的生命是其真实性，即根据事实进行公正的报道。因此，以客观、中立的态度为公众报道新闻事件是新闻媒体应该恪守的基本原则。

　　但是，由于新闻媒体代表的权益主体不同，在报道时可能会带有不同的主观倾向，因此平时人们看到的新闻报道，总是呈现出某种倾向性观点，虽然不一定会决定人们的行为，但在一定程度上会影响他们的观点。换言之，新闻报道并不总是像其宣称的那样公正、客观。受新闻媒体的政治立场以及新闻写作者的观点、态度等多种因素的影响，新闻媒体在报道的新闻事件中都暗含了自身的观点、立场和态度，把意识形态隐藏在新闻报道的字面意思之后，而隐含的主观意识形态会对读者的认知判断造成潜移默化的影响，这种影响在一定程度上构成了报刊的话语权力。由此可见，报刊英语中的语言、意识形态以及话语权力之间存在着复杂的关系。

　　为了客观、理性地理解新闻报道，读者需要对报道话语进行批评性话语分析（critical discourse analysis），它是由 20 世纪 70 年代末开创的批判语言学发展而来的。英国语言学家罗杰·福勒（Roger Fowler）等人在 1979 年出版的《语言与控制》（*Language and Control*）一书中，率先提出了"批判语言学"的概念，开启了批判语篇分析方法。意识形态普遍存在于语言之中，语言同时是社会控制和权力关系得以实现的一种重要手段，并直接参与社会现实和社会关系的构成（戴炜华等，2004）。批判性话语分析为分析新闻语篇提供了重要的理论和方法支持，我们可以基于此对报刊英语中新闻语篇的语言进行分析，剖析语言的特点和规律，揭示出隐含在字里行间的新闻媒体的意识形态，探讨语言、权力和意识形态三者之间的关系。

　　下面两个片段选自《华盛顿邮报》2020 年 8 月 12 日报道的一篇题为 "Trump backers' dizzying response to Kamala Harris's selection" 的新闻，主要涉及美国共和党人对民主党总统候选人约瑟夫·拜登提名竞选搭档一事的评论，具有十分明显的政治倾向性。下面将从词语选择和引语使用两方面，分析该报道如何通过语言渗透，淋漓尽致地表明了《华盛顿邮报》的立场以及共和党对民主党的态度。

- Trump backers' response to Harris' selection has been somewhat **dizzying**. They have mostly painted her as the kind of **radical** that McDaniel did, even labeling her a socialist. But as with the man whose ticket Harris is joining, they have offered mixed messages by also suggesting she is a **disappointment** to Sanders supporters and even a **tool** of Wall Street.

   Fox News' prime-time airwaves on Tuesday night were full of **dire** warnings about Harris' supposed liberal hostile takeover of the party. But on Tucker Carlson's show, he asserted she was, in fact, an **entirely principle-free** politician who would bow to big business. (From *The Washington Post*, Aug. 12, 2020)

本篇新闻的背景为 2020 年美国大选。2020 年 8 月 11 日，民主党总统候选人乔·拜登提名联邦参议员卡玛拉·哈里斯（Kamala Harris）为副总统候选人，《华盛顿邮报》就共和党方面对此的反应加以报道。在词语选择方面，dizzying 体现了《华盛顿邮报》对共和党一贯的不支持态度。同时，在分析共和党对民主党提名反应的部分，词语 radical、disappointment、tool、dire、entirely principle-free 都传递出很强的否定色彩。以上表明共和党出于本党派利益的主观意图，营造了对民主党副总统候选人不利的舆论导向，误导美国选民，以期在总统大选中为共和党派赢取更多选票。

- "Susan Rice is a hardened partisan," Carlson said of another top VP contender who was passed over. "But she is not stupid, and more to the point, Rice has sincere beliefs whether you like them or not—and we don't. But Kamala D. Harris is the opposite of that. Harris may be the single most transactional human being in America."

   "Phony Kamala will abandon her own morals, as well as try to bury her record as a prosecutor, in order to appease the anti-police extremists controlling the Democrat Party," the RNC said. (From *The Washington Post*, Aug. 12, 2020)

引语，尤其是直接引语，通常是新闻记者借助当事人的话来表述自己的立场观点，进而影响受众观点的有力工具或手段。上述第一段引文是塔克·卡尔森（Tucker Carlson，美国福克斯电视台著名主持人）对卡玛拉·哈里斯的负面评论。卡尔森非常鲜明地站在共和党的政治立场，对民主党副总统候选人进行毫无掩饰的语言诋毁，歧视明显。第二段引文来自 Republican National Committee（共和党全国委员会），同样代表着共和党对卡玛拉·哈里斯极为否定的观点。《华盛顿邮报》直接引用共和党代表的粗暴言论的这一做法，表现出该报在政治上一直以来对共和党持有的不友好态度。

新闻报道应该客观、公正地呈现事实，但是美英两国的报刊不仅在本国的新闻报道中会因政治立场不同采取不同的话语倾向，有目的地引导受众，而且在关于他国的新闻报道中也会有意识形态的倾向性表现。一直以来，美国和英国凭借其强大的经济影响力，在国际上表现出非常强势的话语权，而由于中西方意识形态的差异，美英两国的媒体对中国的负面报道居多。尤其是自新冠疫情暴发以来，为转移本国矛盾，美英政府和诸多媒体一直致力于抹黑中国，利用其对国际话语权的控制营造不利于中国的舆论环境，煽动本国人民和西方国家对中国的敌意。在这样的背景下，中国媒体要积极应对，反击美英媒体的恶意抹黑行为，同时努力在国际传播中化被动为主动，提升中国媒体的国际话语权。

因此，在阅读英语新闻报道时，读者需要运用批判性话语分析，提高语言鉴赏及评论能力，透过现象看本质，分析新闻报道中隐含的意识形态倾向和话语权力指向，从而看清新闻报道的事实原貌，做出正确的价值评价。

Text A

导读

2011 年 3 月 15 日，叙利亚内战爆发。动荡局势使叙利亚民不聊生，民众颠沛流离，社会千疮百孔，危机积重难返。

自 2020 年以来，叙利亚的伊德利卜冲突降级区战役进入新阶段。2 月 12 日，叙利亚政府军完全控制了拥有重要战略意义的 M5 高速公路，这进一步激化了国内矛盾。接连不断的叙利亚内战是国内矛盾、国外霸权势力和各种宗派势力三者之间的博弈。本文介绍了俄罗斯和土耳其两国在叙利亚的较量，这一博弈加剧了叙利亚的紧张局势。

Syrian Civil War[1] Enters Dangerous New Phase

Analysts say Turkish-Russian diplomacy is key to de-escalating violence that is fueling another surge in refugees.

By Abby Sewell

BEIRUT[2]—A dangerous new phase has opened in the nine-year-old civil war in Syria, with a major offensive by government forces in Idlib[3], the last major rebel outpost in the country, and an

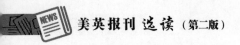

escalation to direct confrontation between the Syrian regime and Turkey.

The conflict in Syria has driven the largest refugee and displacement crisis in modern history—with an estimated 5.5 million refugees outside the country and another 6 million displaced inside the country.

Now recent developments in Idlib have caused yet another mass flight and fears of worse things to come. According to the United Nations Office for the Coordination of Humanitarian Affairs (OCHA), nearly 700,000 people have been forcibly displaced in Idlib province and surrounding areas of northwestern Syria since the beginning of December.

"This is, from our initial analysis, the largest number of people displaced in a single period since the Syrian crisis began almost nine years ago," OCHA spokesman Jens Laerke told reporters in a briefing on Tuesday. "This latest displacement compounds an already dire humanitarian situation on the ground in Idlib and protection, shelter, food, water, sanitation and hygiene, health and emergency education are all urgent priorities."

As part of the Idlib offensive, Syrian government forces, with Russian backing, retook the formerly rebel-controlled town of Saraqeb[4], which is strategically located at the intersection of two highways. The operation put the Syrian government in sight of its goal of once again controlling the entire M5 highway between Damascus and Aleppo.

But it also brought Syrian and Turkish forces into direct clashes—a first during the war, although Turkey has been supporting rebel groups since the beginning of the civil war. After Syrian shelling near Idlib hit a Turkish post on Feb. 3, killing seven Turkish soldiers and a civilian, Turkey retaliated, with Turkish officials claiming to have killed dozens of Syrian soldiers.

Aron Lund, a fellow with the progressive U.S.-based progressive think tank The Century Foundation[5], said that the Turkish reaction was in part a response to the killing of the soldiers, but "also reflects Turkish fears of a new refugee crisis pressing up on its border". Turkish President Tayyip Erdogan[6] said on Tuesday that the Syrian government will pay a "very high price" for the strikes in Idlib.

"There are already 3.5 million Syrians in Turkey, and domestic opinion is very anti-refugee," Lund said. "Erdogan hasn't got much room for maneuver—he needs a quick ceasefire. Escalating like this is his way of slowing Assad's forces and showing Russia he means business."

Initially condemning the Syrian government at the outbreak of unrest in 2011, Turkey's involvement in the country has since evolved from providing military support for Syrian rebels to direct military interventions.

The escalation of violence in Idlib may also represent a blow to Erdogan's hopes of convincing the international community to support plans to send refugees back to "safe zones" in northern Syria. He made a pitch for this proposal at the Global Refugee Forum in Geneva in December.

Idlib has been a base for a patchwork of armed groups, including some considered by the international community to be extremist, such as Hayat Tahrir al-Sham[7], an armed group formerly known as the Nusra Front and linked to al-Qaida. But UN Special Envoy Geir O. Pedersen, in a briefing to the Security Council last week, noted that the vast majority of the estimated 3 million people living in Idlib province are civilians, many of whom have already been displaced before from other parts of Syria.

As the last major rebel-controlled area, Idlib had been the destination for many Syrians unwilling to live under regime rule after the Syrian army reclaimed other areas of the country, including Aleppo and Eastern Ghouta.

Now many of them have fled again, under intense fighting and a Syrian and Russian aerial offensive that has struck residential neighborhoods, hospitals and schools. With the Turkish border now closed, many are living in crowded camps on the Syrian side of the border.

Nour Hajj Ismail was among the civilians who fled during the offensive in Saraqeb, where she had been a teacher in a center run by Women Now for Development, an NGO[8] that provides educational and vocational classes and other services for women and girls at centers in Syria and Lebanon. The NGO reported that the entire teams at their centers in Saraqeb and in the town of Maarat al Numan were displaced as a result of the recent offensive in Idlib.

Ismail, speaking via WhatsApp[9] from the Aleppo countryside, where she and her family have fled, said that in the past, the center staff and students had persisted in the face of danger.

"Even when there were airstrikes, we would come back and open again the next day and with even more determination," she said.

But in the recent offensive, she said, "The bombing became very savage…There were strikes very near to the center, and that affected the students and beneficiaries and us as teachers, because when we were coming and going from the center, we were in danger."

Now, Ismail is unsure when or if she will be able to return home. "We don't want anything but our simplest rights, to learn and live in safety," she said. "We don't want more than that—just to return to our houses without warplanes and without being oppressed."

The OCHA's Laerke called for an immediate cessation of fighting. Turkish and Russian officials met in Ankara over the weekend, but without reaching an agreement on an end to the clashes.

Lund said that Erdogan's relationship with Russia is strained given that Moscow has previously negotiated ceasefire agreements on behalf of the Syrian government "but is now again backing an offensive into the Turkey-protected zone".

Still, he said Turkish-Russian diplomacy will likely determine the course events will take.

"There are constant secret talks, and I think both Putin and Erdogan are concerned that the situation could get out of hand," he said. "They have built a strange, tense, but also mutually beneficial relationship, and neither of them wants to let Idlib destroy that."

（From *U.S. News*, Feb. 11, 2020）

NOTES

1. **Syrian Civil War**：叙利亚内战，始于 2011 年 3 月，至今已延续 10 余年，持续不断的战争和冲突使整个国家陷入动荡混乱状态，一半以上叙利亚民众被迫逃离家园，流离失所。内战的直接导火索为 15 名叙利亚少年因街头涂鸦被认作反政府而被捕，事件持续发酵后引发全国抗议和示威，最终点燃内战。内战的深层次原因是叙利亚由来已久的国内矛盾激化升级，这是各宗教势力、反政府武装和政府军的角逐混战，也是欧美大国在叙利亚博弈的体现。

2. **Beirut**：贝鲁特，黎巴嫩首都，国家政治、金融中心。它位于地中海东岸，连接东西方国家，因其重要的战略位置而备受瞩目。

3. **Idlib**：伊德利卜省，位于叙利亚西北部，接壤土耳其，是叙利亚反动武装在叙境内掌控的最后一个省。收复伊德利卜、结束内战是叙利亚政府一直以来的心愿，但反动武装及其背后的国际力量使这个地区的局势扑朔迷离。

4. **Saraqeb**：萨拉奇布市，位于伊德利卜省的战略要地，M5 公路沿线的一个重镇，也是叙利亚最重要的区域之一。叙利亚政府军于 2020 年 2 月 6 日恢复了对此地区的控制。

5. **The Century Foundation**：世纪基金会，由进步商业领袖爱德华·菲莱纳（Edward Filene）于 1919 年创立，美国历史最悠久的公共政策研究机构之一。世纪基金会是一个进步的、无党派的智库，致力于创造机会、减少不平等、促进国内外安全。

6. **Tayyip Erdogan**：塔伊普·埃尔多安，土耳其政治家，生于 1954 年，2014 年当选土耳其总统，2018 年连任至今。土耳其作为叙利亚的北方邻国，较早地介入了叙利亚内战：支持反政府武装；在与土耳其接壤的叙利亚伊德利卜省设立据点，驻扎军队。

7. **Hayat Tahrir al-Sham**：沙姆解放组织，前身为努斯拉阵线（Al-Nusra Front），逊尼派伊斯兰主义政治组织和民兵组织。

8. **NGO**：全称为 Non-Governmental Organization，非政府组织，是在地方、国家或国际级别上建立的独立于任何国家和政府的非营利性社会组织。它可以提供公共服务，发挥人道主义作用，目的是促进经济发展和社会进步。

9. **WhatsApp**：类似于微信（WeChat）的一个应用程序，外国人使用较多。它使用起来简单方便，除聊天功能之外，WhatsApp 的其他功能也非常强大。

USEFUL WORDS

beneficiary	[ˌbenɪˈfɪʃəri]	*n.*	a person who derives advantage from sth., especially a trust, will, or life insurance policy 受益人，受惠者
briefing	[ˈbriːfɪŋ]	*n.*	a meeting for giving information or instructions 简报；作战指示
de-escalate	[ˌdiːˈeskəleit]	*v.*	to diminish in size, scope, or intensity; to reduce the level or intensity or size or scope of （使）逐步降级；缩小规模；减少（数量，冲突等）
dire	[ˈdaɪə(r)]	*adj.*	extremely serious, urgent or terrible 可怕的；悲惨的
displacement	[dɪsˈpleɪsmənt]	*n.*	the removal of sth. from its usual place or position by sth. which then occupies that place or position 取代；位移
hygiene	[ˈhaɪdʒiːn]	*n.*	practices conducive to maintaining health and preventing disease, especially through cleanliness 卫生
maneuver	[məˈnuːvə(r)]	*n.*	(*pl. maneuvers*) military exercises involving a large number of soldiers, ships, etc. 军事演习；作战演习
patchwork	[ˈpætʃwɜːk]	*n.*	a thing composed of many different elements so as to appear variegated 拼缝物；拼凑的东西
persist	[pəˈsɪst]	*v.*	to continue in an opinion or course of action in spite of difficulty or opposition 坚持；持续
retaliate	[rɪˈtælieɪt]	*v.*	to make an attack in return for a similar attack, especially for revenge 报复；回敬
sanitation	[ˌsænɪˈteɪʃn]	*n.*	conditions relating to public health, especially the provision of clean drinking water and adequate sewage disposal 环境卫生；卫生设备
shell	[ʃel]	*v.*	to bombard with shells 炮轰
strained	[streɪnd]	*adj.*	showing signs of nervous tension or tiredness 紧张的；勉强的
surge	[sɜːdʒ]	*v.*	(of a crowd or a natural force) to move suddenly and powerfully forward or upward 蜂拥而来
unrest	[ʌnˈrest]	*n.*	a state of dissatisfaction, disturbance, and agitation, typically involving public demonstrations or disorder 动荡的局面；不安的状态

EXERCISES

I. Vocabulary

Choose among the four alternatives one word or phrase that is closest in meaning to the underlined part in each statement.

1. The conflict in Syria has driven the largest refugee and <u>displacement</u> crisis in modern history—with an estimated 5.5 million refugees outside the country and another 6 million displaced inside the country.

   A. discard   B. migration   C. remain   D. residing

2. This latest displacement compounds an already <u>dire</u> humanitarian situation on the ground in Idlib and protection, shelter, food, water, sanitation and hygiene, health and emergency education are all urgent priorities.

   A. desire   B. conspire   C. amiable   D. terrible

3. After Syrian shelling near Idlib hit a Turkish post on Feb. 3, killing seven Turkish soldiers and a civilian, Turkey <u>retaliated</u>, with Turkish officials claiming to have killed dozens of Syrian soldiers.

   A. revenged   B. retained   C. sympathized   D. swashed

4. Erdogan hasn't got much room for <u>maneuver</u>—he needs a quick cease fire. Escalating like this is his way of slowing Assad's forces and showing Russia he means business.

   A. military exercises   B. industrial manufacture

   C. military strike   D. economic prosperity

5. Initially condemning the Syrian government at the outbreak of <u>unrest</u> in 2011, Turkey's involvement in the country has since evolved from providing military support to Syrian rebels to direct military interventions.

   A. warfare   B. agitation   C. serenity   D. stress

6. The <u>escalation</u> of violence in Idlib may also represent a blow to Erdogan's hopes of convincing the international community to support plans to send refugees back to "safe zones" in northern Syria.

   A. interruption   B. depression   C. parallel   D. deterioration

7. Idlib has been a base for a <u>patchwork</u> of armed groups, including some considered by the international community to be extremist, such as Hayat Tahrir al-Sham, an armed group formerly known as the Nusra Front and linked to al-Qaida.

   A. consolidation   B. farrago   C. concentration   D. embodiment

8. Ismail, speaking via WhatsApp from the Aleppo countryside, where she and her family have

fled, said that in the past, the center staff and students had <u>persisted</u> in the face of danger.

    A. insisted   B. resisted   C. abided   D. centralized

9. But in the recent offensive, she said, "The bombing became very <u>savage</u>…There were strikes very near to the center, and that affected the students and beneficiaries and us as teachers, because when we were coming and going from the center, we were in danger."

    A. uncivilized   B. brutal   C. neutral   D. indifferent

10. Lund said that Erdogan's relationship with Russia is <u>strained</u> given that Moscow has previously negotiated ceasefire agreements on behalf of the Syrian government "but is now again backing an offensive into the Turkey-protected zone".

    A. collided   B. crushed   C. tense   D. integrated

II. Comprehension

Decide whether the following statements are true (T) or false (F) according to the information given in the press clipping. Mark T or F for each statement.

1. After 9 years of civil war in Syria, the number of refugees in this country has reached 12 million.

2. OCHA is an organization which shows an objective attitude towards the civil war in Syria, but secretly it is in support of rebel groups in this country.

3. Syrian government forces are backed by Turkey, while Russia supports the Syrian rebel groups, which resulted in a more complicated situation in Syria.

4. According to the initial analysis from OCHA, nearly 700,000 people have been forcibly displaced in Idlib province and surrounding areas of northwestern Syria since the beginning of December, and this is the largest displacement since the Syrian war.

5. Syrian government forces and rebel groups fight for controlling the M5 highway, because it occupies a strategic position in this country.

6. Turkey claimed to have killed dozens of Syrian soldiers in revenge for Syrian rebel groups hitting a Turkish post on Feb. 3 which killed seven Turkish soldiers and one civilian.

7. Turkey's involvement in Syrian civil war has evolved from providing military support for Syrian rebels to direct military interventions.

8. Now the three million refugees living in Idlib province are civilians, many of whom have already been displaced before from other parts of Syria.

9. Nour Hajj Ismail used to be a teacher in Saraqeb, before she and her family fled to the Aleppo countryside where she was not sure whether she could still continue to work as a teacher, because the bombing became very savage.

10. Both Putin and Erdogan are concerned about the situation in Syria, because they could benefit from Syrian civil war, and secretly both of them wish Syrian government forces could defeat the rebel groups.

III. Topics for Discussion

1. "We don't want anything but our simplest rights, to learn and live in safety." "We don't want

more than that—just to return to our houses without warplanes and without being oppressed." These remarks are from a teacher in Syria. Please describe what kind of life the civilians in Syria are living currently.

2. Please list the sufferings of civilians during a war. You may cite the evidences from the Syrian civil war, World War I or World War II.

3. "Arab Spring" was a popular term in early 2011, referring to demonstrators' series of protests and uprisings against the government in the Middle East. Some experts regard it just as a challenge of the Arabs' entrenched dictatorship, while others believe it is actually a reflection of the game of world powers in the Middle East. Please refer to the Internet to find more information about "Arab Spring", and critically analyze the reasons behind it.

4. After the outbreak of Syrian civil war, some Syrian refugees fled to Europe, seeking asylum, but not everyone could make it. Is it the responsibility of European countries, such as Germany, to offer unconditional help for them? Please refer to the Internet and find more evidence to support your idea.

5. The Syrian civil war has lasted nine years, while when the war will end still remains unknown. What are the possible results of the war in this country? Please share your ideas with your classmates.

宗教对西方文化的影响——以基督教为例

宗教属于社会意识形态，是人类发展到一定阶段时出现的特定思想与信仰。一个民族文化的形成和演化，往往都跟宗教的发展密切相关。西方文化是指源自希伯来的宗教文化和古希腊理性主义的人本文化相结合而发展起来的欧洲文化，它后来又传到美国、加拿大以及澳洲。基督教作为世界三大宗教之一，始于公元 1 世纪，有 2,000 多年的发展历史，在西方文化中处于核心地位，影响了整个西方思想文化的发展。可以说，基督教的思想已经深深地融入西方文化，维系着西方人的精神世界。

一、基督教对西方政治文化的影响

虽然早期的基督教与政治分离，并受到罗马统治者的迫害，但是在上千年的欧洲中世纪历史中，基督教会借助其掌握的政治力量对欧洲社会实行了全面操控，垄断了思想文化。虽然近现代西方社会实行了政教分离，但是基督教的价值观对现代西方的政治理念有着深刻的影响。

二、基督教对西方道德生活的影响

在社会生活中，法律用来规范人们的外部行为。若要人们自觉遵守社会准则，维持正常的社会秩序，则需要道德的约束。基督教与道德的关系历来密切。比如，基督教提倡要爱人如己，并宣称这是神的旨意和命令；用宗教的语言对其成员提出强制性的行为规范，并启发和要求他们遵守，这些实际上就是对道德提出的要求。在历史上，基督教是西方人们的价值观依据；在现代社会，维系社会的道德则是其主要的社会功能。

三、基督教对西方文学的影响

宗教在西方文学的发展过程中起到不可忽视的积极作用，可以说，西方文学与基督教会的思想和活动密不可分。作为基督教最高神学经典的《圣经》，是人文科学领域的伟大文献和文学作品。它为西方文学作品提供了最基本的素材宝库，使西方文学作品中深深地打着《圣经》的烙印。中世纪的宗教文学，基本上以基督教为题材。之后的文艺复兴时期依旧如此，如但丁·阿利吉耶里（Dante Alighieri）的《神曲》（*Divine Comedy*），被视为世界上伟大的作品之一，蕴含着深厚的宗教哲理。在英国文学史上占有重要地位的著名诗人约翰·弥尔顿（John Milton）的《失乐园》（*Paradise Lost*）、《复乐园》（*Paradise Regained*），也是以基督教的题材为核心的。还有一些作家通过隐喻来表达自己的宗教思想，如美国作家纳撒尼尔·霍桑（Nathaniel Hawthorne）的《红字》（*The Scarlet Letter*）；欧内斯特·米勒·海明威（Ernest Miller Hemingway）的《老人与海》（*The Old Man and the Sea*）则是根据耶稣受难的细节创作而成，他将老人构想成耶稣的化身。

四、基督教对西方教育的影响

若要研究西方的教育史，必然绕不开基督教。在欧洲，许多古老的大学是由基督教会创办的，如巴黎大学就是在大教堂学校的基础上发展而来的。这些由教会创办的神学院为西方近代和现代高等教育打下了基础。西方高等教育中一直沿袭至今的一些传统，如指定学生必须学习的课程、使用教科书、毕业授予学位等，都始于中世纪大学所确立的一些制度。

五、基督教对西方人们日常生活的影响

西方最隆重的节日是圣诞节（Christmas）和复活节（Easter），它们分别是与基督教中耶稣的诞生和复活有关。在一定程度上，这两个节日的庆祝活动已经成为全社会每年的盛事。此外，无论证人在法庭上作证还是美国总统的就职仪式，人们都要手抚《圣经》进行宣誓。在美国的很多城镇，教堂还是各种社会活动的中心。

总之，基督教思想是欧洲文化的重要渊源之一，对西方历史文化的进程起着举足轻重的作用。作为构筑西方文化的重要组成部分，基督教对西方文化的方方面面产生了重要的影响。了解基督教和西方文化的密切关系，对于人们正确、全面地认识西方文化大有裨益。

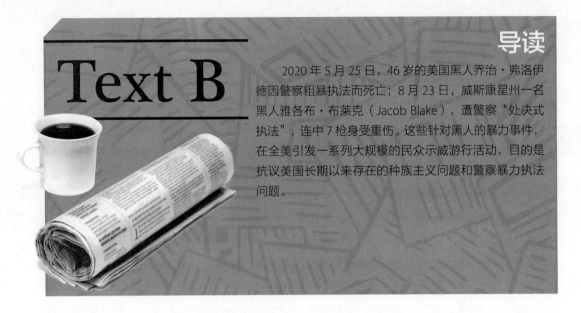

2020 年 5 月 25 日，46 岁的美国黑人乔治·弗洛伊德因警察粗暴执法而死亡；8 月 23 日，威斯康星州一名黑人雅各布·布莱克（Jacob Blake），遭警察"处决式执法"，连中 7 枪身受重伤。这些针对黑人的暴力事件，在全美引发一系列大规模的民众示威游行活动，目的是抗议美国长期以来存在的种族主义问题和警察暴力执法问题。

导读

After this summer's protests, Americans think differently about race. That could last for generations.

A rich body of research finds major events can create sustained changes in attitudes.

By Bryan Schonfeld and Sam Winter-Levy

This summer's Black Lives Matter[1] protests shifted White American attitudes towards race quite significantly. Beginning with the recording of George Floyd's killing[2] at the hands of Minneapolis police on May 25, the protests quickly shifted attitudes considerably, as TMC editor Michael Tesler noted here on June 9. In late May, 57 percent of Americans said police officers were more likely to use excessive force against Black people than against White people, according to Monmouth University's June 2 poll, conducted around the peak of the protests—a big jump from just 33 percent in December 2014. Roughly three out of four Americans called "racial and ethnic discrimination" a "big problem" in the United States—up from only about half of Americans in 2015.

And the protests haven't ended. More recently, protests erupted after a Louisville grand jury declined to charge police officers in the death of Breonna Taylor[3], an emergency medical worker shot and killed at home during a raid in March.

But will those changes in attitudes last—or fade? Over the past few years, political scientists, economists and psychologists have made important findings suggesting that prejudice has deep roots and can be transmitted from parents to children over many generations. That's true for anti-

Black racism, anti-Semitism[4] and any other form of bias. But they've also found that attitudes can shift—and that protests can help those increases in tolerance last.

Prejudice can last for generations

Much of the social science literature on prejudice's persistence explores anti-Semitism in Europe. Findings suggest that ethnic hatred can flourish in certain places over shockingly long time spans. As the Black Death[5] tore through medieval Europe, Jews were widely blamed for poisoning wells. Pogroms broke out across Europe. In Germany, for example, Christians launched pogroms of varying intensities across the country. Almost six centuries later, as the Nazis rose to power, the same places that burned Jews in the middle of the 14th century showed markedly higher levels of anti-Semitism than neighboring towns. They were six times more likely to attack Jews as the Nazis rose to power. And today, municipalities that supported the Nazis more enthusiastically in 1933 are more likely to support the hard-right Alternative for Deutschland (AfD) party[6]. Far-right party vote shares in Germany and Poland are higher in places closer to Nazi concentration camps.

Scholars have found similar results for anti-Black racism in the United States. A 2016 paper found that White people who live in southern counties that had higher proportions of enslaved people in 1860 are more likely, today, to express racial resentment towards Black people, and identify as Republicans and oppose affirmative action. The culture, norms and institutions of the Southern "Black Belt"[7]—the focal point of antebellum slavery, where, according to the political scientist V. O. Key, southern Whites had "the deepest and most immediate concern about the maintenance of White supremacy"—were transmitted within families and across generations. Passed through institutions, families and communities from one generation to the next, prejudice can last for decades, if not centuries.

Increases in tolerance can persist, too

But just as certain historical events can fuel prejudice that can last for centuries, other events can boost tolerance for generations. Take, for example, the interaction between Black American soldiers and Britons during World War II. At the time, around 10 percent of the American troops stationed in the United Kingdom were African Americans. The U.S. Army was strictly segregated, but many Britons resisted official attempts to treat Black GIs as inferior. As a result, U.S. War Department surveys found that while White GIs grew less sympathetic to English people while stationed there, most Black GIs became more positive about them. The feeling was mutual. As Black soldiers visited local restaurants, bars and dance halls, many Britons saw and interacted with African Americans for the first time—and responded positively. "I don't mind the Yanks[8]," one

Englishman remarked, "but I don't care much for the White fellows they've brought with them." Or as George Orwell wrote, "The general consensus of opinion seems to be that the only American soldiers with decent manners are the Negroes."

According to a new paper by economists David Schindler and Mark Westcott, the effects of these interactions persisted long after most U.S. troops had returned home. Schindler and Westcott find that the presence of Black GIs reduced prejudice significantly. The places where more African American soldiers were deployed during World War II contained fewer supporters of the far-right British National Party[9] in 2009. People there display less implicit anti-Black bias and are more likely to report warmer feelings towards Black people. (U.S. troops were stationed in bases in the United Kingdom regardless of local racial attitudes.) The effects were particularly strong in rural, predominantly White areas where geographic mobility has been relatively limited. Direct contact with Black Americans may have shifted British attitudes in a more tolerant direction in the 1940s, with effects that have lasted for decades.

Protests can similarly affect public opinion. The political scientist Soumyajit Mazumder finds that White people who live in counties where the civil rights movement[10] protested are less likely to harbor racial resentment against Black people, and more likely to support Democrats and affirmative action today. "The attitudes propped up by the Jim Crow[11] racial order," Mazumder writes, "can be reshaped through instances of non-violent mobilization." Other research finds that protests in an electoral district lead more people to vote and to donate to political candidates who share their ideological leanings. What's more, protests tend to push legislators to vote more in line with protesters' goals. Sustained collective action can create lasting social change.

We don't yet know whether this summer's Black Lives Matter protests will have a similar effect. But we do know that it's possible to reduce prejudice in a way that lasts for generations; that protests can significantly change public opinion; and that major events can shape political attitudes long after the news cycle moves on. Since the George Floyd-inspired demonstrations may have been the largest in U.S. history, we should expect a lasting impact on American racial attitudes.

（From *The Washington Post*, Oct. 12, 2020）

NOTES

1. **Black Lives Matter**："黑人的命也是命"，美国黑人抗议维权运动中的口号，起源于美国黑人社区，是黑人对长时间以来遭受的系统性种族歧视、暴力等不平等待遇的抗议。2020 年，黑人乔治·弗洛伊德（George Floyd）的死亡事件，把这项运动推向了高潮。

2. **George Floyd's killing**：乔治·弗洛伊德被粗暴执法致死事件。2020 年 5 月 25 日，乔治·弗洛伊德在手无寸铁的情况下，被明尼苏达州警察德里克·肖万（Derek Chauvin）跪压制服时窒息而死。此事件在美国引发反种族主义及警察暴力的抗议活动。

3. **Breonna Taylor**：布琳娜·泰勒，一名美国黑人急救医生。2020 年 3 月 13 日，美国肯塔基州路易斯维尔市的三名便衣警察以搜捕毒贩为名闯入其家中，当时泰勒和男友正在家中休息，泰勒的男友误以为警察是非法入侵者，开枪防卫，遭到三名警察反击，年仅 26 岁的泰勒身中多枪死亡。

4. **anti-Semitism**：反犹太主义。排挤和迫害整个犹太种族的思潮由来已久，历史上，欧洲的反犹主义最严重。

5. **Black Death**：黑死病，又叫"鼠疫"（plague），一种致命的瘟疫，14 世纪蔓延欧亚两洲，夺走了欧洲 30% ~ 60% 的人口。

6. **Alternative for Deutschland party**：德国新选择党，右翼政党。该党派批评、反对穆斯林移民进入德国。

7. **Black Belt**：黑土带，位于美国南部地区，最先因其黑色的肥沃土壤而著称。历史上这个区域是美国黑人奴隶制的中心，黑人的人口比例高，以种植园经济为主。

8. **the Yanks**：（俗称）美国佬，俚语，原指住在美国东北部新英格兰地区的人。

9. **British National Party**：英国国家党，极右翼政党，被认为是英国的新纳粹政党。

10. **the civil rights movement**：美国国内民权运动（1955—1968），以反对黑人种族歧视和争取选举权为目标，著名黑人运动领袖马丁·路德·金是这场运动中卓越的领导人。在 1963 年，他发表了著名演讲"I Have a Dream"，呼吁取消种族歧视，实现种族平等。

11. **Jim Crow**：通常指 *Jim Crow Law*（《吉姆·克劳法》），指针对美国黑人的种族隔离政策，尤其是在公共设施方面，白人和有色人种被隔离对待。

📖 USEFUL WORDS

affirmative	[əˈfɜːmətɪv]	*adj.*	giving assent, supporting a policy or attitude, etc. 肯定的
antebellum	[ˌæntiˈbeləm]	*adj.*	belonging to a period before a war especially the American Civil War （美国南北）战争前的
boost	[buːst]	*v.*	to increase or raise 增加；促进
electoral	[ɪˈlektərəl]	*adj.*	relating to elections 选举的
erupt	[ɪˈrʌpt]	*v.*	to break out 爆发
harbor	[ˈhɑːbə]	*v.*	to maintain (a theory, thoughts, or feelings) 怀有
municipality	[mjuːˌnɪsɪˈpæləti]	*n.*	an urban district having corporate status and powers of self-government 市政当局
pogrom	[ˈpɒɡrəm]	*n.*	organized persecution of an ethnic group (especially Jews) 大屠杀

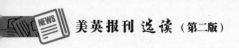
prop   [prɒp]   *v.* to support by placing against sth. solid or rigid 支撑
sustained   [sə'steɪnd]   *adj.* continuing, lasting 持续的；持久的

EXERCISES

I. Vocabulary

Choose among the four alternatives one word or phrase that is closest in meaning to the underlined part in each statement.

1. A rich body of research finds major events can create <u>sustained</u> changes in attitudes.

     A. detained   B. contained   C. lasting   D. penetrating

2. More recently, protests <u>erupted</u> after a Louisville grand jury declined to charge police officers in the death of Breonna Taylor, an emergency medical worker shot and killed at home during a raid in March.

     A. broke out   B. disrupted   C. suspended   D. persisted

3. Over the past few years, political scientists, economists and psychologists have made important findings suggesting that prejudice has deep roots and can be <u>transmitted</u> from parents to children over many generations.

     A. inflicted   B. transformed   C. sent   D. engendered

4. As the Black Death tore through medieval Europe, Jews were widely blamed for poisoning <u>wells</u>.

     A. foutains   B. propriety   C. prudence   D. relevance

5. <u>Pogroms</u> broke out across Europe.

     A. Uprisings   B. Massacres   C. Explosions   D. Plagues

6. But just as certain historical events can fuel prejudice that can last for centuries, other events can <u>boost</u> tolerance for generations.

     A. lessen   B. boast   C. increase   D. balance

7. The political scientist Soumyajit Mazumder finds that White people who live in counties where the civil rights movement protested are less likely to <u>harbor</u> racial resentment against Black people, and more likely to support Democrats and affirmative action today.

     A. generate   B. maintain   C. abolish   D. enhance

8. "The attitudes <u>propped</u> up by the Jim Crow racial order," Mazumder writes, "can be reshaped through instances of non-violent mobilization."

     A. asserted   B. advocated   C. promoted   D. supported

9. Other research finds that protests in <u>an electoral district</u> lead more people to vote and to donate to political candidates who share their ideological leanings.

     A. an area relating to electricity   B. an area relating to eruption

     C. an area relating to election   D. an area relating to elevation

10. What's more, protests tend to push <u>legislators</u> to vote more in line with protesters' goals.

    A. judges   B. law-makers   C. voters   D. candidates

II. Comprehension

Decide whether the following statements are true (T) or false (F) according to the information given in the press clipping. Mark T or F for each statement.

1. It is well acknowledged that police officers in the United States were more likely to use excessive force against Black people than against White people.

2. As for the Black Death in medieval Europe, Jews were widely blamed for poisoning wells, and were killed massively for that.

3. In Germany, municipalities that supported the Nazis more enthusiastically in 1933 are more likely to support the hard-right Alternative for Deutschland party.

4. In World War II, Black American soldiers in Britain were treated equally, even the U.S. Army was strictly segregated.

5. The interaction between Black American soldiers and Britons during World War II vanished soon after most U.S. troops had returned home.

6. The places where more African American soldiers were deployed during World War II in Britain contained more supporters of the far-right British National Party in 2009.

7. This text implies that the civil rights movement was also about the protest against racial discrimination.

8. This summer's Black Lives Matter protests will reduce prejudice in a way that lasts for generations.

9. In the 1940s, direct contact with Black Americans may have shifted British attitudes in a more tolerant direction, with effects that have lasted for decades.

10. Racial discrimination still exists in the United States, even though historically several protests against it have been conducted.

III. Topics for discussion

1. The event "George Floyd's killing" was mentioned in the text. Please visit the corresponding websites to know more about this case, make some comments upon it and share the ideas with your classmates.

2. Martin Luther King Jr., a prominent black leader during the American civil rights movement in the 1960s, was awarded the Nobel Peace Prize. In 1963, he delivered the famous speech " I Have a Dream" , calling for the abolishment of racial discrimination, which also encouraged thousands of people to fight for racial equality. Has the "dream" mentioned by Martin Luther King Jr. in his speech come true in the U.S.? Please illustrate your ideas.

3. By law, public facilities and government services such as education were divided into separate and unequal "white" and "colored" domains. This was a fact before the civil rights movement in the U.S. Do you think this is in line with "justice" belief in this country?

4. "Freedom" and "equality" are the two basic American values, though sound resonant and

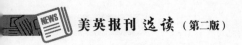

admirable, can be uneasy companions. These two ideas may come into conflict with each other. Please refer to the Internet to find evidence showing the ongoing tension between "freedom" and "equality" in this country.

5. The United States was once compared to "a melting pot" for its cultural diversity, and later with the alternatives like "salad bowl", "mosaic". All of those indicate that this country used to be a nation of immigration. What are the appropriate policies that the government is supposed to employ to fulfill the concept of multiculturalism in the real sense?

《镜报》简介

　　英国的报纸按照版面内容可分为严肃性报纸和通俗性报纸。严肃性报纸通常篇幅较长，刊登的新闻内容深刻、严肃，偏重于社会政治生活的主题，同时也刊登关于高雅文化的评论文章和特别报道，读者多是受过良好教育的中产阶级。通俗性报纸在传统上版面尺寸较小，有更多的图片和醒目的标题，文章篇幅短，内容通俗易懂且娱乐性强。《镜报》（The Mirror）就是英国的一份通俗性日报。

　　《镜报》是英国销量最大的日报之一。该报由"北岩爵士"阿尔弗雷德·哈姆斯沃思（Alfred Harmsworth）于 1903 年创刊，本义是为女性创办的小型报纸，这也是该报名字的来源。"让这份报纸成为女性的一面镜子，既照出女性暗淡的一面，也照出光彩的一面……娱乐但不轻佻，严肃却不呆板"是该报一直秉承的办报目标。此报创立后不久便改为画报，随着版面越来越丰富，目标读者群就不再局限于女性。在内容上，该报的图片占比越来越高，报道范围包括新闻、娱乐和体育等方面。

　　1951 年，塞西尔·金（Cecil King）任《每日镜报》董事长，建立了镜报集团。1984 年，罗伯特·马克斯韦尔（Robert Maxwell）买下镜报集团报业公司。1999 年，镜报集团和三一集团合并成为英国最大的报纸出版商——三一镜报集团（Trinity Mirror），《镜报》于是成为该集团的旗舰级报纸。几经易手和合并，《镜报》已逐渐变成英国有影响的大报，发布的消息被公认为具有较高的可靠性和权威性，其姐妹报纸为《星期日镜报》（Sunday Mirror）。

Bibliography

安义宽 . 2003. 公司债券及其相关品种发展 . 经济管理，（11）：6 – 14.

陈明瑶，卢彩虹 . 2006. 新闻英语语体与翻译研究 . 北京：国防工业出版社 .

陈仲利 . 2013. 最新英美报刊选读 . 北京：中国人民大学出版社 .

储昭根 . 2015. 冷战后美国的经济安全与外交 . 国际观察，（4）：142 – 157.

戴炜华，陈宇昀 . 2004. 批评语篇分析的理论和方法 . 外语研究，（4）：12 – 16.

邓友平 . 2014. 美国"课程现代化"的科学主义内核研究 . 东北师范大学博士论文 .

端木义万，赵虹 . 2013. 美英报刊阅读教程（普及本）（修订本）. 南京：南京大学出版社 .

端木义万 . 2005. 美英报刊阅读教程（中级本）（精选版）. 北京：北京大学出版社 .

高攀，郑启航 . 2016. 美国参议院通过波多黎各债务重组法案 . 经济参考报，7月1日 .

葛密艳 . 2015. 报纸专栏名称与特色表达 . 采写编，（1）：30 – 32.

侯维瑞 . 1988. 英语语体 . 上海：上海外语教育出版社 .

黄萍 . 2006. 新闻英语中新词汇的造词分析 . 黑龙江社会科学，（2）：132 – 133.

李孔岳 . 2006. 科技成果转化的模式比较及其启示 . 科技管理研究，（1）：88 – 91.

理查德·卡特，张民强 . 2004. 现行美国教育体制 . 河北师范大学学报（教育科学版），（6）：
    100 – 102.

廖维娜，杨静 . 2008. 高效阅读英美报刊文章 . 西南民族大学学报（人文社科版），（12）：
    142 – 145.

林克勤 . 2005. 当代报纸专栏的类别及其特点 . 新闻界，（3）：125 – 126.

刘大保 . 2000. 社论写作 . 北京：中国广播电视出版社 .

刘凤鸣 . 2005. 英语报纸词、句特征 . 西南民族大学学报（人文社科版），（3）：305 – 308.

刘燕华，王文涛 . 2013. 第三次工业革命与可持续发展 . 中国人口、资源与环境，（4）：
    3 – 7.

那明 . 2014. 金融危机背景下国家主权信用评级影响因素分析——基于 27 个 OECD 国家面板数据的研究 . 世界经济研究，（10）：28－33.

唐军，李政 . 2011. 我国发展对冲基金的必要性分析及前景预测 . 商品与质量，（1）：43－44.

王劲松 . 2009. 对我国发行市政债券若干问题的思考 . 财政研究，（5）：31－34.

王克俊 . 2007. 报刊英语语言特色研究 . 四川理工学院学报（社会科学版），（1）：109－112.

王明明 . 2009. 跨境贸易人民币结算试点——突破和改变 . 中国金融家，（6）：45－47.

王长勤，纪海涛 . 2015. 科技创新与国际竞争格局演变 . 紫光阁，（11）：29－31.

王振华，马玉蕾 . 2009. 英语报刊选读 . 北京：高等教育出版社 .

隗静秋 . 2010. 中外饮食文化 . 北京：经济管理出版社 .

肖小月 . 2013. 英美新闻标题语言特色分析 . 重庆交通大学学报（社科版），（2）：133－136.

晓晓 . 2012. 英国教育体制：现状、学制、体制、特点 . 内蒙古教育，（3）：38－40.

熊易 . 2016. 国际开放科学数据实证资源及利用研究 . 图书馆理论与实践，（1）：12－14.

徐明初 . 2002. 论英语成语比喻的文化特色及其翻译 . 宜宾学院学报，（2）：59－61.

姚正萍 . 2020. 对英语报刊新闻标题的语法特征研究 . 英语广场，（33）：55－56.

余翔 . 2015. 美国经济增长新特征与前景 . 国际问题研究，（4）：82－95.

张宏菊 . 2010. 美国联邦行政学院领导人才培训的历史与现状 . 华东师范大学硕士论文 .

张卫平 . 2006. 英语报刊选读 . 北京：外语教学与研究出版社 .

赵敬 . 2010. 中美饮食文化差异 . 学术论坛，（13）：227.

周淑真，冯永光 . 2010. 美国政党组织体制运行机制及其特点 . 当代世界与社会主义，（3）：114－119.

周鑫宇 . 2020. 美国政党政治的"十字撕裂"及其未来发展趋势 . 当代世界，（8）：11－17.

周学艺 . 2010. 美英报刊导读（第二版）. 北京：北京大学出版社 .

周学艺，赵林 . 2013. 美英报刊文章阅读（第五版）. 北京：北京大学出版社 .

Rifkin, J. 2011. *The Third Industrial Revolution: How Lateral Power Is Transforming Energy, the Economy, and the World*. London: Macmillan.